Anthony's
Apologies:

Don't read beginning
to end. The
madness will
consume you

Also by Davy Rothbart

Found

The Lone Surfer of Montana, Kansas

FOUND II

MORE OF THE BEST LOST, TOSSED, AND FORGOTTEN ITEMS FROM AROUND THE WORLD

DAVY ROTHBART

A FIRESIDE BOOK
Published by Simon & Schuster
New York London Toronto Sydney

FIRESIDE
Rockefeller Center
1230 Avenue of the Americas
New York, NY 10020

FIRESIDE and colophon are registered trademarks of Simon & Schuster, Inc.

For information regarding special discounts for bulk purchases,
please contact Simon & Schuster Special Sales at 1-800-456-6798
or business@simonandschuster.com.

Manufactured in the United States of America

10 9 8 7 6 5 4 3 2 1

Library of Congress Cataloging-in-Publication data is available.

ISBN-13: 978-0-7432-7307-7
ISBN-10:   0-7432-7307-9

Found is an uncommon tribute to and commentary on everyday life—a collage of disparate "found" items sent in by readers across the nation, ranging from love letters to doodles to shopping lists. Consistent with the entirely random way in which they have been found, no connection, relationship, or association between the individual items included in the book is intended or should be inferred from the manner in which they are displayed. Names and identifying characteristics of certain of the authors and creators of the "found" items and certain people featured in them have been changed.

FOUND

THE ROAD WARRIORS

When we put the first FOUND book together a couple of years ago, my friend Jason Bitner, who started FOUND Magazine with me, pointed out that there were finds in it from every single state. If folks had sent stuff in from every state, it seemed to me only fair to take the show on the road and visit all 50 states, sharing our all-time favorite finds with people and collecting brand-new ones. So I bought a van on eBay, roped my little brother Peter into coming along, and hit the road with him for an 8-month, 50-state, 136-city tour. I couldn't have imagined what an amazing journey it would turn out to be!

CHARLOTTE!
THE FOUND
GUY IS COMMING
TOMORROW, RIGHT
??? 1:00 ???
4:00, 7:00 ???
8:00 Space Gallery
=

13.4545
11/148.00
+ /38
-33
-50
-44 130
55
50

From Alaska to Florida and Hawaii to Maine we held our raucous FOUND parties in every type of place imaginable—bookstores and bars, colleges and prisons, art galleries and army bases, bingo halls and an old ice factory, inside an abandoned train car, and even in the dark grimy basement of a house in Nashville, Tennessee, that belonged to a pair of guys called Roach and Dirt. At each stop, I read my favorite finds outloud to the crowd and Peter played his guitar and sang a few lovely and lewd songs he'd written inspired by FOUND notes. But the most thrilling part every night was when we invited folks to come up and share their own finds with the rest of us—I never knew what to expect and the results were always heartbreaking and hilarious. It was a glorious feeling to celebrate FOUND stuff with people in every city who love it all as much as I do.

continued on the next page!

THE FOUND GUY
FOUND by Richard Wilson
Portland, ME

continued from the page before

At the end of the night we'd climb back in the van, arms full of new FOUND treasures, and burn for the next town. Four in the morning, I'd be at the wheel, driving through the Rockies or the Everglades or the cool Arizona desert, and Peter would be stretched out in the back of the van, reading to me from the stack of FOUND stuff we'd collected that night. There was something sweet and beautiful and deeply affecting about watching America reel past out the window while my brother read from FOUND letters, voicing the hopes and dreams of real Americans. I love FOUND stuff so much—traveling to all these cities, meeting so many kindred spirits, and getting all this incredible FOUND stuff, I felt like a kid in a candy store. Or no—a kid on a 50-state *tour* of candy stores!

This 2nd FOUND book is a collection of the funniest, spookiest, weirdest, and most crushing FOUND notes that we've collected on tour and that you guys have mailed in to us. At home in Michigan, it's so cool how much wonderful FOUND mail lands in our mailbox every single day—a smorgasbord of finds. And they come not just from the U.S., but from all over the world—in this book there's finds from Scotland, Taiwan, Australia, Honduras, England, Canada, and the Virgin Islands, among others. This book in your hands, it's the product of an unbelievable collaborative effort—thousands of people across the globe scouring the ground, taking a second to pick something up, and if it's interesting, sending it in to us. If you've already sent us your finds, thank you so much, keep 'em coming! And if you haven't yet, please join in! We're excited to check out what you've found, and to share it with everybody else.

Okay, word, thank you *thank you* for reading this book and being a part of FOUND—now please keep your eyes to the ground and send in your finds!

Peace out for now—see you on the road. Love and respect—

— DAVY

DAVY ROTHBART
point guard, FOUND Magazine

MICHIGAN
HG LFE
GREAT LAKES

2

photo by Dorothy Gotlib

If you decide
that
you love me
anytime today
Please
call me

ANYTIME FOUND by Anna Caramanna, Phoenix, AZ

I'm just glad
my son wasn't
here to witness
a fireman make
such a shameful
outburst, even if
you were provoked!
– observer

FIVE-ALARM OUTBURST

FOUND by Bruce, San Francisco, CA

To the finder of
this note,
WELL DONE!
You have successfully
completed the
first task
of this enchanted
quest. Hellooooo !!!

TO THE FINDER

FOUND by Lisi Stoessel, Edinburgh, Scotland

NOT A BOMB

FOUND by Mike McCaffrey, Oakville, Ontario

DON'T BE
FRIGHTENED
IT'S NOT A BOMB
OR BIOHAZARDOUS

FOUND Magazine. You have successfully
completed the first task of this enchanted quest.

3

FOUND

is presented by

FOUND Magazine's

point guard

DAVY ROTHBART

& power forward

JASON BITNER

with

PETER ROTHBART

DAVID MEIKLEJOHN   ARTHUR JONES

Dec. 1972

BRITTEN STRINGWELL   SARAH LOCKE   LAUREN HART

NOT PICTURED:
JAMES MOLENDA
ANGELA PETRELLA
JAVAN MAKHMALI
MOIRA SALTZMAN
AARON WICKENDEN
MIKE DIBELLA
DAN TICE
AMANDA PATTEN

photos on this page FOUND by (clockwise) Mike Rothbart, Madison, WI; Brande Wix, San Francisco, CA; Eleanor, Rochester, NY; Nina & Katie, St. Louis, MO; Lisi Stoessel, Charlottesville, VA

FOUND Magazine's Davy Rothbart (right) and Jason Bitner (left) during the company's annual Ice Fishing extravaganza.

Cynthia Ellen Masa

IF YOU THINK FOUND MAGAZINE IS SUPER-KEWL, PUT YOUR HAND IN THE AIR!!

& jillions of FINDERS worldwide!

TIMMY SMITH

BRANDE WIX

MIKE HELFERSTAY

4

Newton's Julia

Todd,

You..... you make me happy. I Don't Know if you Know how much I love you. If you Don't its Allot. You Are My Brother. you And fletch

Love

—Kevin—

Copyright (C) 1994 Art Matrix, Ithaca, NY USA (607) 277-0959

this book is dedicated to sarah locke.

Thank you

BLESS the U.S.

The finds in this book come from many countries, but the lion's share of them come from the United States. Check the handy guide below to see which pages contain finds from your home state!

AL 11, 62, 146, 185—AK 241—AR 68, 113—AZ 3, 31, 202—CA 3, 4, 8, 9, 12, 13, 16, 19, 21, 33, 38, 54, 63, 64, 65, 67, 71, 74, 77, 83, 93, 96, 99, 101, 102, 103, 109, 122, 123, 125, 129, 135, 139, 141, 143, 144, 148, 149, 155, 159, 172, 178, 182, 183, 185, 191, 201, 211, 215, 217, 220, 221, 222, 227, 229, 236, 239, 240, 241—CO 36, 84, 85, 137, 139, 203—CT 27, 205, 218—DC 129, 130, 139—DE 187—FL 10, 53, 103, 116, 179, 181, 191, 239—GA 112, 128, 202, 216, 236, 242—HI 15, 176—ID 32—IA 182—IL 7, 37, 48, 49, 52, 82, 96, 104, 105, 106, 107, 117, 118, 119, 140, 141, 192- 95, 225—IN 72, 139, 170, 172, 173, 181, 193, 207—KS 187—KY 25, 66, 67, 176— LA 39, 40, 41, 44, 45, 46, 47, 151, 201, 225, 226—MA 58, 59, 228, 238—ME 1, 24, 71, 82, 154, 182, 184, 217—MI 1, 5, 14, 18, 28, 29, 52, 60, 63, 67, 69, 76, 92, 93, 98, 126, 127, 137, 134, 140, 165, 167, 168, 169, 177, 197, 219—MO 4, 5, 27, 54, 71, 129, 154, 199, 236—MN 16, 140, 152, 180, 200, 220, 239—MS 225, 241—MT 177—NC 6, 97, 113, 123, 208, 212, 218—ND 31—NE 203—NH 86, 87, 88, 89, 90, 91, 237— NJ 68, 125—NM 30, 33, 71, 76, 140, 146, 154, 174, 175, 185, 204, 223— NY 4, 17, 25, 30, 34, 42, 43, 50, 51, 61, 63, 94, 97, 121, 124, 129, 155, 166, 173, 179, 196, 206, 207, 208, 209, 210, 211, 212, 224, 246—NV 60—OH 23, 30, 37, 52, 114, 130, 131, 134, 135, 172, 173, 192, 198, 223, 228, 251—OK 6—OR 13, 21, 31, 32, 114, 120, 129, 197, 214-15, 244, 245— PA 35, 70, 77, 116, 129, 208, 218—RI 119, 199—SC 115—SD 27—TN 17, 110, 111, 113, 150, 151—TX 18, 25, 26, 32, 56, 73, 92, 96, 155, 216, 230, 231, 232, 233, 234, 235, 240, 242, 246—UT 30, 57, 141, 208, 209— VA 4, 20, 113, 119, 197, 216, 217—VT 136, 137—WA 25, 27, 30, 67, 92, 128, 130, 171, 190, 211—WI 4, 20, 38, 39-41, 98, 134, 183, 191, 204— WV 130, 252—WY 205

this photo album page

FOUND by Ron Buechele & Tracy Varley, St. Louis, MO

5

The Condom made a mistake and broke.

PLAYING THE BLAME GAME

FOUND by Olisa Corcoran

Durham, NC

this photo FOUND by Lori Daniels, Shawnee, OK

6

I, Al Burian, being of reasonably sound mind and body, do hereby deliver my last will and testament, on this morning of November 3, 2001. Should I die under circumstances other than the total collapse of civilization, i.e., if it's at all possible to arrange a funeral, I would like it to happen in the following manner: I'd prefer to be cremated, then have my remains laid into the earth in a ceremony where "Another one bites the dust" by Queen plays over a public address system. That should put people in a jovial mood and hopefully a good party will follow.

Signed,

AL BURIAN

witness *Liz Daidel*

7

These three faxes rolled off of our office fax machine in the middle of the night. Who's Gigi? A dog, a cat, a child? Why is Gigi being held captive? I love the last page—oops—my bad! —G.

THE 2ND FAX

Aug 25 05 02:43a

41588963

p.1

This is cruel and emotional abuse. No wonder you drive the women you're with crazy -(insane) They either join cults or want to kill thamseves + not get out of bed for months, + have to take anti-depressants. Be a man for once in your life.

The world doesn't revolve around you. Just let me have Gigi now. I can't believe you are even doing this, I will come get her. If not I'm calling the police

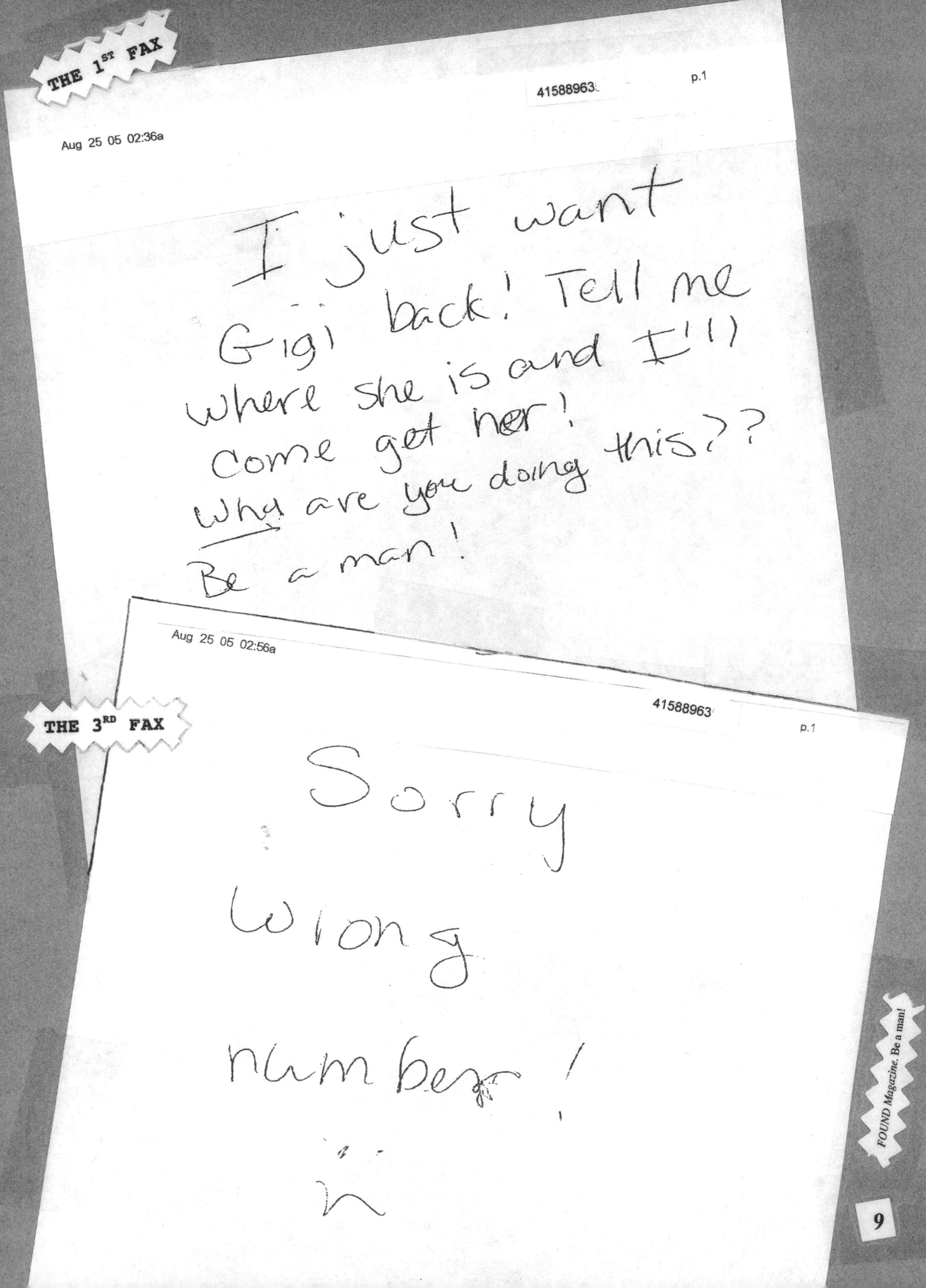

41588963   p.1

Aug 25 05 02:36a

I just want
Gigi back! Tell me
where she is and I'll
come get her!
Why are you doing this??
Be a man!

Aug 25 05 02:56a

41588963   p.1

Sorry

wrong

number !

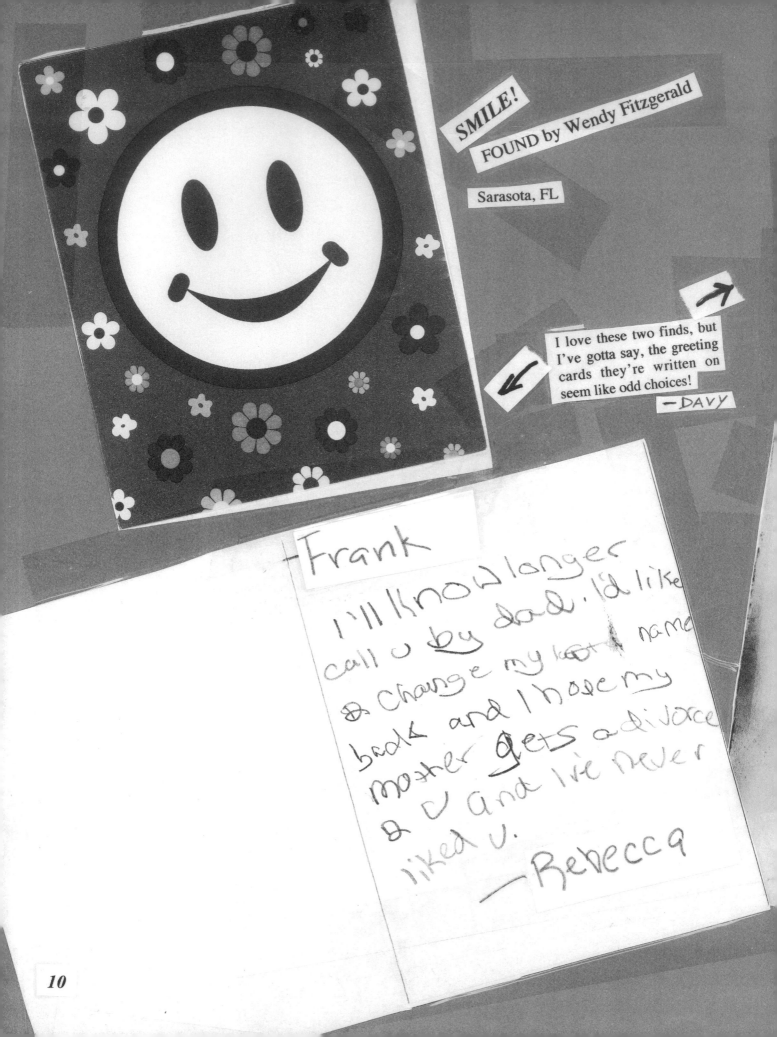

SMILE!

FOUND by Wendy Fitzgerald

Sarasota, FL

I love these two finds, but I've gotta say, the greeting cards they're written on seem like odd choices!

—DAVY

Frank

I'll know longer call u by dad. I'd like to change my last name back and I hope my mother gets a divorce & u and I've never liked u.

—Rebecca

AIN'T DOIN' NOTHIN'...

AIN'T DOIN' NOTHIN'

FOUND by Mike Smith
and Dakota LaCroix

Dothan, AL

This is probably my favorite thing I've ever had a part in finding. The friendly card. The estranged Jehovah's Witness couple. The sinister dad who almost certainly murdered his whole family shortly after writing this. My friend and I found this in an abandoned house in Alabama—the place had huge holes bashed in the walls, food mashed into the carpet, stuffed animals ripped up with their innards strewn from room to room. It seemed as if the inhabitants had left in a hurry.

—M.S.

...BUT THINKIN' OF YOU!

Hi Kids,
I AM ALWAYS THINKING OF YOU AND PRAYING FOR YOU. MOMMY WILL CERTAINLY HAVE TO ACCOUNT TO JEHOVAH FOR NOT TAKING YOU TO THE MEETINGS. THERE IS NO EXCUSE. ALSO IF YOU STAY THERE AND DO NOT GO TO MEETINGS OR OUT IN SERVICE YOU WILL SURELY LOOSE YOUR LIVES AT ARMAGEDDON. I LOVE YOU AND WANT YOU TO LIVE. DO NOT LISTEN TO EXCUSES. THEY ARE FROM SATAN. I AM ANXIOUS TO SEE YOU. IT WON'T BE LONG NOW.
Love always,
Daddy
(your only)

11

TRAPPING CATS #1
FOUND by Dan Tice
Ventura, CA

I found these two notices among other papers and debris in the trunk of an old Chevy I bought in suburban L.A. —D.T.

There is a person in our immediate area who is trapping our neigborhood cats and I have no idea where he is taking them. I am effected because between my across the street neighbor and myself, we have 5 ferile cats who are all spayed and neutered, and we feed them. Noone in the neighborhood objects to the cats except the person who is doing this terrible deed. I have received a letter of complaint from the city which I have responded to. Last week, I noticed one of the cats gone. I was afraid it might have been hit by a car, but there were no traces. The missing cat had only 1 eye, as I had to have an operation on him years ago, since the cat had such a bad infection, it was blind in that eye anyway. The cats are all from the same litter in 1998. At any rate within the last 2 days, another cat is not showing up for meals. Yesterday morning I was walking my dogs when suddenly I noticed this neighbor had an animal trap with cat food set in it. The trap was in his front yard mostly covered by bushes. I took pictures of the trap in front of his house. I confronted him with the disappearances today, and asked where he took the cats. He just said, "Did you see me take your cats. I don't know what you are talking about." I am so upset having raised these cats from kittens in the neighborhood, that I don't know what to do. I contacted the animal shelter and when they get around to it, they will send an officer to see if he has a permit, which I'm sure he doesn't. If everyone could write him imploring him not to do what he is doing, that may help. I am so afraid the officer might get there after all the cats are gone, and God only knows where he is taking them. I just found out that another neighbor is missing a cat. I am leaving his address in case someone can pass this on to anyone who can help. Thank you. The person who is trapping the cats is...

Frank Talbert
3663 Baytree Blvd.
San Luis Obispo, CA 92609
(805) 316-48

12

6/25/2004 9:26 AM

Dear Neighbor:

It has come to my attention that my neighbor has sent out a memo throughout our community stating false information about me.

I can assure you that his accusations are absolutely not true. He has stated in his memo that I am trapping cats. This is not true. I have not - nor do I ever intend to trap cats.

I set out a humane rat / gopher trap which is what my neighbor saw on my property. The trap has always been empty in the three days that it was set. I did not catch gophers, rats or any other animals. I assured him that I am not targeting his cats or anyone else's cats. He was so irate that I have since thrown the humane trap away.

However, since the sending of my neighbor's anonymous letter giving out my address and phone number, I have received voicemail messages to my home threatening to poison and shoot my dog. I have turned over the recorded messages to the police department.

The purpose of this memo is to assure you, my neighbors, that I am not trapping cats. Please feel free to contact me if you have further questions or concerns.

Thank you,

Frank
(805) 316-48

The person who is trapping the cats is… FOUND Magazine.

HARMONY OF THE WORLD

FOUND by Michael Svoboda

Portland, OR

GOD & OUR DOCTORS

FOUND by Sean Santos

Lansing, MI

7/29/03

Meg,

You can no longer live here or even stay here, per court order. I have cleaned out all of your things. You and everyone else need to leave Jake, me & Naomi alone. We are a family and do not need anyone's help but God & our doctors.

-Christine Hunt

Kyle, well you Really Fucked me over this time you ASS.

I Have been Robbed AGAIN!
THIS TIME my PASSPORT And CHECKS As well As Lube.

YOU Are A LIAR + A THIEF And you Are out of Here.

I have had the Police over And Filed A complaint. I can't believe how you Have Played me. Your Drug buddy came by And Spilled the beans about your Sex/Drug Party the other NIGHT. I Found my DVD's + the Other Items of mine In your Room. As well As Drug Paraphernalia (leave the keys on the MAT)

Their are two
Perfect spider webs
on your bike Really big
spiders about this big
take a look before you
distroy them also the spider
cant be to far away if you
cant see them

FOUND by JoEllen Martinson & Rob Davis

St. Paul, MN

EXPECTATION
=
DISAPO

Im glad I
lost my virginity
with you. It
felt so good.
thank you for
the wonderful
night ya gave
me honey

FOUND by Alexis Koren

Hollywood, CA

FOUND by Dorothy Fox

Fontana, CA

⚡FOUND⚡
IN LIBRARY BOOKS

Librarians are one of our best sources of FOUND stuff—it's amazing to read through all of the notes tucked into books that have been returned to the library. But notes aren't the only things folks are using as bookmarks. Stokley Towles, an artist in Seattle, polled librarians at the King County Library System about the stuff they'd found in returned books. This is the list they came up with!

— DAVY

-band-aid
-tissue
-drinking straw
-blank Post-it note
-yarn
-paper clip
-piece of grass
-feather
-phone card
-lottery ticket
-unused plane ticket

-insurance plan
-strip of condoms
-leaf
-bobby pin
-bag of marijuana
-comb
-restraining order
-wedding photograph
-seven $100 bills
-IRS refund check
-Dear John letter

-toothpick
-cashier's check for $5,000
-postage stamp
-a raisin carefully placed at the edge of the page, its tip sticking out the top of the book
-silver spoon
-pair of chopsticks
-savings bond
-valid passport
-snapshot of a family on a roller coaster, everyone screaming
-origami swan
-a raw strip of bacon

-two-inch carpenter's nail

-pencil

PASSPORT

Pay to the order of

For

BANK OF OAK R
Oak Ridge, Tenn.
FOR DEFENSE AND FOR HUMAN
SERVING THE

"What else can I do to thank you?" said Maggie. I was done with my story; the fever had cooled; we were in the den with the two TVs, but at some point she'd shut them off. "What would you most want? Anything, just tell me, out of curiosity."

"But I stole your bag," I protested. "I'm just giving it back."

"He did steal your bag," Noah agreed sleepily, his lids hanging low.

"And you gave me a tape," I added. "That's a lot."

"Yup, baby," said Noah, "you did give him the tape."

The woman stared at me with owl eyes.

anging on every pause and intonation.
ame back in and asked me for my
me and the name of his unit, then disap-
wn the hall. Here and there Maggie
strummed ___ itar for a bit and hummed, as though to gently accentuate the action in the other room. I was twitchy with nervous excitement. Every time I heard Noah dialing another number, I imagined my brother at a command post in some dark, hot room deep within his ship—the kind of red-lit chamber in submarine movies where people shouted things. I pictured a phone clanging to life in the middle of a vast circuitry board, and my brother picking it up and saying, "This is Mabry," the same way he'd answered the phones when he'd worked at

17

BOCCI

is good for letting go of your problems. It is a beautiful day, let go of your problems as you let go of your balls. Clutch the balls and really work them over in your palms until you have gathered up all of your negativity and let the balls spread it back into the earth. The earth is there for you to talk to and let go of your balls on.

LETTING GO

FOUND by Britten Stringwell
Ann Arbor, MI

FOUND Magazine. Clutch the balls and really work them over in your palms.

this photo FOUND by Lori Daniels, Roanoke, TX

Boccie is an Italian form of lawn bowling.

Teenagers: what in your life is most satisfying?

Well heres my Top 25 Bitch! + 1 and a 200! !!!!!

(1) Nothing! - except needing alchohol to be the asshole I really am! (or shouldn't be)

(2) listen to mixing

(3) Evil hardcore gabber acid techno - Die motherfuckers!

4 The feeling of wanting to destroy this fucked up world.

5 Freaking out the rich motherfucks with hardcore techno.

6 Reading Victorian Novels. - Jane Austin, Anthony Trollope, Brontës

7 Looking at my Audrey Hepburn Poster. - Days of Wine + Roses!

8 Getting stoned and listening to space rock. Fuxa Windy/Carl Flowchart

9 getting stoned in the park with my buddy Josh.

10 Going to insane hardcore raves and taking lots of drugs.

11 Mentally raping every girl/woman I see! as long as shes not fat!

12 Thinking bad thoughts about all the trendy superficial fucks.

13 Buying Music

14 Listening to the shit I bought.

15 Fucking the shit out of my girlfried -especially in the ass.

16 Telling lame ass punk rockers (punk rock is dead!)

17 Spitting on all the socialites. - Fuck you! your all a bunch of sheep.

18 Buying a 40 oz. for the homeless man in our neiborhood

19 Hoping someday to be vegetarian. Don't kill the animals, kill the humans.

20 Dreaming of WW3. - Not really, but it would be nice to see a Nuke go off!

21 Being disrespectful to god! Whos god is it anyways! Fuck all!

22 Sticking up for the ones who really need it! I see to many so called winners, stepping on the so called losers! Fuck All!

23 Saying fuck you to Satan! He is an asshole.

24 Reading about Religion- Buddhism, Hinduism, Tainism, isms

25 Thoughts of suicide. Who really cares anyway? Just kidding.

26. Peace love anarchy!

Feeling Negative. - Fuck your positive bullshit, it's only prolonging the inevitable. Total war, to destroy 2000 years of Culture. Fuck yes!

oh, yea tell Erin Thorson to give up on the voting bullshit. She a sheep and should be slaughtered! Tell Laureen to Fuck off! christ is fuckin dead you assholes.

#GOOD

MORNING SON

I WAS IN THE AREA AND THOUGHT I'D SAY HI BUT ITS LIKE 6 FUKIN THIRTY, SO I LEAVE A NOTE INSTEAD. BEING SOBER AINT BAD ~~AS TEMPTATION KEEPS REARING IT'S HEAD, SO I'VE BEEN STAYING AWAY~~ FROM THE BARS. BUT I STILL NEED TO SEE MY FRIENDS. I MADE A DECISION TO COME IN TO WAL-MART TODAY AND SEE WHAT HAPPENS

OVER
↓

OR IF NOTHIN ELSE TO CLEAN OUT MY LOCKER. EITHER WAY I WANT TO BE IN GOOD STANDING SO I CAN GIVE IT A SHOT AGAIN IN A YEAR. RIGHT NOW I'M BACK IN THE TEMP FIELD. STOP DOWN OR CALL THE ANCHOR AFTER WORK. I GOTTA PLAY SOME PINBALL. SAY HI TO B---

I LOVE YOU

DAD

HIYA FOUND,
MY BOYFRIEND FOUND THIS NOTE IN THE HIGH SCHOOL FOOTBALL FIELD NEAR OUR HOUSE.
I SURE WISH MY OWN DAD COULD FIND THAT "BEING SOBER AINT BAD". CURRENTLY, MY DAD IS SLOWLY "LEAVING LAS VEGAS" (IF YOU KNOW WHAT I MEAN)
—CIAO—
WZGC.

DAD:
You're Really Lucky
THAT THE SHIT you've
Been Spreading About
Me, Doesn't Really
Bother ME, But
IF I Hear Anymore
Of your Fuck'N
Lies ABout Me, TRust
Me I WILL BE BACK
TO DROP YOUR ASS.
I'M NOT KIDDING
→

Not

I WILL NO LONGER
Be THE SCAPEGOAT
FOR THIS FAMILIES
Fucked up Life. I
DO NOT WANT TO
Be CONTACTED BY
ANyONE EVER
AGAIN.
P.S. you DID THIS
NOT ME, I WAS
VERy GOOD TO you
AND you SHIT ON
me AGAIN, But NEVER
AGAIN

FOUND Magazine. You did this not me.

I work as a professional hospital chaplain. Yesterday I was cleaning up the chapel after services and found this note crumpled in a ball in the corner of the room. —M.T.

Dear god,
my dad is very
ill, and is dying
give me money
dammit

FOUND by Kagan McLeod

Toronto, Ontario

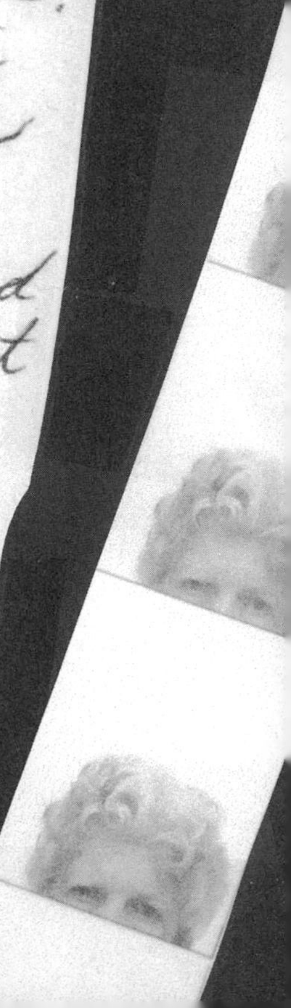

Feb 14, 200_

Dear Sean
Have a
great day!

Well Sean, hope you are losing some weight. Jan put a $100.00 in your bank account. It is from Gramma Jeannette for Valentine's day gift so you can afford diet & healthy food. fresh vegetables? apples instead of sugar stuff. I am worried about you gaining weight. You are too heavy. Time to stop it now. I hope Jan weighed you before you left on Monday.

Love You
Gramma Jeannette.
X O X O X O

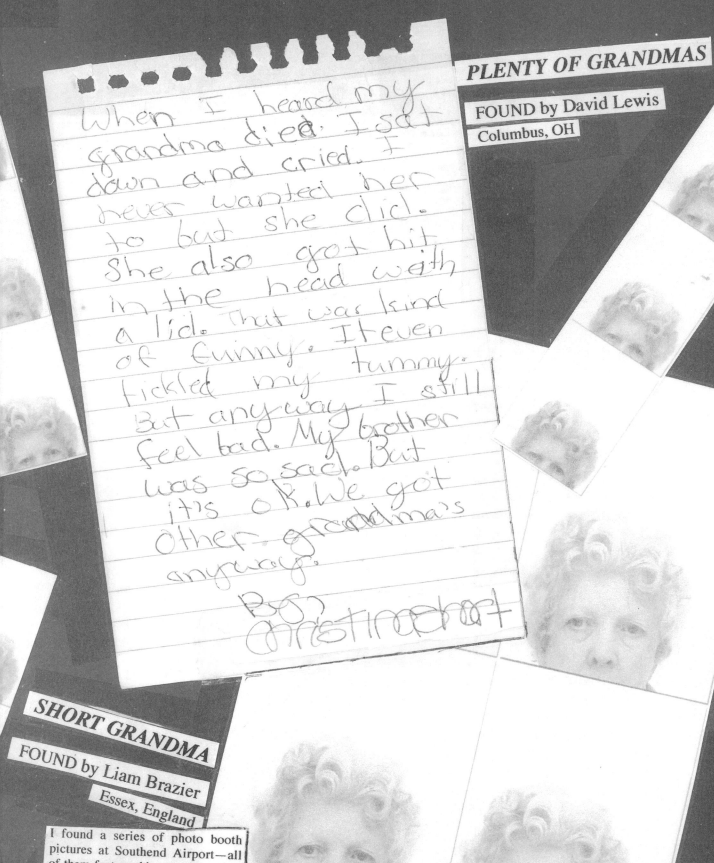

When I heard my grandma died, I sat down and cried. I never wanted her to but she did. She also got hit in the head with a lid. That was kind of funny. It even tickled my tummy. But anyway I still feel bad. My brother was so sad. But it's O.K. We got other grandma's anyway.

By Christineahart

SHORT GRANDMA

FOUND by Liam Brazier
Essex, England

I found a series of photo booth pictures at Southend Airport—all of them feature this woman, and in all of them a part of her face is missing from the frame. My hope is that she eventually figured out the mechanics of the height-adjustable seat. —L.B.

23

 Reward

$100.00 for the return of laptop stolen **2nd floor Room 734** Upton, No questions asked!!!!!!!!

$500.00 for information leading to the arrest and conviction of person or persons involved with the theft

(ladies welcome to stop by at anytime, with or without information)

Call - 207-678-12⬤ or leave note under door

WITH OR WITHOUT INFO

FOUND by Sarah Treible

Portland, ME

Umm, is this guy looking for his laptop or a date?!
(Read the fine print.) ~DAVY

FOUND Magazine will quickly destroy your yard.

LOST DENTURES

LOST DENTURES ON 5/7/05

DRAVUS AREA
CALL (336) 945-71

LOST DENTURES FOUND by Dan, Seattle, WA

LOST DUCK FOUND by our friends at Book People, Austin, TX

Lost Duck!!!

Call: 457-89

find Me!

find! him!

Scuby is lost!

$Rward$

(he peeps a lot, and he is yellow, with some white on his head)

Lost Dog
Mid-Night

**Large Black Dog, Very Ugly !!!
Not sure what breed she is. Definitely MIXED ! Appears to be a cross between a Lab, Greyhound, Border Collie and a Deer. Extremely Fast !!!**

Very good with Children, but extremely destructive to the Yard (excellent pet for children, but lots of work for their father). If you find her, please place her in your garage immediately (as she will quickly destroy your yard). Also, make sure that you remove everything from her reach as she likes to chew and will destroy anything she can get too.

Please call immediately as we miss her and would really like to have her back (I know, it's hard to explain, but we love her)　(859) 384-35

Reward $ 0.05

(I know it's not much of a reward, but trust me, if you survive 1 day with her you will want to pay me to take her back)

FOUND CHIHUAHUA FOUND by Joe Schumacher, New York, NY

LOST VERY UGLY DOG FOUND by Brad Denham, Union, KY

! LOST!

Small, female Chihuahua
4.5 yrs old, spayed
name Jaden,
Please call us if any

FOUND!

(616) 498-11

Missing since: 4:30pm 12/22/05

25

Good news! Not only has the Chihuahua been found and returned to its owners, so has Scuby the duck and Midnight the Very Ugly dog. Sadly, at the time this book is going to press, the whereabouts of the missing dentures remain a mystery.

—DAVY

To: THAT BITCH
ALICIA

Dear Alicia,

What were you thinking?! fucking Ben in the next room while I was sick w/ mono. UR A DIRTY BITCH and I rebuke you!!! I thought we had something special, but clearly you didn't. I hope you enjoy "tramping it up" and fucking half of Austin.

Please die

Sincerely,

Roger

THINGS TO DO

~~GET A NEW skateboard deck~~

~~think of band names~~

~~GET LAWN-MOWING SERVICE GOING~~

Hook-up wITH JEN

MAKE IT TO 6th GRADE

Sell guitar

~~Buy boots~~

Buy laundry detergent

Buy hooks for towels

Kims perscription

Sex w/ Dave

Buy new jeans

BILL OF SALE

This Bill of Sale will transfer ownership of one 1973 Ford LTD from Mr. Nigel Dang to Mr. Terrance Dang as of January 9th, 2004 in exchange for US$100 cash. This sale does not include the title for the vehicle, which was lost in the great sub-Saharan petroleum fires following the overthrow of the Congolese government in 1998, however Mr. Terrence Dang will receive full ownership of the vehicle. The vehicle is sold as is, with no warranty or possibility of return expressed or implied.

Signed and Dated:

Mr. Nigel Dang _____ 09.

Mr. Terrence Dang _____ J

FOUND Magazine. Lost in the great sub-Saharan petroleum fires following the overthrow of the Congolese government in 1998.

Name Ben-11   Date _____

Planning a Story About Yourself • I

I will write about the time when I ___got a gun Held to my head.___

I will begin my story this way. ___One day I was walking down the road with my friends, and two boys were walking by with a pitbul. So we went to hide couse it was lose with No chain on it.___

In the middle part of the story this will happen. ___But then they draged us out, and let me go. but chassed My friend So I went to run and tell Someone. But when I did they grabed me and Held a gun to My Head. And he said don't move are say anything or I'll blast your Head off.___

I will end my story like this. ___Then he Let me go and said I'll give you money if you don't tell. So I refused it and ran home told my parents and they called 911___

I will include these details in my story. ___What he did to my friend and details on speacial things.___

Unit 2 • Prewriting Master

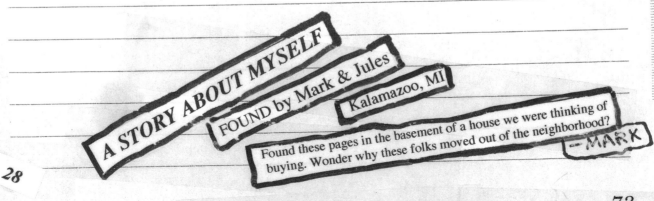

A STORY ABOUT MYSELF

FOUND by Mark & Jules

Kalamazoo, MI

Found these pages in the basement of a house we were thinking of buying. Wonder why these folks moved out of the neighborhood?

—MARK

28

Name _____   Date _____

Planning a Story About Yourself • II

Imagine these squares are photographs of important events from
your story. Make a rough sketch in each one. Then when you write
your story, use these "snapshots" to help you describe the events.

FOUND Magazine. Details on special things.

29

The Writing Process, Step 1: Ideas for Getting Started, p. 63, "Brainstorming"

Cedser dressing

Sugar free *fucking* syrup

Sugar packets

mop heads

bagels -

9 X 95

FOR THE DUMPED
FOUND by Brian Hare

Bowling Green, OH

This Wal-Mart receipt, found inside a book at the BGSU library, seems to include the quintessential items for a woman after a breakup.
—B.H.

```
ALWAYS LOW PRICES ALWAYS WAL-MART
            MANAGER JEFF

ST# 1927 OP# 00002689 TE# 17 TR# 04818
CHOCOLATE   007726000001 F      4.97 D
HAIR COLOR  007124918409        7.83 J
HAIR COLOR  007124918430        7.83 J
SHAMPOO     007278506688        1.64 J
ULTRA GENTL 007704310562        3.68 J
PEARL ROSE  003772479102        2.87 J
BATH PEARLS 003772479028        2.87 J
                    SUBTOTAL    31.69
        TAX 1   5.750 %          1.54
                       TOTAL    33.23
                   MCARD TEND   33.23

ACCOUNT #6961-07
APPROVAL #000408
TRANS ID -
VALIDATION -
PAYMENT SERVICE - N
                     CHANGE DUE  0.00

     # ITEMS SOLD 7
        ***CUSTOMER COPY***
```

TWENTY-EIGHT DAYS LATER
FOUND by Jonathan Shipley, Vashon, WA

Found this in late January in a 7-11 parking lot. My guess is that someone's New Year's resolution to eat healthy is starting to wear a little thin.
—J.S.

- Diet Coke
- Water
- Tonic
- Tampons (maybe times)
- Popsickels
- Red bull
- Frozen Healthy shit
- Vitamins/ diet pills
- wine?

SEX BOOKS AND BIBLE
FOUND by Mike Smith, Las Cruces, NM

Lap Top

Tags

mics

stands - speaker + mic

bass

copy music for david.

Human sex Books

Bible

MISSION ACCOMPLISHED!
FOUND by Shannon Booker, Salt Lake City, UT

I found this picture—Mormon missionary holding a jug of mysterious liquid—tumbling down the sidewalk in downtown Salt Lake.
—S.B.

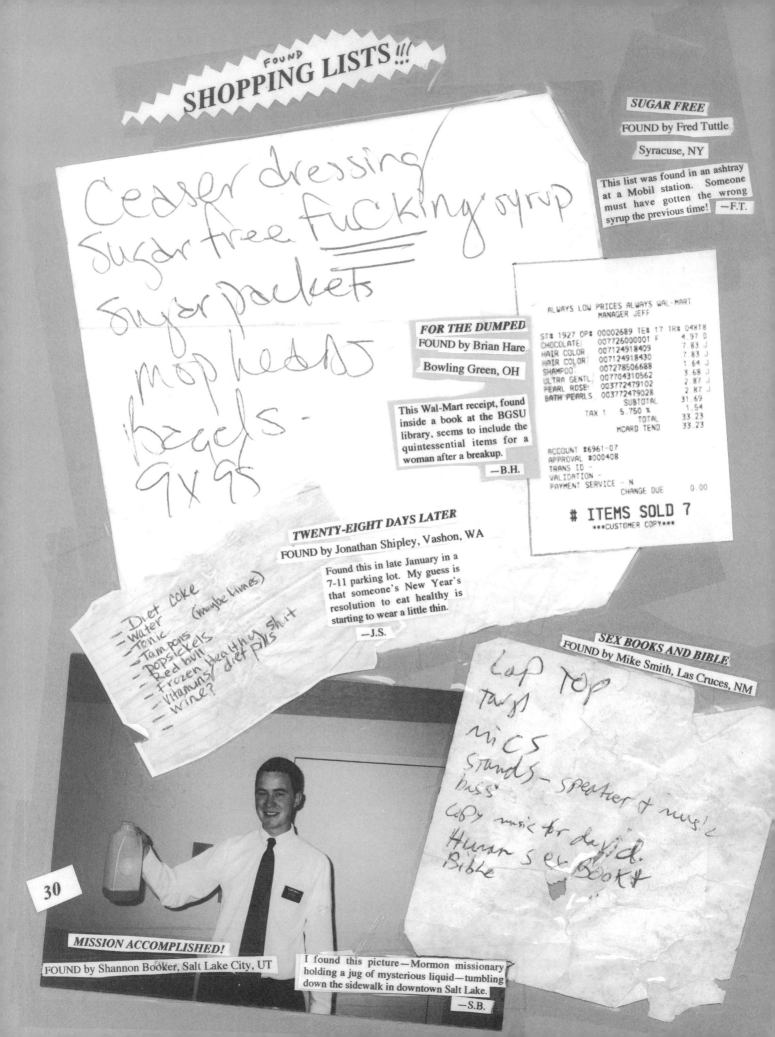

JEF

Tampons

PERIOD FOUND by Chris Willis, Portland, OR

Bread
cheese
milk
pack of DVD's
smelly candle
CD/DVD case.
Dish Soap

SMELLY CANDLE FOUND by Chris Willis, Portland, OR

paper towels Kleenex
paper plates (dessert)
ice cream
2 Sympathy Cards

TWO FOUND by Chris Willis, Portland, OR

Coffee Creamer.
flour
Celentro - green onion
Milk 2%
restroom dec.
~~Soda~~

When you are honest you are free

FREEDOM FOUND by Chris Willis, Phoenix, AZ

cookies
dried fruit
powdered milk?
canned food: meat, soup
gravy
cereals
vitamins
tea
frozen stuff? bread
casseroles? soups
peanut butter
crackers pb
popcorn
dried potatoes
packaged cheese: velveeta
hot chocolate

rice

Wows
baked beans
~~crabs~~
juice
milk
health bars
flashlights
coffee pot
outside grill
gun?
batteries
candles
kerosene heater

Y2K CHECKLIST FOUND by Ray Haque, Minot, ND

I picked up a book called *The Millennium Bug* at a thrift store. Inside was a list detaling what someone was planning to stock up on to prepare for the impending "disaster."

—R.H.

On the FOUND tour last year, Peter, Javan, David, and I spotted this secret treasure map—burned edges and all—lying in the grass in front of a restaurant called Thai Gourmet. We were happy to see that our mystery buccaneers had made it to their destination.

—DAVY

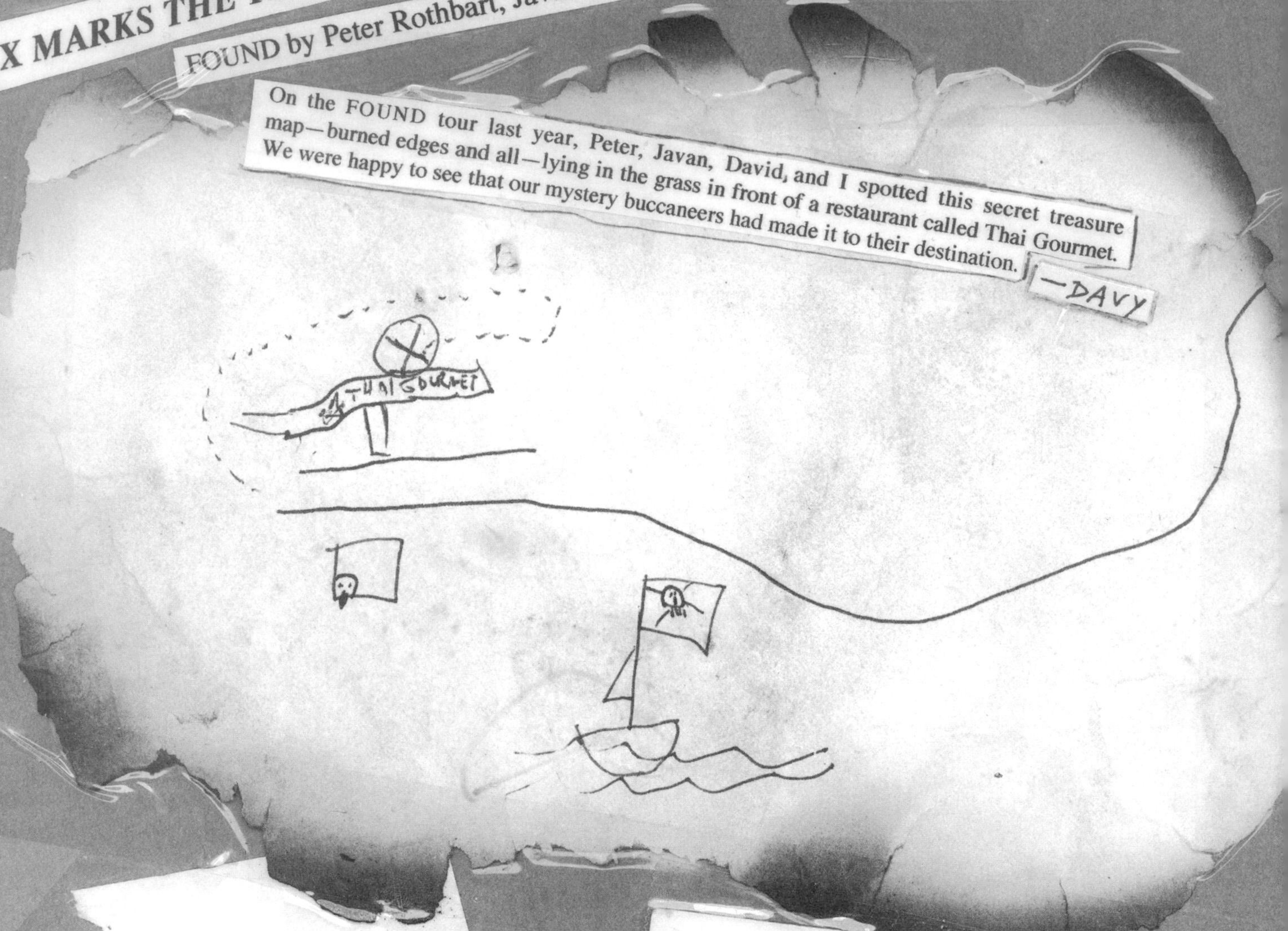

THAI GOURMET

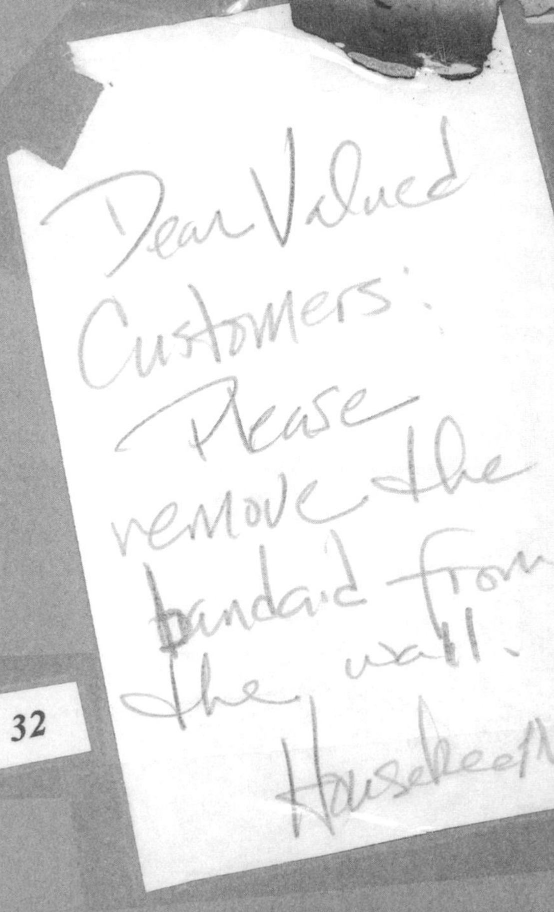

Dear Valued Customers: Please remove the bandaid from the wall.

Housekeeping

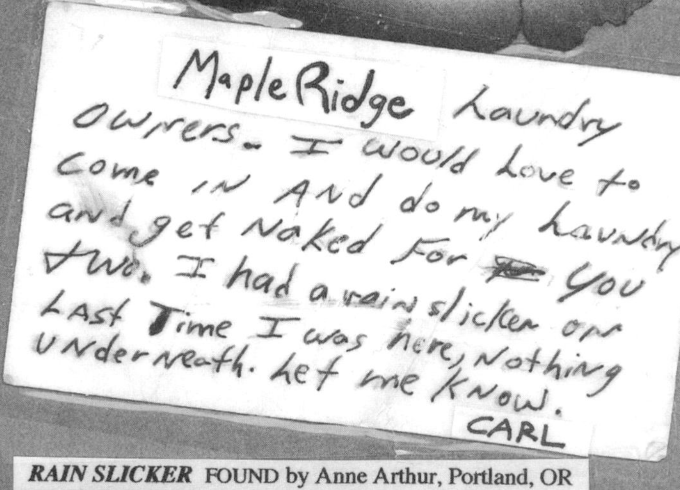

MapleRidge Laundry owners— I would love to come in And do my laundry and get Naked For you two. I had a rain slicker on Last Time I was here, Nothing underneath. Let me KNOW.

CARL

RAIN SLICKER FOUND by Anne Arthur, Portland, OR

DO NOT DISTURB FOUND by Ginger Chase, Moscow, ID

32

FOUND by Scott Denning

Bernalillo, NM

this drawing FOUND by Kelly Frazer

Taipei, Taiwan

TO THE WEMAN OF BERNALLIO COUTION

THERE IS A STORY I NEED TO TELL , I HAD A HUSBAND THAT I TRULY LOVED , AND TRUSTED WITH MY ALL , AND I'M SHUR YOU WEMAN OUT THERE DO TO. AND ALL I CAN SAY TO ALL OF YOU IS TO KEEP YOUR GUARD UP FROM A LOOSE WOMAN CALLED   MARGUERITE PENA   SHE RUNS AN ICE CREAM PARLOR IN THE SUMMER. SHE IS A SLUT .SHE HAS USED HER PARLOR FOR HER OWN INTERTAINMENT SHE PERSUADES MARRIED MEN WITH A FLIRT MOCKING THEM WITH BODY MOVEMET , A CELL NUMBER TO CALL .MY HUSBAND TOOK TO WHAT SHE OEFERD HIM AND THEY BECAME INTIMATE AND HAD AN AFAIR FOR SEVERAL MOUNTHS ,   PETER LEIX WAS MY HUSBAND I GAVE HIM UP WHEN I FOUND THEM TOGETHER IN A MOTEL ROOM , I ALSO LOST THE CHILD I WAS GOING TO HAVE MY BABY ,BUT SHE HAS NO MORALS FOR HER SELF OR OTHERS , WHERE WAS HER HUSBAND IN THE SUMMER OF 2002 , SHE WAS SEEN AT SEVRAL BARS , AT THE HYATT AT SANTA ANNA MORINOS, SILVAS , JOKERS PUB, MIDNIGHT RHODEO, AND NOT ONLY WITH MY HUSBAND . A MAN THAT HAS A MEAT MARKET , A MAN THAT WORKS AT THE CEMENT PLANT , A MAN THAT WORKS AT A WELDING SHOP ALL OF THEM FROM BERNALILLO . MY HUSBAND ASKED HER TO LEAVE HER HUSBAND AND HER REPLY WAS HE TOOK THE CANDY LIKE ANY OTHER MAN KEEP YOUR GAURD UP WEMEN .

FOUND Magazine. Took the candy like any other man.

LOVE YOU Dad GET JOB JUST JOKING

Divorce Papers

Use blanks below or unprinted sides for your own headings.

MARRIAGE PPRS.

NO POINT IN WASTING PAPER

FOUND by Mike Smith   Las Cruces, NM

Someone gave me an old filing cabinet. Many of the files still had tabs on them. When I pulled them out to replace them, I found that written on the back of the one labeled "Divorce Papers" were the words, "Marriage Pprs." Funny how easy things can change. Funny… and horrible at the same time.

—M.S.

A GOOD POSITION AND A COMFORTABLE SALARY WILL BE YOURS
02 13 17 25 28 51
NEVER !

NO FORTUNE FOUND by R.J. Sakai, Los Angeles, CA

33

11.15.02

To Whom it May Concern:

This letter serves as my plea of "NOT GUILTY" with respect to the enclosed parking violation. My reason is as follows: The evening of October 23, 2002, I drove to 68 Hicks Street in Brooklyn to meet a friend who would be subletting my friend's apartment which is located in that building. I met her in front at 6:00 pm to give her the keys. I turned off the car when I arrived and waited for her to show up. After our brief meeting, we both got into the car because I offered to drive her to the nearest subway station. When I tried to start the car, nothing happened, not even one little sound. My friend stayed in the car with me while I called my boyfriend for help. The weather was turning colder and we were freezing in our thin jackets, so we went up to the

You know how after you get a parking ticket you can write in and contest it and try to explain why you shouldn't have to pay? It usually says right there on the ticket that it's pretty much got to be some kind of life-threatening emergency or forget about it. Somehow I don't think all this talk of thin jackets and subletting apartments is gonna stand much of a chance...

DEATH IN FAMILY

A better strategy is to strike first, before you get the parking ticket in the first place. After Julie gave me this FOUND note in Philly, I've been sticking it on my windshield every once in a while when I need to leave my van parked illegally for a couple minutes, or, okay, yeah, a couple of hours. I love this note for its frantic succinctness. I mean, those parking cops can be bastards, but can you imagine how ruthless they'd have to be to give someone a ticket with this on their windshield? Ain't got one yet!

—DAVY

Carrie found this page with these sage words of advice tucked into a book that had been returned to the school library where she works. I wish someone had clued me in to all of this when *I* was younger—it might have saved me a whole lotta turmoil!

—DAVY

Remember

To always listen to what ever the elder has to say, wether Its Dumb shit or If Their right. Because their always right at least thats how they feel and told alot of the times they are right and alot of times their not, but the point is you cant ever change how they think, because your young and Ignorants, So why should they. When it comes to any conversation Let them say what they have to say and say youll try to do better If their wrong you still say sorry, because why) Because what ever words you say wont change their minds, But Saying youll do better will be something theyll not be able to argue with, but you gotta actually do it, not just say it. So just let them say what they have to say, you cant change how they think no matter what so deal with it, Dont argue even If their rong, you cant change what the think say your sorry youll do better then theirs no fight, nothing you said that was stupid that you. regret, so just chill let it go and take note and try harder.

FOUND by Teresa Mikulan
Cleveland, OH

This summer I found a nightstand on the side of the road. I carried it home and set it on the porch. For some reason the drawer wouldn't shut. I pulled the drawer out; lodged behind it was a dildo, a condom wrapper, and a Cleveland Metroparks zoo pass. I like to think the previous owner would go to the zoo and then follow it up with some vigorous sex. —T.M.

M.Hunter
N-Dawen #2R
Chicago IL 60647

USA 37

FOUND
MAGAZINE?
3455 Charing Cross Rd.
Ann Arbor, MI
48108-1911

#6 Any woman who says they don't masterbate is a fucking liar.

#5 Any woman who denies owning a dildo has at least 5! in different colors.

SIX SEX SECRETS!

FOUND by Maurice Hunter
Chicago, IL

Hey—don't leave us hangin'—what's the #1?!
—DAVY

#4 After SEX we don't need to alway "snuggle" sometimes we want you to leave us the fuck alone

#3 One night stand sleep overs are never a good idea. Women don't It's better to leave wasted and remember us as hot with an awesome body & great tits!

#2 All women @ one point want to bang another Chick!

#1

37

FOUND by Danny

Delton, WI

Happy Fathers day to you, even thoug you told me I can't cook and the pie I made sucked.

MOTHER'S DAY

FOUND by Kate James

Davis, CA

Happy mothers day! and I hope you and me get to go to India!! Look AT The RAPING! I LOVE YOU A LOT!

38

David Antanaitis
Speech
November 23, 2005

Influences on Life

Everyone's life begins with the positive and negative influences they come across from time to time. It is how they look at and approach these influences that carry them on to their future. Many people have made an influence on my life, but there is nobody who has affected my life more than my step dad. When I was younger, my parents separated when I was in the third grade. I was then given custody to my mother and did not have a father figure in my life for quite sometime. It was very hard for me to deal with not having my father there, but I just kept my head up and didn't let it get to me. My mom would go on a date every now and then but she really never found anyone. Then, one day, this guy came to our house for dinner. At first I was kind of shady towards him cause I didn't know him very well at all, but then I got to know him and we began to get along very well. When he was growing up he didn't have a dad either. His dad passed away in his arms when he was just a little kid on the farm. So right from the start we had something in common. Jerry has always been very athletic, even to this day, and played many sports in high school. He would come over and we would play basketball out in the drive way and throw around the football. Before I knew it he was kind of like my dad. He would come to my basketball practices and help out with the team when the coaches would not be able to make it. At the time I was a little fat kid that was super slow and couldn't run fast even if you paid me. He would sit there and rip on me all day and just tell me how slow I was. "If you want to be a good athlete you have to be faster," he would say. Its just like when Jeri Truhill from Mercury 13 told her family that she wanted to be a pilot. Her father told her "Honey, girls don't fly airplanes, that's MENS work".

CONTINUED ON THE NEXT PAGE →

UP THE SIDELINE

FOUND by Lindsey Simard

Oshkosh, WI

this picture FOUND by Missy & Neff, Baton Rouge, LA

BEARS 61

39

After hearing that quote from my step dad it lit a fire inside of me to prove him wrong and show him that I could be fast and compete with kids my age. I think that it relates to my approach. Jeri worked hard and became what her father told her she could never be, a pilot. I did the same thing. I surrounded myself with the right friends, friends that would push me to run and lift. So my best friend and I would do just that, we ran and lifted everyday to become faster and stronger. With high school right around the corner, I was getting ready for the football season and my step dad was still ripping on me for being slow. The season was almost done and we were playing kettle moraine, a team that was highly respected in the Classic Eight Conference. The score was tied in the fourth quarter and they were punting the ball from their forty yard line. I was back to receive the punt when I saw it was a short punt. It took a big bounce and everyone told me to get away from it. I picked up the ball and turned on the jets up the sideline; nobody could catch me. I smoked everyone right up the sideline for the game winning touchdown. After the game, I was so happy. I couldn't wait to get home and tell my step dad that I out ran everyone on the sidelines to win the game. I got home and I walked right up to him and told him what happened and he just looked at me and said "see, all that ripping on you paid off." He was right, I took him telling me that I was slow and that I couldn't be fast and used it as fuel to make me work harder, just like all of the girls from mercury 13. They used everyone telling them they couldn't do something as fuel to make them work harder. Jerry didn't only influence me in sports, he also influenced me with making the right choices in life. He always told me, "if you want something to happen Davey, make it happen". That is a quote I live by now, cause when I want something to happen, I know it can happen if I really want it to. Last year I wanted to go deer hunting with my real

David Antanaitis
Speech
November 23, 2005

father and my mom was completely against it. She didn't want me going anywhere near my real father cause they do not get along and she doesn't want him and I to have anything to do with each other. So I asked jerry what to do and he told me "David if you want it to happen, Make it happen". So I sat down with my mom and talked to her about it. After a long talk and telling each other how we both felt about it, she said that I could go. I was real happy cause I got a chance to see my dad that I hadn't seen for about 2 years. It ended up being a great weekend, I didn't get the chance to shoot a deer but I got a chance to see my dad and spend some time with him. My step dad doesn't get along with my real dad at all but he still told me that it was a real good thing that I went up north that weekend. He always tells me that you only get one dad and you should try to spend as much time with him as you can cause he could be gone at anytime. Like I said before, my step dad lost his dad when he was real young, so he knows what it's like not to have a dad. I have a lot of respect for him to tell me to go see my dad even if he didn't like my real father. My step father is the one guy I know I can always go to if I were to ever need anything. He always is willing to do anything for anyone and will never put himself before anyone else. Growing up with him in my household has made the biggest influence on my life. Today I see my self doing the little things that he does. Jerry has rubbed off onto me. That's why I thank god that I was blessed with such a good step father. Not everyone is lucky enough to get a guy like him as a second father.

FOUND *Magazine*.
If you want something to happen, Davy, make it happen.

SEAT 29-E

FOUND by Alex Wagner
New York, NY

12-21-04
Flt# ___ / SDO → Houston
SEAT # 29E

RECEIVED
APR 13 2005
CUSTOMER CA__

Dear _____ Airlines,

I am disgusted as I write this note to you about the miserable experience I am having sitting in seat 29E on one of your aircrafts.

As you may know, this seat is situated directly across from the lavatory, so close that I can reach out my left arm and touch the door.

(2)

All my senses are being tortured simultaneously. Its difficult to say what the worst part about sitting in 29E really is? Is it the stentch of the sanitation fluid that's blown all over my body every 60 seconds when the door opens? Is it the wooosh of the constant flushing? OR is it the passengers asses that seem to fit into my personal space like a pornographic jig-saw puzzel?

(3)

I constucted a stink-shield by shoving one end of a blanket into the overhead compartment. while effective in blocking at least some of the smell, and offering a small bit of privacy, the ass-on-my-body factor has increased, as without my evil glare, passengers feel free to lean up against what they think is some kind of blanketed wall. the next ass that touches my shoulder will be the last!

④

I am picturing a board-
room full of executives
giving props to the young
promising engineer that
figured out how to squeeze
an additional row of seats
onto this plane by putting
them next to the LAV.

29E

I would like to flush his head
in the toilet that I am
close enough to touch from
my seat.
          ∧ and taste,

⑤

Putting a seat here was
a very bad idea. I just
heard a MAN GROAN in
there! THIS SUCKS!

29E

DEPICTION OF MANS BUTT IN MY
FACE.

Worse yet, I've paid over
$400.00 for the honor of
sitting in this seat!

⑥

Does your company give
refunds? I'd like to go
back where I came from
and start over. Seat 29E
could only be worse if it
were inside the bathroom.
was located

I wonder if my clothing
will retain the sanitizing
odor.... what about my hair!
I feel like I'm bathing in
a toilet bowl of blue liquid,
and there is no MAN in a
little boat to save me.
I am filled with a deep
hatred for your plane designer
and a general dis-ease that

⑦

May last for hours,

We are finally decending,
and soon I will be able
to tear down the stink-
shield, but the scars will
remain.

I suggest that you
initiate immediate removal
of this seat from all of
your crafts. Just remove
it, and leave the smouldering
brown hole empty, for a
good place for sturdy/non-
absorbing luggage maybe,
but not human cargo.

Signed, Passenger #29E

HURRICANE KATRINA FINDS

New Orlean 17 St Levee
74A
BOR-NO-
Depth 23.2/24.0   -05U
PB   10■20■05

this little tag FOUND by Abram Himelstein, New Orleans, LA

DAVY EXPLAINS:

*T*en days after Hurricane Katrina destroyed New Orleans, I drove into the city with my friend Abram, who teaches high school there, to try and rescue some treasured personal items that belonged to him and his family and friends, and also to check on the condition of some of his students who hadn't made it out before the storm. Roaming around town was one of the most eerie and surreal experiences I've ever had. The city, which had always been so alive and bustling, was now a ghost town, populated only by stray dogs and soldiers—a debris-strewn wasteland, cars and boats stuck in trees, buildings caved in.

*C*an you imagine the way a swimming pool, left unattended for months, might collect a layer of dead leaves on the surface? The streets of New Orleans, filled with rubble and sludge, had a similar layer on top, but this was all people's scattered possessions—toys and Nerf footballs and old photographs and letters and clippings from magazines and the Bible. Sifting through the mess, peeling apart the pictures and papers, revealed intimate glimpses into the lives of the people who'd been forced to flee by Katrina. Something about looking at this stuff—even the most ordinary homework assignments, love notes, and Polaroids—made the tragedy hit home for me. I began to comprehend the full magnitude of all that had been lost—not just people's stuff, but also their simple day-to-day existence in a place that had always been home.

this photo FOUND by Davy Rothbart, New Orleans, LA

OUR NEW WARD

FOUND by Adam Peltz

New Orleans, LA

Davy ♡

I know you are upset with me for making you stay for all the meetings ♡ I am sorry ♡ you But I'm doing this because I know what's best for our family. I am nervous too, even though you probably don't think I am. Sometimes meeting new people and making new friends can be really tough. But this is our new ward, and we will be here for a long time. It's important that we try our best to get to know people. Even though it's hard. I really do understand. But Heavenly Father wants this for us too, and he will help us if we let him. He loves you Davy, and so do I ♡

For those who returned to New Orleans, many had to move to other parts of the city since their old neighborhoods were uninhabitable. This find conveys a small sense of the post-Katrina difficulties. There's something especially striking about seeing a FOUND note with your own name on it!

—DAVY

photos on this page by Javan Makhmali

For Sale
RE/MAX
DEREK WESTLEY
908-3650
RE/MAX
real estate partners inc.
398-9900

45

A couple of months after Katrina, our FOUND Magazine tour brought us back through New Orleans, and it was buoying to see the city begin to get back on its feet.

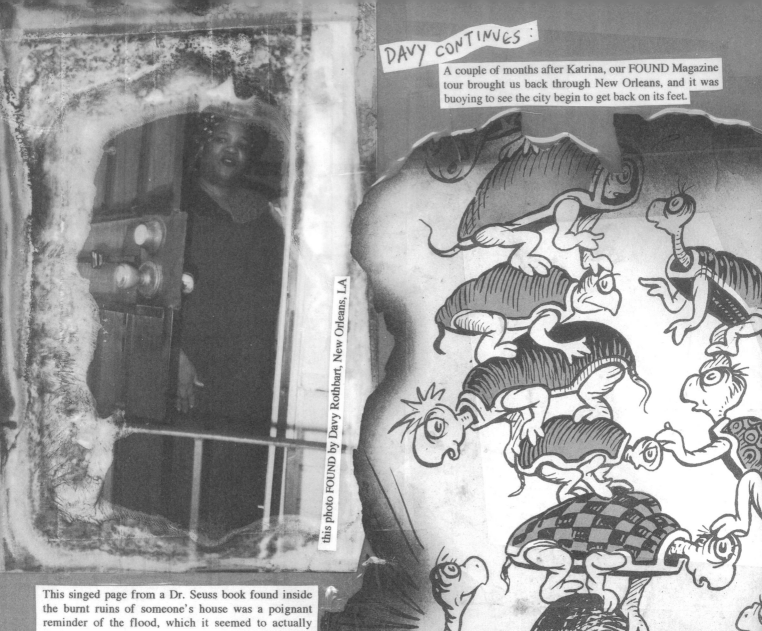

this photo FOUND by Davy Rothbart, New Orleans, LA

This singed page from a Dr. Seuss book found inside the burnt ruins of someone's house was a poignant reminder of the flood, which it seemed to actually depict. Meanwhile, a typical move-your-car parking note found on the street was the surest evidence that things in New Orleans were beginning to return to normal, though its talk of Yankees subtly voiced the concern felt by many residents that their city, in its revival, would undergo a demographic transformation.

this page from a Dr.Seuss book FOUND by Megan Harris

this photo by Javan Makhmali

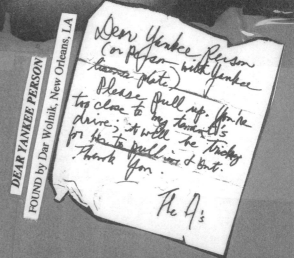

DEAR YANKEE PERSON
FOUND by Dar Wolnik, New Orleans, LA

Dear Yankee Person (or person with Yankee license plate.) Please pull up. You're too close to my tenant's drive; it will be tricky for her to pull in & out. Thank you.

The A's

THE NEW ME

FOUND by Princess Ramona

New Orleans, LA

Mom! Greetings from New
Orleans! I have a confession
to make. I didn't go on
vacation to party it up. Two
days ago I had some plastic
surgery done at Tulane - a
brow lift, lip job, ear tuck,
and some lipo in my backside.
It all went well although I'm
a bit sore and wonky on the
Vicodin. Dan always talked me
down about this stuff, but
now that he's out of the

picture, it seemed like a
good time to go for it.
Hope you like the new me
when I get back. ♡ Jen

Vicki Morrison
1207 Tyler Ave
Cincinnati, Ohio
45220

This postcard, stamped and ready to go, was found in my friend
Ramona's bike basket late one night. Jen's mom must have
been happy that her daughter escaped the hurricane safely, but
she must have had quite a surprise when she saw her!

— DAVY

47

I used to work at the House of Blues, and found this folded letter while sweeping up the stage after a Lil' Kim concert. I'm happy to see that its author made it in to the show and was close enough to toss this onstage; I'm just sorry Lil' Kim never got it.

—S.C.

March 24, 2003

Whats up Kim,

Hey its your nigga hitting you from Chicago, I wrote you a while back, but I dont know if you read it or not, but I know it didnt come back. Well if you aint get it oh well. My name is Elijah aka EJ. Ma I've been holding you down in Chicago. Every one been bumpin your shit. you did a good Job on your new C.D. You need to pat your self on the back, also give it up to "Bee Hive". Man I wish I could be on your promotion team or something. I'm a 22 year old electrician Local 134. But one day I will promote artists, give ideas for videos you know shit like that. Well enough with that Congratulations on your C.D. Its like you really felt me. I was wishing you and twista came with some shit. In a matter of fact today I saw Twista in Kenwood Liquors, him and his buddy money T, well when I rode up I was bangin thug luv that shit tripped me out. So when I went in I gave him his props, I live in the Jeffery Manor and twista is in the hood all the time.

Today is March 24, 2003 and you'll be at the House of Blues friday. I wanna come see you bad, but I have to work. I was going to take off but these white folks at work be trippin. Well I'm happy you did business with Styles and Swizz. Shut the game down baby especially that Hater EVE. She was cool at first, Then she just flipped her whole stello. But you 10 steps ahead of all those hoes. A I saw you on In The Basement. I hope you aint giving my love away to tigger! I'm Just Kidding ☺, You showed Chicago luv, Thanks! Plus you spoke on some good shit.

So you up on that illuminati, 666, New World Order shit? I think you are. Spit some knowledge about that, I wanna know what you think. But Kim my hand is starting to hurt plus I'm starting to get writers block. You are the Queen Bee fuck all the haters. Hey you know black folks always want something. If there is any chance you can hook it up for me to see you in concert?

Also before I leave I wanna say sorry about BIG my pops died March 9, 1987 on my 6th birthday so that a very special day for me too. So if your in Chicago and you wanna kick it

FOUND Magazine. Thanks for taking time out on your busy schedule to read this letter.

with your biggest fan and be on some real shit, then get in touch. Tell Hilliary & The Bee Hive keep that shit coming. Thanks for taking time out on your busy schedule to read this letter.

Love Ya
EJ
Chicago Luv

P.S Excuse me if I spelled some stuff wrong. I'm not dumb. Also I'm leaving you my telephone # and address Just in case you wanna shoot the shit.

Elijah Kennedy
322 E. 95th St.
Chicago IL 60617

773-993-71
or
773-242-97

49

FOUND by Johanna

Rochester, NY

I NEED A HAIRCUT.

illustration by Amy Thomas

ATHOMAS'05

4/29/99 Needs haircut

needs
hair
cut

4/5/99 Said he was Dracula — he + sister
adopted from Pennsylvania (Transylvania)
Adoptive mother pregnant with human
child asked if he told parents yes what
did they say — They were surprised

4/12/99 Told him that Dracula talk
was a good story — denied it a story
may have led him along — Said
if Dracula can make new baby
go away. — Pursue this

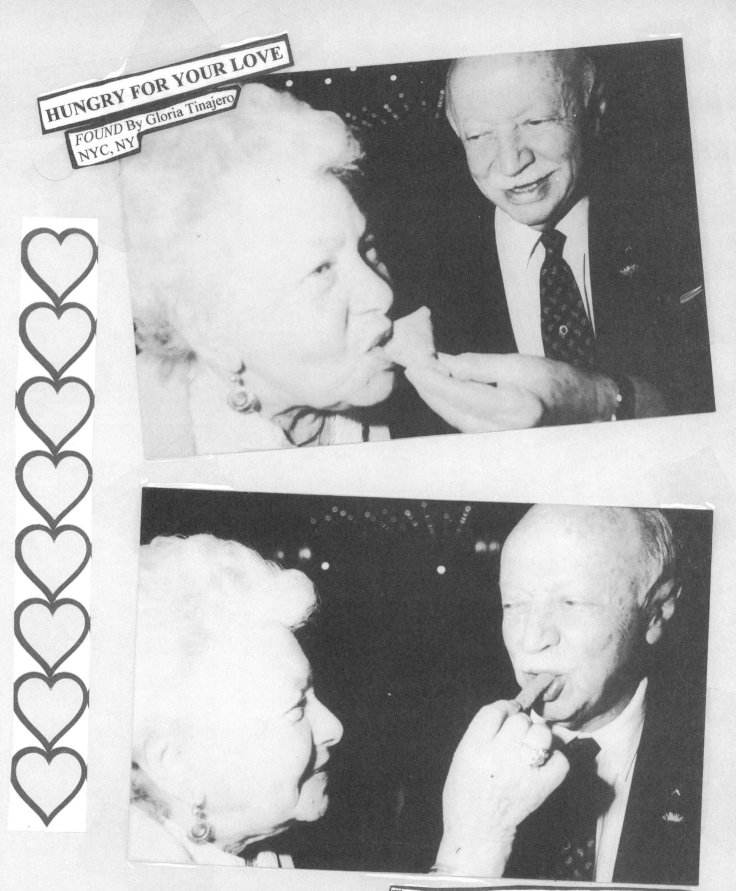

The new owner of a cottage style Bayside Queens apartment was going to throw everything out—furniture, clothing, etc. Gloria went there and pawed through some abandoned treasures. In a cigar box she found these photographs.

—DAVY

FOUND by Jason & Erica Muxlow

Chicago, IL

My whole family knowes about what me and my man... u know, and they let me stay with him.

Dats so cute. So what does he think is he sad cuz wut happened. ???

He doesn't know! He thinks I never was!! Shit, Girl are you gonna tell him.

My husband and I found this little note on the sidewalk outside a local corner store. Sounds like someone was pregnant and is now possibly hiding a secret about terminating the pregnancy.

—E.M.

this photo FOUND in an abandoned house by Colleen & Dave Errington, Toledo, OH

FOUND Magazine. Gritty drama.

Here is a Free ticket to the Thursday, Jan. 22nd performance of EMU's gritty drama, In the Blood.

We hope you can attend and enjoy the show!

Sincerely,
Billy, Angela, Dave, Misty, and Chris
... And Jesus.

52

JESUS LOVES YOU (AND WANTS YOU TO ATTEND A PLAY AT EASTERN MICHIGAN UNIVERSITY ON THURSDAY)

FOUND by Liz

at the Denny's on Washtenaw, Ann Arbor, MI

Dear Mrs. Dionne,

   I am so, so sorry about your husband. I want you to know that It was not my fault. I left Dragon's Tongue, Nick Trenkle and Dorn Walbridge did most of what was done. Andy is a great photographer. I saw you at the trial, and I wanted so terribly much to say something to you. To tell you how sorry I was. How sorry I am. I am so, so sorry.

Sincerely,
Mike McAfee

THE DRAGON'S TONGUE

FOUND by David O'Gorman

Gainesville, FL

This is one of the most cryptic, intriguing FOUND notes we've ever received. "Most of what was done..." *What* was done?? We may never know.

—DAVY

53

I work at a small independent movie theater called the *Tivoli*. One day someone put copies of this letter on every car in the surrounding parking lots. I wonder if Jenny ever found Derek, and if he wanted to be found.

—M.M.

Hi my name is Jenny. I am a long time Lee's Summit resident and I personally need your help. On November 26, 2004 I was having my bachelorette party at Denim and Diamonds. I met a guy named Derek and took him home with me. I had to cut my party short because he was married and had to be home by 3 or 4 am. I called him a lot after that first time and I know the wife answered at least once. We slept together again and I just knew I was in love and needed to be with him. I called him everyday and told him I needed to see him.

He said his phone was through work and was being taken away. He would get a new cell phone and call me back with the new number. I know he probably still wanted to call me but maybe didn't have my new cell phone number or lost my old number. I know he has a 5 year old kid and he was dark haired and rode bulls. Well if you know of such a guy please PLEASE call my new number at 816-354-12.... I know he has probably talked about me and is trying to find me.

You can also try my sister Veronica McKinney.

54

these pictures FOUND by Heather Cann, San Francisco, CA

FOUND Magazine. Rode bulls.

FRANTIC LANDLORD

FOUND by John Weidz   Toronto, Ontario

My girlfriend and I found these plastered up all over the place on our evening walk. What the hell is the story here? We couldn't come up with a single satisfying explanation. —J.W.

FOUND by Burns Waggener

San Antonio, TX

Jud:

I will make a deal with you:
Let me take you over to Bike World,
Broadway Bicycle Show or B and J and
we will look for and purchase for you
a nice bicycle you can ride and use
for transportation. You will find
that with a bicycle, you can ride
through most smaller areas, they
require little maintance on your part,
and most important, you do not have to
buy gasoline for bicycles, only foot
power and bicycle riding is good for
your health as well. Not only that
you do not need to buy license plates
and a vehicle inspection sticker each
year as well. Also you will need a
helmet even though it is still not a
state law in Texas but we are working
for a law like that regardless of age/.

illustration by Dan Tice

"2"

There are several types of bicycles
today such as the mountain bike like the
one you brought home and I had the
pleasure of test riding the bike
briefl6y if you remember, along with
xxxxxx hybrid bikes, and mountain bikes
come in both single and dual suspension
bikes as well as the famous rigid frame
bikes. You also can bring a bicycle
easily into your house instead of
parking the bike outside like you have

to with a car, I would like to see
someone try to bring a car into their
house and park the car right in their
living room, or where ever inside a
house. I have never owned a car in

"3"

my entire life and am not going to
start now and I am 54 years of age.
I did take drivers training in high
school because my mother and father
wanted me to and I took it to please
them yet I let it known to them I am
never going to own a car. Also with
a bicycle, you do not polute the
air and we are hearing more and more
on "the green house effect" and
"Global Warming" more and more these
days. There are times I wonder what
most Americans would do had Henry
Ford's mother and father never gotten
married or elected to have an
abortion. Americans nho doubt would
be much better off. Take care.

Alex

FOUND by Sam Miller and Jake Trimble

Salt Lake City, UT

The internet is worse than t.v. because if you fall asleep watching t.v. it's fine. But if you fall asleep at the computer. Your head will hit the keybored and the computer will start beeping at you and will wake you up. Also a computer screen is usualy smaller so you cant really see whats going on. Also computers can break alot easier. Another thing is that there is alot of bad stuff on the internet like pornography and stuff. Also the internet is way to confusing. The tv is alot easier to use cuz all that you have to do is push buttons. It is also alot of fun. It can also be a great time waster. Also in my opinion time seems to go by alot faster when whatching t-v. But the most important thing you cant watch family guy or simpsons online.

illustration by Dan Tice

57

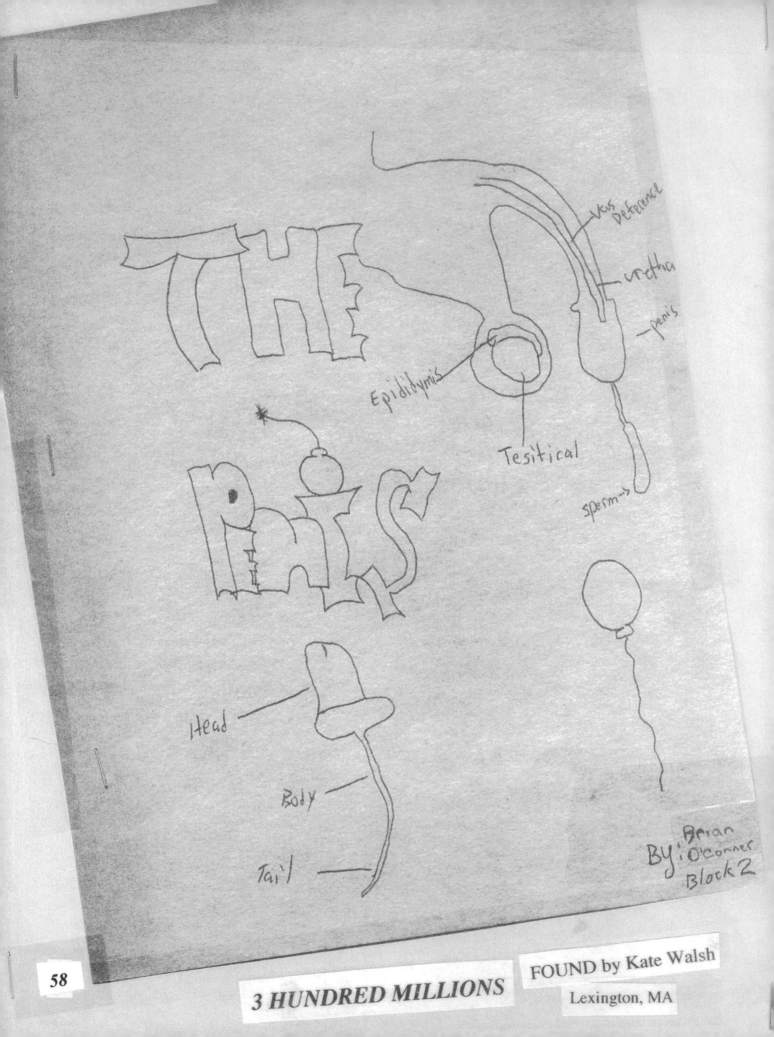

THE PENIS

Vas Deferance

urethra

penis

Epididymis

Tesitical

sperm→

Head

Body

Tail

By: Brian O'conner
Block 2

3 HUNDRED MILLIONS

FOUND by Kate Walsh

Lexington, MA

Brian

Table of Contents
Need Intro

Structure

The penis is a structure that helps to spurt out the sperm. Now I'm going to tell you all the things that help the penis, the scrotum is the soft sac of skin that covers the testicals and hold the testicals in place. The testicals are two ball which in the inside the testicals produces sperm The epididymis is a little muslee that on the top of a testical. The vas deferenec is a long skinny line which the can go threw. The semial vesical help the gall-bladder do it job which is to realese the urine. The penis looks like a lot of tissues produce into muslee which looks like along muslee.

confusing
need more

Brian   funtian

The penis lets out of a while sexual intercouse. This is how sperm goes threw a mans penis. First at puberty the brain tells the testicals to produce testoterone and sperm. Sperm travel to the epididymis where they mature and travel thought the vas deferenec, past the semial vesical and prostate glan though the urethra, and are spruted out the tip of the penis. The penis look like a lot of tissues put together that looks like a long muslee. Every day each an adult produces 3 hundred millions of sperm.

are you sure

Brian   connetion

It helps by produceing and leting out some sperm, and the things that help it are the organ that are inside of your body. Every thing help each other so that they can relate to each other, and help out.

Didn't tell the anything

Brian,
Your writing need a lot of work. This paper is confusing and doesn't say much

C-/D

59

11/3/05

Hey Grandma,
You crack me up. I'm going to be 20 years old in a couple months and my grandma is still sending me 5 bucks for Halloween. Hey, don't get me wrong. I appreciate it but seriously you don't have to. Honestly I would rather you sent me a letter telling me what you have been up to and how you are doing than 5 dollars. But thank you so much anyways. Looking forward to christmas in TC.

love
[signature]

↰ 5 ON IT FOUND by Beth Simon, Traverse City, MI

Poring through all the great finds that folks have sent in over the past few years, these three notes stood out as striking anomalies. We've received tons of FOUND notes in which kids beg their parents and relatives for money—this young man (left) says he'd really rather have a nice letter from his grandmother instead. Below, an extremely polite parking note among a sea of angry ones. We've also seen plenty of teachers, in these FOUND notes, reprimanding their students for being late or missing class. Here (opposite) the tables are turned.

—DAVY

Hey man, we were wondering if you could please move your car one car length back or into the driveway. It's difficult to maneuver our vehicles into our driveway since some have a bad turning radius and we don't want to accidently run into your car. Thanks

BAD TURNING RADIUS FOUND by Amy Brennan, Reno, NV

FOUND Magazine. You crack me up.

Dear Mark,

Since it is Friday and you haven't showed in the past 20 mins. The class divided to leave but we left you our papers. Which I think is a bad Idea, because you may never show and everyones paper's will be lost to the Janitor Staff

from

Chris H. + Class

P.S. Since there is test tuesday, I am very upset with you not showing. I will probably leave you an email for questions on the exams.

Sunday March 12, 2000

Dear Lilah:

Per our psychic conversation I am writing you to let you know that I am now aware, since I am writing you this letter, of your current address. You told me that you don't have a phone, so I guess it may be kind of hard for you to contact me by phone. At any rate, when you can, give me a call at 454-9987.

This is a rather difficult letter for me to write, since I haven't talked to you directly. I want you to know that I think that we have a very special relationship, one made in heaven. I have never been in touch with such a nice, sweet person.

A little history. The first and only time that I saw you was when you worked at Show and Tan Video in Dothan. This must have been three years ago. You struck me as the prettiest, sexiest girl that I have ever seen, and I never forgot you. I guess that it is just luck that God decided to put us together like he has. I know that you realize I call you "Sho-Tan", and I hope that it does not offend you. The only reason that I do this is because I didn't know your name for such a long period of time. **Lilah**, I am so happy to be able to write you a short letter, and I pray to God that this letter reaches you.

Monday I am going to try to contact the Department of Corrections for the state of Florida in hopes of finding a job somewhere in the state of Florida. I am counting on you going to my new job site with me. I hope that we can establish a relationship in time to allow us to get to know one another before it is time for me to leave. I hope that you will now seriously start to consider moving with me. I realize this may be a little premature on my part. Please excuse me.

I am going to cut this letter short. I have more to say but I will do so in the next letter. Goodbye my sweet girl and please call me as soon as possible.

Your psychic friend and love,

Rob

Mom —

6/76

This is not the best shot of Fred, but what can you expect after a party. This was taken the night that you called and Jimmy, Sam, Fred we were all doing it up. Remember?

It will still give you an idea what my baby looks like.

FOUND by Jared Mark

Brooklyn, NY

TO DO

~~Sam~~

How To Improve My Self Confidence

1. Dress for success
2. ~~Consciences~~ of voice
3. Watch & follow role models
   a. Watch Joe Pesci
   b. Watch star
4. Identify other self confident role models in the business & write them down
5. Maintain eye contact w/ everyone I get to.

"FUNNY LIKE I'M A CLOWN? I AMUSE YOU?"
FOUND by Christopher Kostrzak, Los Angeles, CA

GUEST LIST   FOUND by Dan Zatkovich, Lansing, MI

St Joan of Arc
St Nicholas
Scooby Doo
Bambi
Pope
~~Jesus~~
Scrooge
Father Ed
~~pastor of et~~

63

book (not real)
fairytale

FOUND by Nina Vlanin

San Francisco, CA

Miss Greta Gahler
228 Bingham
San Francisco,
Calif.

...rton.

I found this 1932 letter while Dumpster-diving many years ago and it has become a keepsake. It speaks of a gentle, bygone era but is filled with playfulness and even a touch of mischief. Greta Gahler was a minor radio star of the time.

—N.V.

Wednesday night

Darling!

Well here we are, having arrived about 3 o'clock, made our beds, had a few drinks (don't tell Helen), etc. Everything is going swell so far, and Al and I have been quite loquatious. I'll tell you one of our subjects later. About 5 we went to the store, and bought some provisions and for dinner we had oodles of steak, potatoes and fried onions. Al cooked them and he's a swell cook. Then we came up stairs and listened to Cecil and Sally. ~~to one~~ You were swell, darling; I was quite proud of you — and, by the way, Al tells me that Dan was ribbing you this morning when he told you you were lousy. Al claims he ~~prob~~ probably didn't even listen to the skit.

And now, here is one of the subjects Al preached to me about. Sexual intercourse between you and I. He recommends it ~~highly~~highly and he says that he and Helen are both agreed that we should do it whether married or not. — We'll discuss the problem when you arrive. But don't tell Helen I said anything about it. However, you might pump Helen as to her opinions on the subject.

I hope you can read this letter. This business of writing by hand is terrible. And consequently this letter is going to be very short. But believe me, I'll make up for it when you get here! Even though this isn't such a hot letter I be thinking long and hot thoughts about you when I go to bed tonight. I sure love you darling, and I'm praying for you to keep loving me. Be a good girl, darling, and think of me as much as I'm thinking of you. Good night sweetheart.

Ralph

X

BIGGER IS BETTER

FOUND by Sara Todd

Louisville, KY

Dear People of FOUND Magazine:

I found this letter in the parking lot of my local Walgreen's here in Louisville, Kentucky. It was on the ground next to my car and when I first saw it, I immediately thought of your magazine & when I opened it up it was better than I ever expected! I don't remember the date I found it — sometime in late July 2004. I thought it was hilarious when I read it but & I felt a little bad that Kristy might miss the opportunity to meet with Dan and also have, well, read on...

Thanks!

—Sara Todd
Louisville, KY

KRIS
READ

PLEASE
HELP YOUR
SELF TO
THIS NICE
WOOD!

NICE WOOD
FOUND by Jonathan Greenbank
Liverpool, England

Changing Attitudes About Sex

Until the mid-1900's, most people did not openly talk about sex. The subject was masked in giggles, blushes, and "dirty stories." Today, however, sex is much more frequently discussed as a normal part of human life.

Hi Kristy, I had to go back home before I planned. Just wanted to tell you I met a guy at the bar last night. HE HAS THE biggest COCK I HAVE EVER SEEN. I remember you telling me how DAVE doesn't satisfy you and how you dream about being with a MAN that is well hung. It is not only long but it is thick to. Belt down a few drinks and give him a call. His # is 381-52... Ask for DAN. Don't pass up on your dream. I had the most intense orgasm in my life. Call me and let ME know how it went.

Love ya
Steffany

FOUND Magazine.
Don't pass up on your dream.

66

SAP

In Memory of Edgar

I'm so sorry for the loss of your chameleon, Edgar. Losing a pet is always difficult, regardless of their size or age. Edgar was lucky to have such a loving home while he was with you.

Please let me know if there's anything I can do for you.

Take Care —

Jacey

OP PICK-UP LINE

UND by Christopher Westcott

Los Angeles, CA

IN MEMORY OF EDGAR
I found this in the freezer in our garage—I'm not sure how it got there. The sympathy for such a small animal is really cool, & I wish more people were nice like this.

—J.C.

I Dont Know you But I like you call me My Number is 911 thanks have a good day. Jimmy

Poodle! dooodle!

Small Changes

DAVY ROTHBART
FWND!
3455 CHARING CROSS RD.
ANN ARBOR, MI 48108

Poodle Doodle

this drawing FOUND by Kelly Frazer, Taipei, Taiwan

PRO

Gentleman
handsome
great with kids
very active
trustworthy
saves money

CON

sometimes wussy
knows it
doesn't want kids
But tennis?
but doesn't trust me
kind of a tight ass

THE

GOOD good in bed

polite great kisser
Kind
good gift giver
thoughtful
funny
considerate

BAD

continued good - complains too much
- Kind of grumpy
- doesn't brush as much as I want him to.
- has to be guided in his bathroom cleanup.
- sometimes smokes
- too comfortable in his small town
- I am "not his type"
- afraid of marriage

- think I am too bossy
- makes too many analogies between Brenda and I and he and Nate
- may not like my mom

CONTINUED BAD

FOUND by Stephanie Y.

Hillsdale, NJ

I found this note folded on a counter in a Laundromat.

—S.Y.

this photo FOUND by Sarah Arteaga, Conway, AR

FOUND Magazine knows it.

THE MEN IN THE TRUCK

FOUND by Karen Turner

Royal Oak, MI

Take BACK the Bimbo's Mailbox!

5 AUGUST 2005

HELLO "FOUND MAGAZINE"!,

WE SAW YOU ON A LITTLE SEGMENT ON I THINK, CNN, NEWS THIS AFTERNOON AND I THOUGHT YOU MIGHT LIKE THE FOLLOWING FOR YOUR MAGAZINE:

SOME MONTHS BACK I DID A HOUSE CLEANING OUT AND DECIDED THAT INSTEAD OF A GARAGE SALE I WOULD JUST DONATE EVERYTHING TO ONE OF THE CHARITIES. IT WAS NOT SALVATION ARMY BUT I WON'T SAY WHO IT WAS. I PUT EVERYTHING ON THE PORCH IN CLEAR VERY LARGE PLASTIC BAGS ABOUT 30 OF THEM! ON EACH PLASTIC BAG I PUT A LARGE PIECE OF PAPER WITH THE CHARITYS' NAME. WHEN I GOT HOME FROM WORK.....MY VERY LARGE WOODEN MAILBOX, THAT WASN'T IN A LARGE CLEAR PLASTIC BAG & DIDN'T HAVE A LARGE PIECE OF PAPER WITH THEIR NAME ON IT, WAS GONE!!!

SO! I GOT ON THE PHONE AND CALLED THEM, EXPLAINED WHAT HAPPENED AND SHE SAID SHE'D CALL THE MEN IN THE TRUCK AND HAVE THEM BRING IT BACK OR CATCH THEM IN THE MORNING.

THE NEXT DAY, WHEN I GOT HOME FROM WORK, THERE WAS MY LARGE WOODEN MAILBOX ALL BACK SAFE AND SOUND!

THAT EVENING MY HUSBAND TOOK OUR LABRADOR FOR A WALK. A FEW HOUSES AWAY ... AT THE CURB ....HE SPOTTED A YELLOW POST-A-NOTE AND COULDN'T RESIST PICKING IT UP. IT SAID:

"TAKE BACK BIMBOS' MAILBOX!"

YOU CAN HAVE THE NOTE...FOR I'LL NEVER FORGET IT HAHAHA....I HAD TO LAUGH AT IT BUT MY HUSBAND IS STILL LIVID ABOUT IT AND THE KIND OF GUY WHO ALWAYS WILL BE LIVID ABOUT IT! NOW I ONLY CALL ON "SALVATION ARMY" FOR CHARITABLE PICK UPS.

MOST SINCERELY,
Karen
KAREN TURNER

PS..WHY DO I STILL HAVE THE NOTE? I THOUGHT IT WAS WORTHY OF MY SCRAPBOOK. HAHA

Are you a pirate?

Do you enjoy swashbuckling, plundering, and generally being a scourge of the seven seas? Then you're probably not interested in renting a room in a two bedroom apartment for only 400 bucks a month, deposit is just two hundred and fifty, all the utilities are paid for, its within walking distance of a grocery store, next to seven buslines, and there four different ethnic restaraunts in the area! That and the guy looking for the roommate isn't a jerk. Seriously, I've ran polls on this and people have confirmed I'm not a jerk. If your interested call 742-71 , if you just want to give me money for some reason, call 742-71 . If you just want to cuddle, call someone else.

SWASHBUCKLING ROOMMATE
FOUND by Mike DiBella, Philadelphia, PA

this drawing FOUND by Janelle Parsons, Prague, Czech Republic

FOUND Magazine. Scourge of the seven seas.

70

— E.D.J.

Later editions of this flyer contained the word "cancer" after "breast."

October is Breast Awareness Month.
****
In recognition of this, the Work Life Council is sponsoring on-site mammograms for the third consecutive year.
****

MAMMOGRAM SIGNUPS
September 24, 25, & 26
11:30 – 1:00
Atrium

Dates for Mammograms:
October 7
October 22
October 23
December 4
****

State Farm Group Insurance:
Age 35-39 One baseline mammogram
Age 40+ One per calendar year

Group Health Plan:
One baseline mammogram per calendar year after age 35.
Participants should contact GHP for prior authorization if they've had a mammogram in the past 12 months.

For questions, contact: Ka_____ ___tha_ ___ ___ Kath___ ___
Work ___e Council Mem___ __s

— DAVY

Two excuses are always better than one!

TODAY IS MY GRANDMOTHERS 100 BIRTHDAY

AND

THERE IS A RACOON IN MY BATHROOM.

WILL OPEN AT 3PM

Thanks

"Dude, how are we gonna find some girls to hang out with? Wait, I know!"

— DAVY

Sugar Dady

Looking For Roommit
Luissianna and TRumbll
free For femite
free Rent and utilites
for More INF call
sugar Dady at 713-2__

H.P. Entertainment

○ Make some real

Summer $$$$$$

H.P. ENT. is conducting its 1st annual *LATINA Model* search in the L.A. County. Are *you, your sister, cousin or friend 18 years or older* and look good in a *swimsuit, jeans, small tops, &/or shorts* this is for you.

Come to our *Bar-B-Q* in Cudahy **Sunday June 13th 2004** from 12 noon to 9 pm, we will have *Scouts* from <u>H.P. Entertainment</u> on location, <u>FREE</u> food and drinks.

Must have a California Picture I.D.

RSVP:
Tevis @ 310) 366-98__
E-mail: _____
Brandon @ 323) 485-79__
E-mail: _____

Please leave boyfriends, haters, and CB's at home.
There will be Security (off duty COPS) on site.

Underground Reciprocals
716 N. Fifth Avenue
ste. 21   thousand Oaks,
Ca 92092

Daforce is a new and up coming rap star who'll be around for a
very long time. You see Daforce has a great free-styling
abillity and knows how to motivate the crowd by any means
necessary. His musical career is on a uprise rapidly, Daforce
has a very unique style and can't be compared to anyone. He has
opened up for acts like Too Short, who he has respect's,
Redman and keith Murray, Biz Markie....You probably can hear all
the different influences in his music.Hip Hop is a great form
of art and needs to keep growing, first run DMC came along and
blew it up, Rakim, Kane, P.E. Now we have Snoop, Naughty,Tupac,
Busta, West side connect,Hip Hop has been taken to a next level.
Now Daforce is going to continue the legacy. After hearing the
poverty and riches cd, you will have no choice but to agree that
the 1st step has all ready been taken. da luv of money will have
no problems getting airplay, so don't be fooled lets see, you'll
trip on how different it is, taste the flavor. Daforce is a new
a addition to hip hop. Blazed is a song only a few can understand
you might have to look through your 3rd eye. The year 2020 is a
futeristic song,and what's the racket is about those fake mc's
who take away the realness that the brothas be trying to kick.
Most of the album was a challenge for Daforce, because his boy
jayze had made a $500 bet that he wouldn't be able to freestyle
on the Ep, which he lost the bet.Daforce knows the streets are
wild and you better know your shit and back it up if you preach.
Music does funny things to people, everything you've ever ate
i am sure didn't taste great the first time you taste it,
some how down the road it's all good, trust me.

CONTINUING THE LEGACY

FOUND by Jason Henn

Richmond, IN

This odd press release was mailed to me six years ago. Sadly, it's the only correspondence I ever received from Underground Reciprocals.

—J.H.

Lucas Richards

illustration by Lucas Richards

I found this note in a trailer on a property belonging to my employer, Big Sur Land Trust. A squatter had illegally taken up residence there before we bought the property, and when we did, my boss wanted the now-empty trailer hauled to the dump. Inside was tons of rat shit, dirty dishes, rotted clothes, and a pitted drug-cooking spoon that I washed and use to this day. I felt bad for whoever the occupant had been, especially when I found this note among the feces and junk.

—S.D.

DEAR ADAM AND KRISTY,
I KNOW YOU ARE PROBABLY SURPRISED TO HEAR FROM ME. IT HAS BEEN A LONG TIME. I AM IN BIG SUR, CALIFORNIA RIGHT NOW. I HAVE TRIED TO CALL AT THE RIGHT TIMES, MAYBE GRANDMA HASN'T BEEN HOME AS MUCH.
I REALLY MISS YOU GUYS A LOT. YOU HAVE GROWN SO MUCH, I KNOW, MY FEELINGS ARE BETTER FOR RIGHT NOW I DON'T HEAR THE SAD VOICES AS MUCH.. I FEEL THAT YOU GUYS REALLY ARE AT HOME SAFE - WITH YOUR FATHER. I hope THAT THIS IS TRUE. I HAD ANOTHER DREAM. I HAD A DREAM THAT I WAS IN A BIG COLLISIUM OUTSIDE. LIKE A PLACE WHERE PEOPLE GO TO WATCH A LIVE CONCERT OR SHOWING. I KEPT HEARING YOUR VOICES BUT I COULDN'T SEE YOU. THEN I REALIZED THAT YOU WERE IN A PLACE UNDERGROUND THAT WAS UNDER WHERE THE PEOPLE STOOD TO WATCH THE SHOWING. IT WAS HARD TO FIND YOU GUYS OVER THE LOUD CROWD, BUT I DID.

I am not myself. I have become Vincent, an old classmate of mine from highschool and am appearing on television as part of a preview for an upcoming blockbuster film. On the screen, I am wearing a white suit there is grease in my hair and I am surrounded by a circular pattern of computer animated stars.

Watching the television is a six-foot tall banana with arms and legs sitting in a straight-backed timber chair. The banana stares on in silence, gets up stiffly and walks out the door.

HOLLYWOOD DREAM

FOUND by Chris Sullivan

Toronto, Ontario

I work at a large record store in downtown Toronto. We regularly find strange notes and lists that have been left behind; this one appeared today.

—C.S.

illustration by Dan Tice

Feb 12th 97

Dear Sir, Madame

I am returning this book to you, as I ~~stole~~ it from you in the first place. Since I've read DIANETICS my life is changing for the better.

Thank You

Ryan S. ~~Grant~~

Edwards/Randolf

12:57 - 1:06
Offered a better deal than ~~asked for~~
Very nice and precise
Not ~~busy~~, 1 car
Area clean
Bag on speaker holding together?
Speed below average - car in front at window ~~speaker~~ for at least 3 minutes
Less than a minute with me - Very good
Very nice all around

I

4

76

THE COOLEST THING I EVER SAW

FOUND by Maurice Reeder   San Pedro Sula, Honduras

I was on a city bus on the outskirts of town when the guy in this picture climbed on board. I was sitting near the front, but my Spanish isn't too good, so I couldn't totally follow the conversation between this guy and the driver. They started arguing, maybe over the amount for bus fare or something. Things got really heated really fast, and suddenly the guy in this picture pulled a two-foot machete out of his belt and started waving it around menacingly in the air. In a flash, the driver produced an enormous bullwhip, turned halfway toward the machete guy, and whipped the whip with a sizzling crack, snapping the blade right out of the guy's hand, *and all of this while still steering the bus!*

Finally he pulled the bus over; there was a brief scuffle and both guys crashed to the floor, and then the machete guy plucked up his machete and dashed off the bus. The driver dusted himself off and got back behind the wheel with surprisingly little fanfare from the rest of the passengers, which made me wonder if this was a commonplace occurrence. I noticed that a few papers and pictures from the machete guy's breast pocket had scattered into the aisle—I kept this little passport shot of the guy himself, a souvenir of the coolest thing I ever saw.

—M.R.

COAST

FOUND by Paula Hatfield
San Francisco, CA

COAST for
next 6 months

I found this card in the gutter outside my apartment. It struck me as odd that someone would need to write a note reminding himself to chill out. Then it occurred to me that instead he was limiting himself to just six months of coasting before getting his act together. Then I flipped it over and saw that it was written on the back of a business card for a marriage counselor. What kind of advice is that?   —P.H.

LIL JIN(
I'm in CYOTIE
(CROSS STREET

GETTÍN
WASTED!

NAAA! J I'M CALLIN

YOU CUZ IT'S 1:00

GETTIN' WASTED

FOUND by Sue Eggen
Pittsburgh, PA

Found (then lost)

Often, at our FOUND events, folks tell me about something amazing they once found, and then they say, "Yeah, it would've been perfect for *FOUND Magazine*, I wish I hadn't tossed it." This kind of conversation always twists a knife in my heart—it's thrilling to hear about the find, but disappointing that the original find is gone.

Melissa Gardner, from Washington, D.C., told me about some favorite finds which have passed through her hands over the years. Since she no longer has the originals, she offered to at least draw some pictures of them and share her remembrances!

—DAVY

This Note

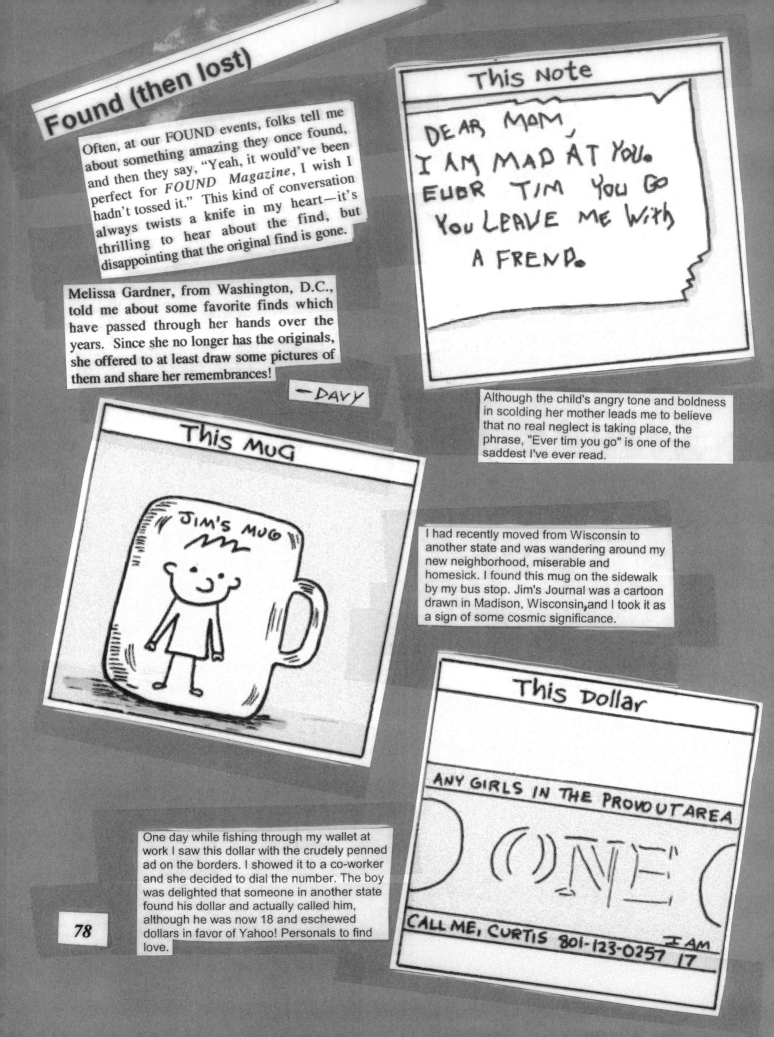

DEAR MOM,
I AM MAD AT YOU.
EUOR TIM YOU GO
YOU LEAVE ME WITH
A FREND.

Although the child's angry tone and boldness in scolding her mother leads me to believe that no real neglect is taking place, the phrase, "Ever tim you go" is one of the saddest I've ever read.

This MUG

JIM'S MUG

I had recently moved from Wisconsin to another state and was wandering around my new neighborhood, miserable and homesick. I found this mug on the sidewalk by my bus stop. Jim's Journal was a cartoon drawn in Madison, Wisconsin, and I took it as a sign of some cosmic significance.

This Dollar

ANY GIRLS IN THE PROVO UT AREA

ONE

CALL ME, CURTIS 801-123-0257 I AM 17

One day while fishing through my wallet at work I saw this dollar with the crudely penned ad on the borders. I showed it to a co-worker and she decided to dial the number. The boy was delighted that someone in another state found his dollar and actually called him, although he was now 18 and eschewed dollars in favor of Yahoo! Personals to find love.

78

This Notebook

This was an amazing tome I found in college. The notebook consisted entirely of back and forth notes between a couple, chronicling the entire relationship from beginning to end, not to mention all the highs and lows in between. In fact, every event was so diligently recorded ("Oh My God! I can't believe we actually did it last night!!!") that my friends and I wondered if it was actually a work of fiction. Eventually we decided it was legitimate -- the scribbled letters full of tears, trauma and typos were just too genuine.

This Porcupine Fish

I found this weird, lacquered fish at a garage sale. I guess it was kind of gross to keep the brittle blown-up carapace of a fish around, but it fascinated me for some reason. I kept it on a shelf for years until I accidentally dropped it and it shattered into a million piecces.

This Polaroid

Other enthusiasts may argue whether or not this old Polaroid of a girl theatrically sucking on a joint while being calmly observed by a mellow-eyed hippie is a true FOUND Item. One, because I found the Polaroid in my mom's drawer, and two, because the mellow-eyed hippie is my dad.

Melissa Spence Gardner

China's Flag was adopted in 1949. The large star and four small stars stand for the Communist Party and its members.

The State Emblem of China is framed by wheat and rice, the nation's leading agricultural products.

I hear a lot of fantastic stories from folks who've got FOUND pets—discovered at the park, in the street, in junkyards, in Dumpsters, at the beach. There's a common thread to all of these stories, this sense that their pet is all the more precious because of how it came into their lives. They didn't just go to the pet store, they *found* this animal, or in a sense maybe their pet found them. It's like they were guided together. The serendipity seems to make it sweeter. And by finding their dog or cat or ferret or iguana and taking them in, they've rescued them from a bleaker, uncertain situation. No surprise, I love these kinds of stories.

So when I first talked to Kathleen Lavey, a newspaper writer in Lansing, Michigan, and she told me that she had two FOUND *daughters*, I was riveted. Here's the conversation we had:

Davy: Wow! So, where were your daughters found?

Kathleen: Both of my girls are adopted from China, and both were found abandoned on the street. My older daughter, Julianna Xisi, was left under a bush by the gates of an orphanage; my younger daughter, Ella Yuemei, was left on the sidewalk of a busy street.

Davy: Who found them?

Kathleen: An orphanage worker found Julianna, and Ella was found by a passerby on their way to work in the morning. China started their one-child-only policy in 1979. As I understand it, in many segments of Chinese culture—if you only have one child—you want a son. A son carries on your family's ancestral line. If you have a daughter, she has no obligation to support you in your old age. For peasants and small-town folks, it's especially important to have someone to look after you when you're old. Sons are better; that's what people want. A lot of baby girls are abandoned. Typically, mothers will drop their babies off in high-traffic areas and even hide out and watch to make sure someone finds them. A lot of them are left near orphanages, police stations, and hospitals.

Davy: When were your daughters found?

Kathleen: Julianna was found on January 2nd, 2000, she was plucked out of the bushes, reeled in from the cold. She'd clearly just been born the night before, New Year's Day. Now she's five years old, about to start kindergarten. Ella is three. Ella was found in a box on the street, wrapped up in a little cloth, a little packet of powdered milk in the box beside her. She was already ten days old when she was found, which makes her story a little murkier. Stirs up a lot of questions.

Davy: Yeah—what were those ten days like for her mother? Trying to decide what to do, maybe terribly torn? It's intense. Do you ever wonder what it was like for this young mother to leave her baby behind?

CHINA

CHINA is a huge country in eastern Asia. It is the world's largest country in population and the third largest in area. About a fifth of all the people in the world live in China. The country covers more than a fifth of Asia. Only Russia and Canada have more territory. China's vast land area includes some of the world's driest deserts, highest mountains, and richest farmland.

Chinese families traditionally valued sons far more than daughters. A husband could divorce his wife if she failed to give birth to sons. In some cases, daughters were killed at birth because girls were considered useless. Today, girls as well as boys are valued. This change came about partly because the Communist government strongly supports the idea that women should contribute to the family income and participate in social and political activities. Women do many kinds of work outside the home. Many young husbands share in the shopping, housecleaning, cooking, and caring for the children to show that they believe the sexes are equal. However, equality between the sexes is more widely accepted in the cities than in the countryside.

Kathleen: Every freakin' day! You know, the anonymity factor is a big reason why a lot of people adopt from China—there's no chance the parents will ever materialize and come looking to claim their kids. It's supposed to ease the anxiety and concerns about who the birth mother is. But it's had the opposite effect on me. I think about Ella's birth mother, and those ten days, and I feel such a kinship with her. It's hard to get my head around it. I love her, too. She gave her baby an opportunity in a culture where abortion is encouraged. Maybe she couldn't afford her, maybe there were social pressures, but I appreciate her generosity, going through with it, giving birth. I feel a kinship with her that transcends everything. Julianna's mother, too. These are the kids' other mothers. There's a little ritual I started with the girls, before they could even read and write. At church there's a place where you can write down prayers—so, we've been writing prayers for their birth mothers, for their health and safety, to let them feel our love.

Davy: Think you guys will ever go to China and visit the town where they were found?

Kathleen: We're planning to go. In five years, I think, when they're eight and ten; they'll be old enough by then to comprehend it all and remember it, but not teenagers yet, calling out what's great and what sucks. I've got the address where Ella was found. It's not her mother's house or anything, just a random building on a busy street. We'll go visit that address, check out that square of sidewalk where she was found.

A lot of us adoptive parents who've taken in kids from China are, well, okay, a bit over-educated and neurotic. And it's a question: what's the best way to preserve the kids' cultural identity? One way is language. Starting this fall, we're all learning Chinese together. All those years in college I struggled through Spanish—but Spanish was easy it turns out!

One thing I've heard is that the word we translate as "abandoned" in regard to these kids is more precisely translated as "placed in order to be found." Here's the way I hope all of this will make sense to my daughters when they grow up—they were born in a very poor place by people who couldn't take care of them; by the seeming randomness of being left somewhere and then stumbled over—*found*—they ended up growing up here in Michigan, with me.

We're all very lucky.

Kathleen Lavey with Julianna and Ella

SMELLING THE SNEAKERS

FOUND by Richard Wilson

Portland, ME

I would Like to Smell the Altarboys Sneakers and boots that did the Altarservice on January 7, 1995 At saint PAUL's church in Portland. I think that the Altarboys Name is Victor. I think he is a neat guy. I Realy do Like him alot

these pictures FOUND by Connie Launuen. Normal, IL

Have you ever done something that seemed weird to everyone else because you knew it was what God wanted?

PART OF HIS PLAN

FOUND by Sam England

Urbana, IL

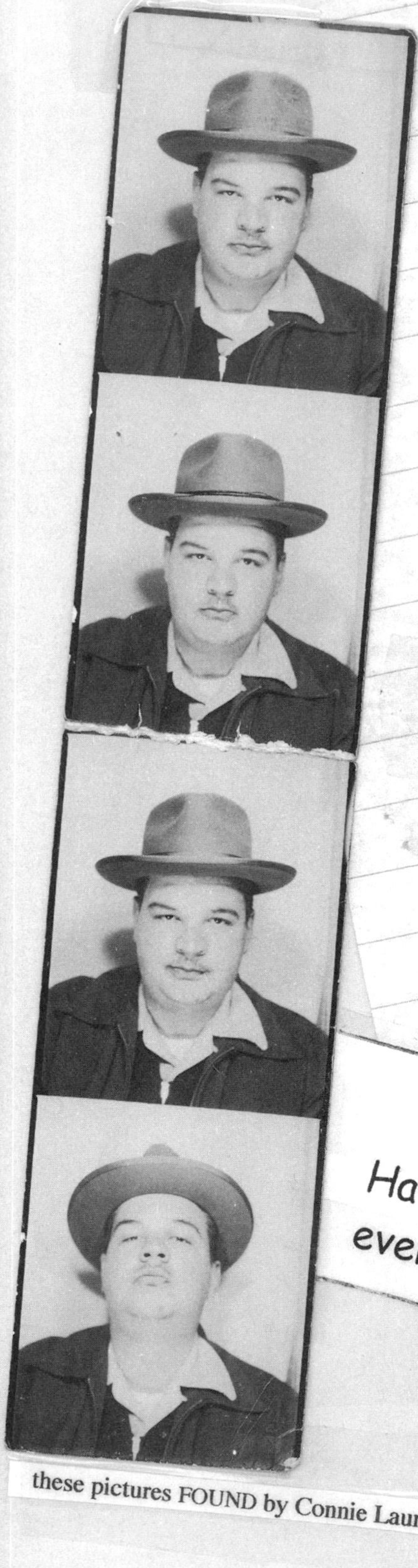

Dear God,
I'd like to say thankyou
for all you've done for
me and did just like to
ask you to help me have
a great day tommorrow
going down the water slides and
help me have a journey at
the end of the day to
Australia. Amen

A. THOMAS

illustration by Amy Thomas

83

MR. PERFECT

FOUND by Jerry Riddle

Denver, CO

Found this in a copy machine. I'm amazed by the idea of such a list going up to 291!   —J.R.

257) Will make love in a car

258) Looking for plain, old fashioned security

259) Immensely attracted to me physically by the tone of my voice, the scent of my perfume, the touch of my skin when our hands accidently brush

260) Must be patient, understanding and easy-going

261) Doesn't care how long it takes to bring me to the state of sexual extasy that his own sexual natures crave

262) loyal and loving partner, someone who values security.

263) Truly believes that best relationships are often those which takes longer to start off but become more and more contented as the years go by.

264) Who is independent but unlikely to stray for the sake of a fling with someone else.

265) Gentle, caring honest soul who truly believes in the sanctity of home and marriage, of permanent relationships, of living happily ever after.

279) Does not have the Peter Pan syndrome

280) Determined to get what he wants

281) Does not settle for someone he doesn't feel will be there for keeps

282) Enjoys a challenge

283) Not a loner

284) Loving father, uncle etc...

285) Leave no stone unturned to discover what is going to make me happy

286) Be able to turn my gloomy moments into laughter

287) Does not rush headlong into a relationship without thinking about the morrow

288) Senses what makes me tick

289) Not selfish in bed

290) Takes care of his responsibilities

291) Hates the idea of break ups and divorce

292)

DEAR ADAM SANDLER

FOUND by Gulliver Gold

Nashua, NH

When Gulliver moved into a house close to Manchester, New Hampshire—Adam Sandler's hometown—he discovered a drawer full of letters written to the movie star. Had the star of *Billy Madison, Big Daddy,* and *Happy Gilmore* been the previous tenant? Turns out it was a completely unrelated Adam Sandler who'd been receiving fan mail for years. I find these letters—in their openness, sweet hopefulness, and sheer presumptuousness—to be oddly touching. —DAVY

Dear Mr. Sandler:

My Name is Phil Klein and I am from Coopersville, a small city in Michigan. I recently graduated from Central Michigan University with a degree in Education and some background in broadcasting. I have enjoyed all of your work from SNL to all of your work on the big screen. I write you today for you help and advice on a movie script that I have recently completed. The movie is a combination of Days of thunder meets Joe Dirt, with a little Waterboy and Happy Gilmore attitude. To tell you the truth the main character, "Rusty Civor" will be one of the biggest icons in the near future. I have a felling that Happy Madison Productions might dig this one.

I am currently an unemployed teacher in California and trying to live out a dream of mine since a child. Instead of college I should have tried out for Second City. I figured I would do something with my time away from work instead of nothing. I know you have been involved in the writing process of many comedies in the past, which is why I am sending this information on to you. I would like you to take a look at the work that I have completed. To tell you the truth I don't know where to start. I am about to head to Hollywood blind and hit every agent and movie studio that I can locate. I would like your opinion on what I should do as the next step to sell the script.

I am a very enthusiastic and energetic person who is full of originality. I look forward to starting a career in the movie industry. Enclosed is a copy of the movie script on a disk. If you would be so kind to review the script and notify me on what has to be done to get this in Hollywood. I am clueless on the next step of the process after writing the script. You can contact me at anytime by phone (831-778-63___ ___) or by e-mail (_____@hotmail.com) Thank you in advance for your interest and consideration. Any help would be grateful.

Sincerely,

Phillip M. Klein

MR. ADAM Sandler
5420 Worster Ave
VN, CA. 91401

9140145431

Dear Adam Sandler,
    I am one of your b1 biggest
Fans I am writing you a
Letter because we are doing a
big School project.
    we are writing letters to
People to ask for ther
help. Do you have any missing
Socks? we think everyone
Loses a sock and we
wonder where they go!
Please send me a sock
that you can't find the
mate for. Also, we are
trying to help the homeless
people in our area with
this project because they
need socks too. Please put a
quarter or a dollar into
the toe of the sock.
    I hope you can gave a sock
with money to help the homeless.
and If you can, would you
Send me an auto graph
picture. I'd appreciate it.
    From your biggest fan, Kevin

87

Mr. Sandler,

My name is Julio Ruiz. I'm writing to ask for your help. I understand that we don't know each other, but please, I beg you, read this letter.

My girlfriends, and mine, favorite movie is "the wedding singer". She's fallen in love with "Grow Old With you". The movie is a lot like our story.

Last year I wrote a few additional lines about the two of us and our future together. It would mean the world to me and be such a wonderful surprise for her if you could come to the wedding and play for us.

I don't know how you handle requests such as this or if you will even recieve this letter personally. I have been trying to find a way to contact you since I proposed to her last November. (2002) ↑sorry..😊

I also don't know what you would ask for in return. But whatever it is... I'll do it. But enough of that. If you'd like to look at the verses they are on the next page. PLEASE get back to me. I can make sure I'm the only one to know about this should you decide to make an appearance and play. That way you wouldn't have to worry about people crowding you.

PFC Ruiz. USA

Julio Ruiz

In case you were curious about the wedding here's the info.

when: July 2, 2004
at: Fairmont Park Baptist Church (The receptions close by)
Probably around 7:00 p.m.
La Porte, TX

Operation Iraqi Freedom II

82ⁿᵈ Airborne Division\ D-Main
HHC 307ᵗʰ Engineer Battalion
APO AE 09384

Dear Mr. Sandler:

September 23, 2003

I would like to start of with saying thank your for taking the time to read this letter. I am a member of the 82ⁿᵈ Airborne Division currently deployed to South Western Iraq. Since arriving here we watch a movie or two once our 12 hour shift ends to help wind down and your movies tend to be the most requested DVD's each day. I believe that your movies provide a way of escaping our daily missions and gives each of us a chance to laugh together. Our favorites include; Billy Madison, Happy Gilmore and Big Daddy (my favorite).

Thanks for continuing to make your own special type of movies and I'll keep buying them on DVD. Sorry for the low ratings for Punch Drunk Love.

Sincerely,

Sergeant Arthur Han

November 14, 2003

Dear Mr. Sandler:

I am writing to beg a favor of you on behalf of the Manchester YMCA. We hope that you would consider doing a twenty-minute talk/comedy routine at our Reach Out For Youth Auction, which is being held on January 29ᵗʰ at the Executive Court Club on the Manchester/Londonderry line.

I know that you frequent the "Y" when you are in town, and I hope that I can appeal to you to make this event if possible. Your presence would equate to thousands of dollars for the fundraiser. Since I am in charge of the program, and it's my ass if it fails, I thought I would reach for the stars and contact the city's favorite celebrity: you! The staff of the "Y" does not know I'm doing this, because I know that they have too much class to try and pressure your relationship. I, however, do not.

We cannot, of course, afford to pay you. However, I would personally pay for a limo and hotel, and could possibly come up with first class airfare by whacking a few of our trustees.

I could give you all the high ideals and BS that goes along with begging for your time. The bottom line is this: you have the power to use your fame and success to help the Manchester YMCA make the city a better place for the thousands of disadvantaged children who benefit from the Y's various programs.

If you want to do it, we'd love to have you.

I pulled this address and another off of a web site, so I will send this letter to lots of places in the hope that you receive it. If you're in, have one of your folks call me at 603 -359- 89   and I'll work out the details.

Thank you for your consideration.

Sincerely,

Chadwick Smith

89

Dear Adam Sandler, I'm
My name is Noelle. I'm
half Jewish. I'm an artist
and an experimental musician
I also wrote some comedy
about my hilarious deadhead
parents.
   I burned you a mixed CD.
It has some of my music
on it. The Symbolic Correlations
Pixy is a drawing and a
piece of music that go
together. The colored notes
correspond to the colors in
the drawing. I'm putting some
of my comedy on the CD
too. (My Parents, My First Puff,
the Beyotch Guy)
   It would be good if I
could get some of my music
or writing published. I have
an idea for a comedy
movie. It would be about
two poets who meet at an
open mic and fall in love
and go on a spiritual quest
together and get initiated
into Surat Shabd yoga
and at the end get really
inspired to do lots of art,

Most of the movie (or a
large portion of it) would
consist of different characters performing at
open mics. And I don't
have to be the main cha-
racter but I could perform
comedy about my parents
at an open mic or some-
thing. I could play the
weirdo acid freak who
everybody yells stuff at.
You could play the orthodox
Jewish singing clown who
does gymnastics. You could
be the gymnastics teacher of
one of the main characters
son or daughter and you
could perform at that kid's
birthday party. Your character could have a gymnastic
center and an album of
children's music. (Your character would be primarily
based on Five-ish the clown, the
first person to ever do a
double flip on the uneven
bars back in the seventies,
and who would have been

in the olympics had he not
sprained his ankle that
year) You could have a stunt
double or use special effects,
another option is to have
parts of the movie ani-
mated so all the storers
can appreciate your cartoon
self.
   I'd love to help write a
screenplay. I'm a really
prolific writer and have lots
of ideas of things that
would be good in a movie.
I'm sending you some of
my writing. This particular
piece of writing is a little
bit dark but it has it's
humorous parts too.
   I would love to live in LA
and be in movies or TV.
I need to rent a video
camera and try to be on
the real world or something.
I also want to live in a
big city because there's usually an open mic every
night of the week. I just don't want to be

90

a starving artist forever. I
want to make money. I want
my music to sell and stuff.
I also do paintings and
make jewelery. I also have
bipolar disorder and have a
lot of convulsions. They haven't
diagnosed if it's epilepsy yet
but I've already had an MRI
and an EEG and I'm taking
epilepsy medication.
   A cool name for a movie
character would be Pearl
Cheesepuff. And Shakes Bipoles
should be someone with
epilepsy and bipolar disorder.
I've been called Shakes before.
My friend Ty calls me
Shakes sometimes.
        Noelle Hosdick
http://   tripod.com
         @yahoo.com

P.S. I really appreciate the
song about all the different
people who are Jewish.

Bea Goldman

Hey Adam,
Whaz up?? I'm a huge fan of yours. I also like Mel Brooks alot. Incase you are wondering, I am a Jewish boy. I'm 14 and live in Knoxville, TN. I like hockey, detective work (Sherlock Holmes stuff)(you should make a movie out of it), boxing, commedy, and, of course, chicks. You know, the really hot tan ones. Oh yeah, tell your wife hi. If you could meet anyone ever, who would it be? I said you, Moses, & Godzilla. Email me at   @msn.com. What do you do for fun? No like stereotype, but really. I would really like to hang with you someday. I'm enclosing a picture of me and a report I did in class. (you'll like it). Talk to ya later. Bye
                                                Your pal,
                                                Ben Goldman

Refers   6-16-03

Egupt, the TV, the bmo butt, the copter, the jorpak
football. Musik, scare barding dirt biking
the coach, a liter flat Pigesbays.
Antidishastblishmtryusemi.

Ah, this brings me back to my early grade-school days when everyone envied Dan Zatkovich because he knew how to count to 200, and Mike Kozura was the shit because he knew the longest word in the English language: antidisestablishmentarianism. The word was mystical, grand, elusive. Every day we'd ask Mike to repeat it a dozen times, but we couldn't quite get a handle on it. "Come on, say it again, say it one more time!" Then David Pfeiffer found out that there was an even longer word, something relating to a coal-miner's disease, and for a short time this new word was the flavor-of-the-month. But the new word was completely unpronounceable and ridiculous, and soon enough lost its luster. Antidisestablishmentarianism was back in the fold. I'm thrilled to see that somewhere the tradition continues.

LOVE AND WAR

FOUND by Victor Sanders

Bellingham, WA

Oh my goodness. I really do
miss you. When you didn't sit
by me when we ate I was sad
but thats okay. I get the feeling
that Bryan might have a crush
on you. Kinda buggs me really.
When I think of you my chest
gets really heavy and I start
getting ⬤⬤ bigger breths.
It's going to be hard when you
move. I never thought I could
feel this ⬤ way about someone.
Wow this makes me feel like
your off at war ⬤ in the olden
days and me writing love ⬤ letters.
                    If ⬤

Jimbo kelly
is a
christian
scientist.

JIMBO KELLY
FOUND by Erin Goodell
Seattle, WA

45 +

AGING HIPPIES VOLLEYBALL!

3:00 PM THURS SAND COURTS

1
2
3
4
5
6
7
8
9
10
11
12
13
14
15
16

I hope one day to see this sport on ESPN.

—DAVY

YEAH, I'M LOOKING FOR A LITTLE SOMETHING SPECIAL FOR MY AGENT SOMETHING SUBTLE, YET PAINFUL THAT SAYS HEY, REMEMBER ME... FUCKER.

A LITTLE SOMETHING SPECIAL

FOUND by Brian McCloskey

Venice, CA

While sorting through some of my deceased fathers' personal items, I came across this photograph. On the back there is a Los Angeles, California address and "July 1975" date that precedes my parents' divorce.

Thinking that this could be a long-lost relative, I showed it to my mom. She responded by saying it might be the secretary my father had an affair with. What affair?! The family stories always differ, so I didn't pursue that question.

Anyhow, my father did not seem the type to have an affair, too bound by duty, family and responsibility, but it was the '70s in California!

I like to think this oh-so-'70s babe was saying to my dad, "Ease up, Ed, and enjoy the ride." —Kara

this photo FOUND by Kara Barton, Los Angeles, CA

UNDERGROWN ESCORT SERVICE

FOUND by Jed Lackritz

on the L train, Brooklyn, NY

UNDERGROWN ESCORT SERVICE

SEEKing DESPRATE WOMAN
TO ESCORT. RICH WEATHY
MEN AROWND TOWN
ALSO WE ARE LOOKINg
FOR STRIPERS. AND PRIVET
DANCERS FOR VERY PRIVET
PARTYS. FOR MORE
INFORMATION CALL
MR. ANTHONY GARZA
ON MY BEPPER 15248
OR MY MESSAGE BEPPER
1800 48970 . PIN 58.
LEAVE NAME BRIFE
MESSAGE WITH PHONE. NUMBER
AND WE WILL GET RIGHT BACK
TO YOU

95

To the police who arrested me at Burger King,

I am very sorry any bad behavior I may have showed.

Blake Sheilds

Blake

Nov. 2, 1995

Dear lunch lady,

we are sorry for our behavior. We acted like animals. We won't do it again. I know I was bad. I won't never do it again and I an sorry lunchlady. I won't do it again sorry lunch lady.

Sorry

Danny Brown

96

To cashier:
Will you please sell my son one pack of Newport Lights

Thank you for your help

[illegible]

"MY SON" FOUND by a dubious Carla Kucinski, Greensboro, NC

Ah yes… I remember this gambit!

—DAVY

Sara was at a doctors appointment on

Sara was at a doctors

Sara was at a

Sara was

SAR SAR

Sara was

Sara was at a doctors appointment

Sara was at a doctors appointment on Friday.
Please excuse her from her absence.
Thankyou, NANCY L.

FIRST-TIME FORGERY FOUND by Caitlin Elena, Victoria, British Columbia

I hope Sara got away with it!

—DAVY

OR ELSE

FOUND by Michelle Skinner

Lansing, MI

Mom you should leave me like $5 for gas

—Billy

OR EISE

IF LOOKS COULD KILL

FOUND by Julie Hon

Madison, WI

Dear Blue Hair Gentleman-

I decided to Voice my
Support For you in the
Current Dryer Wars. Everyone
Knows that only one dryer works
and that you should not have to
Wait For Someone to remove
their items in order to dry your
own. This is Not why I am

writing this though. The marvelous
editing you provided the First writer
was excellent. My questions comes
down to this. IF I leave letters
and other items here Can they be
Proof read and Corrected as well?

Yours Truly-
Get over it they are
Clostures

City of Westminster

Department: Education and Leisure

Director
Assistant Director (Leisure and Libraries)
Westminster Libraries Information Services Manager

B.A., M.I.P.D.
.L.A., M.I.P.D., M.I.L.A.M.
B.A., A.L.A.

Direct Line:
Fax   :   0171

Your reference :
My reference

Date
19th August 1996

Dear Sir,

I understand from the Library Staff that last week you were verbally requested to leave the library and not return until your personal hygiene becomes acceptable. In spite of these requests you have continued to come into the library.

Your physical condition is in violation of Section 4 of the City of Westminster Public Libraries and Archives Byelaws. You will be excluded from the use of any library of the library authority until you no longer contravene this section of the Byelaws.

Yours sincerely,

Angela Petrella

Angela Petrella
Information Services Manager

SECTION 4

FOUND by Kelly Sweeney

London, England

This note was folded up and stuck beneath a table leg at an outdoor café on Tottenham Court Road.   — K.S.

100

NAME (LAST, FIRST, MIDDLE) OF PERSON GIVING STATEMENT
SIMS BARRY M

RESIDENCE ADDRESS / CITY IF NOT SAN FRANCISCO
TREAT AVE.

ZIP CODE

DOB / AGE
05-23-58

RESIDENCE PHONE (DAY / NIGHT)

BUSINESS PHONE (DAY/NIGHT)
( ) 67

BUSINESS ADDRESS / CITY IF NOT SAN FRANCISCO
SFPD

ZIP CODE

DATE OF STATEMENT
03-20-03

TIME STARTED
2040

TIME COMPLETED
2050

LOCATION WHERE STATEMENT TAKEN

STATEMENT TAKEN BY (NAME / STAR)

AT SCENE ☐   OTHER: **OFFICE**

IN PRESENCE OF

WHILE WORKING A CROWD CONTROL ASSIGNMENT ON 03-20-03,
OUR PLATOON WAS ASSIGNED TO STOP A RIOTOUS CROWD
WHICH WAS E/B ON MISSION ST. FROM 7TH ST.
OUR PLATOON FORMED A SKIRMISH LINE ACROSS MISSION
ST. AND PROCEEDED W/B. WHEN THE VIOLENT
MOB OF RIOTERS CAME INTO CONTACT WITH OUR
LINE I VERBALLY TOLD SEVERAL OF THE CONSPIRITORS
TO REVERSE DIRECTION OR THEY WOULD BE STRUCK.
MOST OF THE MOB BEGAN TO MOVE W/B ON
MISSION ST, BUT SOME INSISTED ON TESTING
MY RESOLVE. ONE WHITE MALE 22 YRS OLD, BLACK
JACKET, PANTS & BANDANA OVER FACE ATTEMPTED
TO GRAB MY BATON. I SKILLFULLY PARRIED HIS
MOVE AND STRUCK HIM TWICE IN ZONE ONE
OF HIS BODY. THE COWARD THEN RAN INTO
THE CROWD.

ZONE ONE

FOUND by Seth Meisels

San Francisco, CA

The day after George W. Bush declared that war on Iraq had
begun, huge protest marches swept through downtown and the
Mission District. I found this in the street a few days later.
—S.M.

I DECLARE, UNDER PENALTY OF PERJURY, THIS STATEMENT OF _____ PAGES IS TRUE AND CORRECT TO THE BEST OF MY KNOWLEDGE.

SIGNATURE OF PERSON GIVING STATEMENT

RUBBING CHEEKS

Arcata, CA

FOUND by Scott and Acacia Cocking

Hey Poochini,
I have missed you today cause
you are so sweet to sniff and
so nice to look at. I will give
you kisses for dinner
cause I cant get enough
of your sweetness. sorry I am
being silly, you're silly too
though. Yogurt would be
a good thing to eat today
I think, or there is also
chai chocolate, both
would benifit our mouths
& tummies. Some might say
you are my hunny bear
but I would say your are
my lovely poodle. I want
to rub cheeks (face & butt)
because yours are so soft &
warm, and I want to kiss
your jaw spot, the one that
makes me squeel like a little
ninny noo nooo. I just
made that up. Remember

I'm not quite sure—is this woman writing to her boyfriend or to her dog?

—DAVY

when I got all that spicy gum and I couldn't stop eating it, not even to save my own mouth; how silly was that!!

this photo FOUND by Wendy Fitzgerald, Sarasota, FL

One of my favorite places to find stuff is in the computer centers on college campuses. There's always a huge stack by the printers of stuff that students have printed out but left unclaimed—juicy emails, half-baked poetry, and high-brow academic reports on movies like *Dumb and Dumberer*. This essay—cruel yet strangely endearing—turned up in a computer center in Chicago. —DAVY

Ned Kozlowski

July 31, 2003

Linda Baskey

The Ballad of the Danger Mouse

I'm eighteen years old, its summer, and I hate this town. August in State College, Pennsylvania offers a unique work opportunity. Between the second summer session and the beginning of the fall semester many houses and apartments are vacated by the transient student population. What this meant to me is lots of hideously filthy places to clean. This period of time is affectionately known as Hell week. It is two weeks of six-teen hour days culminating in a thirty-six hour day; the only reason anyone would agree to this type of work is the massive overtime one makes.

It is the morning of the first day of work, ~~my friends~~ Rick and Mark and I show up bright and early at seven in the morning, ready for hell. Because we have a tendency towards stupidity we've shown up a day early. All of us just want to go back to our homes and sleep, but we decide to stay up, in some kind of demented preparation for the hell that will follow.

Between us there was very little in the way of entertaining stuff to do that day. I think we had half a pack of cigarettes and about three dollars. So we start aimlessly walking. Something occurred to me; we had spent the last few weeks spending time at our friend Dante's house playing with a three-man slingshot. This thing was strong; we would shoot apples, eggs, potatoes, and the like up to three-hundred yards in random directions from his back porch. We had no care for what or who we may be damaging.

1

104

The entire time we'd been playing with this thing I had been coming up with various bad ideas of things to launch, one thing I had wanted to do is shoot a mouse at the neighbors house. Now I don't mean just towards the house, I wanted it point blank straight into their house. I was not going to be happy unless I reduced something to nothing more then a thick red mist hanging in the summer air.

My friends and I had been walking for a bit and it was decided that we owed it to him to wake Dante up, because he was such a good friend. So while Rick, Mark, and I are walking to Dante's I speak up and tell them I'm taking a detour and I need our three dollars. Since I'm such a trustworthy character and I promised them big fun I got the money.

I high-tailed it to the Hamilton Street Plaza where I knew there was a reputable animal merchant. At first I thought I would have trouble explaining why I wanted to buy two white feeder mice, but I decided I must be feeding my pet snake and all went well. Now I was two dollars less the rich and I had a paper bag filled with mice. I decided to peek into the bag on the way to Dante's house, those mice were some cute buggers and I resisted the impulse to name them. It seemed unwise to name my ammunition.

When I made it to Dante's where Mark and Rick were waiting for me I found out that some of my friends indeed do have some kind of moral compass. I found the slingshot and explained that I had plans to launch my mice; I wanted to fire one straight up and see if we could catch it, and the other was to be vaporized. The owner of the slingshot thought this was a very bad idea, took the slingshot from me, and drove away in his car.

illustration by Amy Thomas

continues on the next page ——>

← continued from the previous page

Stuck with two mice and no slingshot I had to develop an alternate plan. Luckily Rick was there, because he was armed with the information that his room mate had just acquired a kitten. What could possibly be better then a kitten versus mouse battle? Eager to see some carnage we raced to Rick's house.

I was very glad to find that his room mate was a fun loving type like me; he thought mouse fights were a great idea. We crowded into his bathroom and placed the kitten, whose name is Oscar, and a mouse in the bath tub. The cat looked at the mouse, the mouse ignored the cat, they both walked around for a bit. Much boringness ensued. What was wrong with this stupid cat, why wasn't Oscar into hunting? Maybe we were making him nervous. So out with mouse number one, and in with number two; even less happened, and we were so bored we watched for even longer.

I hadn't been paying any attention to what Rick's room mate had been doing while I was watching mouse number two fail to interest Oscar the cowardly kitten. He gets my attention and shows me he's used hair dye to color mouse number one purple. It was terribly cute, the mouse even fashioned himself a little mohawk, before he dried off. Figuring the mohawk was a sign that he meant business, he was given another go at Oscar. Well, we were right, the first thing the purple mouse does when he's back in the tub is jump up and bites down on Oscar's nose. It took Oscar a few seconds to get the mouse off his nose, and when he did he was bleeding. What kind of lame kitten can't mess up a mouse?

I decided I was losing interest in my mice and gave them one last chance to provide some real entertainment. We journeyed to the Fraser Street parking garage. I went to the eighth floor, Rick and Mark stayed on ground level. We were going to see if

3

Our intrepid FOUND detectives tracked down the real Ned Kozlowski to ask him a coupla questions!

NED KOZLOWSKI DEFENDS HIMSELF AGAINST CHARGES OF ANIMAL ABUSE: "Christ, I have pets from animal shelters. I don't abuse animals, feeder mice don't count as they *exist* as a foodstuff. Do you think getting eaten by a snake is a humane death? But yes, this paper is nonfiction. I wrote it for my freshman creative writing professor. She wasn't too pleased—violence did not seem to make her as happy as it does me. Still, it was the only class I ever got an A in."

(via email)

mice could take an eight story drop. I didn't really believe they could, but my interest was waning and I wanted some serious gore after being disappointed.

I held my arm straight out in the air and let go of the white mouse's tail. From my vantage point he fell very slowly. Mark looked like he was going to catch the mouse, he missed. I couldn't see from where I was, though I'm told the mouse broke its front legs, and was trying to pull itself along. It was coughing a good deal of blood. Since we are very humane people we did the right thing, Mark crushed the mouse with a brick.

The mouse from a tall building thing was not going well, and I had one mouse left. It was the purple mouse's turn, I held it out, and dropped it. To our surprise it hits the ground from eight stories and takes off running. Rick had to catch him and put him back in the pet store bag. My friends and I are all very impressed by this feat and the purple mouse if from then on the Danger Mouse.

Celebrations were in order; we were carrying a bag filled with the toughest mouse in the world. We needed to show this mouse how much we appreciated him so we went back to Dante's house and got him drunk. I think he was drunk at any rate. Mark bought him a wide-mouth forty of Budweiser, the wide-mouth was so the mouse could go swimming. When he was fished out he was walking pretty funny.

I washed him off and found him a warm towel to burrow in. He also got his own aquarium. Dante ended up keeping the Danger Mouse for several months. The problem though was that he kept escaping and needing to be recaptured; luckily purple mice are easy to spot. It became time for Dante to move so Danger Mouse needed a new home. One of our buddies' girlfriends thought he was so cute that she was going take care of

4

5

him. Apparently Danger Mouse didn't like her too much and escaped from her right away.

Having not been heard from since I would like to think Danger Mouse is alive and well somewhere doing obscenely dangerous things. My days of mice as entertainment are over.

This piece of shale was found at the top of a high mountain pass in the Whitegoat Wilderness area in Alberta in August of 2003. It's just east of the Jasper – Banff border and is a very wild area indeed. This pass does not have a name and is exceptionally difficult to get to. It requires expert route finding (read: no trails) and several days' time to get there, and the climb up it is not much fun either. The catch is this: I was the one who had left it there three years before this picture was taken. I know that finding one's own things may not qualify as Found material, but consider this: this piece of shale, on which we had casually scribbled our names in August of 2000 when we stayed for a night on the pass, had survived intact at about 1000 feet above treeline in this area for three years. That's three Canadian winters, buried under a dozen feet of snow. That's innumerable storms (I've sat through a couple of doozies in the vicinity) and rain showers that could have easily wiped those names off of there. And after three years, it was still within 10 feet of where I originally left it. It's also worth noting that I'm not the only person to find it. Two brothers had inscribed their names on the flip side in 2001. In my excitement to find this, I neglected to photograph – or remember – their names. Yes, it may be a stretch to be considered Found material, but the odds of finding it again seem so tiny that I figured it's worth sending to y'all, at least as an interesting little story.

Love the magazine; keep up the interesting work,

Russell White, Edmonton, Alberta

NEEDLE IN THE HAY

FOUND by Russell White

Whitegoat Wilderness Area, Alberta, Canada

FOUND
by Steve Heiug

San Francisco, CA

IF I GO 2 geT A beer
I'll miss the bus home,
I'll have to walk. oh, A
Long walk
IF I geT the bus I won't
have time 2 geT a beer.
no beer after 2:00, no
beer::
bus or beer

bus or beer...

I walk, I walk

I walk with beer

cLose 2 my heart. I
hold her, she hAs not been
opened yet. I walk—
could it be? yes! yes!
THE BUS! Ave never been
so hAppy for A bus 2. B Late!

illustration by Sarah Locke

Hi Baby,

This is a lot safer than E-mail. I don't know if we should go off today even though we probably will. I want to so bad, but I don't want to risk what I've been striving for this whole time. After last night I see why we have rules for I-week. It is not just to bust our balls. It is way more than that. It is because we should be concentrating on Omega Chi and nothing else. I kind of knew that before but I didn't know why. I did not know that this fraternity went so deep into you that it could grab you from the inside and turn you inside out to make you a better person. I know why we Haze - it is so we can break you down and mold you into a better person. Pledging only went skin deep as far as I am concerned. I-week Has penetrated my whole body. I always Hear of people "seeing the light" and finding a better way. I could never envision that Happening to me. But now I have seen How I can be a better person. I hope this doesn't sound weird but I know now what matters and who I have to prove it too. I cannot wait until I am done because there is some cool shit that I want you see. I can show this because it is Not ritual - it is not even close to ritual and it has had a Great impact on me. All in All it makes me realize why I should devote this whole week to Omega Chi and nothing else. I cannot wait until I can Hold you in my arms and express my love to you in the many ways I know I can. I am confident that I will be able to head my life in the right direction, and I Know that I want you there with me so I can share it with you. I can actually see me as a Father one day preaching some of these things to my Kids to better their lives and I Know that it will. I hope you don't feel bad at all if I say I want to wait a couple more days to be intimate with you. The truth is I don't WANT TOO WAIT AT ALL. I WANT YOU NOW!!! AHHH!!! but I Know that I should wait because it is only a couple of Days. But that will not stop me from thinking of you. I want you to Know that during Ritual you will be in my mind and in my heart and when it is all over hopefully you will be in my pants. I love you baby and I Am so looking Forward to Having you ~~wear~~ my letters.

Love always and Forever,

Jake

P.S. You Mean The World To ME.

Say, To the Bro. with the Gold Teeth, I saw where you Expressed Intrest, IN my Pit.

Ofcourse, However iF you Are Serious About the Dog

~~Do call me, Any Time.~~

You see, I'm a Registered Nurse, Here at a Local Hosp. I truly can Not spend the Appropriate Time, to which She is Titled.

Thus, it is, in the Best INterst of the Dog that some one, of good Title, intent, Love, And Care — 4 — Dog.

Sincerely,

Alberto

P.S. Call A.S.A.P.

(705) 946-7

112

Stolen
Hot Pocket

Color: tan, Goldish, brown
age: just a few seconds old
type: Chicken Bacon
&
Cheese

Hot Pocket
Reward

Non-Party Things to Do:

✓ Pick haircolor for Amy
· Devise plan for world peace
· Host Post-Party ND/Board Game Party
· Get Manicures
· Sew button on to coat

PRIORITIES   FOUND by Elizabeth Schnell   Richmond, VA

this drawing FOUND by Alexis Moore, Conway, AR

DEAR BRO   FOUND by Shyan Silva   Nashville, TN

Jan. 20. 2004

Dear Bro,
Lets hang-out!
Please, I really
love ya so
when you can
call me at home.
Love-
Justin

Mike,
Please call
Justin he
loves you and
we misses you!
love,
Mom. ♥

#351-4080

113

2-28-2004

I couldn't live with it any longer
The meds were really messing me up.
I had to end the pain
Tell the kid I am sorry

Tracy

LEAP YEAR
FOUND by Casey and Mariana
Gambier, OH

this picture FOUND by Damon Smith & Jesse Faciana, Portland, OR

FINDS THAT DEAL
WITH SUICIDE

Feeling suicidal? Call the Hopeline! 1-800-784-2433

114

Sue,

Hey hun,

Do you know this is exactly a year from the day Ash and I broke up. She walked out of my life, didn't look back, took the engagement ring didn't want anything to do with me any more, a year went bye not even a call, left her a message when grandma died nothing. I let it eat away at me for a year now, along with everything else I couldn't handle it any more. I loved her more then I loved life its self. She was the one for me the only one, but she got scared and let being scared win over how she really felt. Life isn't fair. I learned that the hard way to many time to hold on to any hope. I hope you don't hate me right now. I know you have all the reason in the world I promised I would call I promised I wouldn't try or succeed but I lied I just couldn't out of anyone I would hope you could understand that. If you can't I am sorry. I really don't know how to say this. You and I have bean friends since we were young, 3rd grade when you beat me in the 50 yard dash for gym. I was amazed that a girl could run as fast as us even faster. Do you remember the look on Dukes face not to mention Howie I thought he was going to drop dead right there. You have always bean one of a kind Sue. Ever since we met I new you were different I new you were going to be someone special in my life. Yes I new that at the age of 9. Hun, I have always loved you, for you the good the bad, the person you were and most important the great person you have become. I know when you get this I will be gone, that my plan to kill my self would have worked. I left this for   Joel to give you once I was gone. I am sorry. I hope you can understand that I needed to go on to a better place now. My parents and I haven't bean getting a long, I still had a year of school no money to move out work sucked, after grandma Sadie died I felt like I lost my best friend, she was there no matter what thick or thin, I couldn't deal with it all any more. When I was in the hospital I tried that once to kill my self, I told them the day before they let me out I still wanted to die, but they thought I just wanted to stay in the hospital not go out and deal with the world. I know I am only 22 and I would have my life a head of me, I also know that if I would of called you I would still be a live right now, but please don't blame your self for this Sue, this is what I wanted this is how I wanted my life to end. I didn't want a bc talked out of it, I know that you are hurting a lot right now, and I am sorry that I did this to you, but please no matter what your feeling right now don't follow in my foot steps. My family has lost grandma Sadie and now me, I know they would be devastated to hear they lost you to, as would your family, if things get hard think of you beautiful nieces and how you need to be there for Betty's surgery. Look at all the good your meant to do in the world. You are meant for greater things that's why God wouldn't let you die when you wanted to the times you tried almost succeeded her pulled you back, this was my time to go, I don't want a see you in hell. Live life be happy and live each day to the fullest. Know I always loved you and always will.

Love
Eric

HOPE YOU ARE HAPPY

FOUND by Brenda Durkacs,
Tamarac, FL

this drawing FOUND by Mike Montedoro, Jr., North Versailles, PA

B,

I'm sorry I haven't told you this before. I was just affraid that you wouldn't consider me your best friend if I were to tell you the truth. But I can't really keep this secret from someone I love dearly and someone I trust with my life. I'm sorry I have kept this from you and I hope you will understand where I am coming from. Just let me read this and let me know how you feel. I had to at least tell someone and I figured why not my love, my sister, and my best friend. Again I appoligize for keeping such a big secret from you when I know you have been so honest with me. I love you and I hope you will understand.

THE BEGINING

I'm a fraud. I have lied to myself and everyone I love. I wanted to die. I wanted to kill myself so I wouldn't have to deal with all those jerks at school and the pain at home. I started thinking, I was only thirteen and I was in my own little world. As ~~~~ say ~~~~ in my Dark Place.

I couldn't deal with all the name callings and the fake friends. Me being labeled, "The Fat Funny Gurl," was more

this note continues on the following page ⟶

continued from the previous page

hurtful when I heard it when no one thought I were listening.

When people I thought were my home gurlz and home boyz would talk shit behind my back, I would think, "I can handle it," but I really couldn't.

I felt like tearing myself apart piece by piece. I felt like taking Advil, the medicine I'm alergic to, and just lay there till my throat got so swollen that I wouln't be able to breath and I'd just die. I tried It once but I just ended up in the hospital because I blew up like a turkey and I couldn't handle the itchyness so I paged my mom, my sister, and Aunt, and of couse they rushed me to the hospital. My lips were so big I could't hardly even talk.

I actually tried to look for the bottle of my mothers pills so I could kill myself, but this time no one was home and I wasn't going to call anyone for help. I didn't find the pills so instead I took my sisters enhaler and I took about 30 or more inhalations to see what would happen. I started to feel dizzy, hot and cold at the same time, and faint. I started saying to myself "I wish I hadn't done this. I wish I would have just went to school."

But eventually it wore off and I wasn't dead, so I did it again but this time instead of it wearing off it gave me a little buzz, not a very good buzz at that, for the whole day

THE ANSWERS

FOUND by Pete Dybdahl

Roanoke, VA

I was writing an email at the public library when I struck the paste command by mistake and got this. —P.D.

Well things here are great. We were able to have Ammon week last week. It was great. On Thursday we ended up cleaning a couple of houses, then on Friday we finished cleaning a house and raked two yards, and helped clean another house. On Saturday we cleaned a house and raked four yards. Needless to say by Sunday our arms were like jelly. It was so much fun to be able to help people out physically as well as spiritually.

One of our investigators Thea came to church again. We are so excited for her. I really hope all goes well she is progressing so much. I really love the people that I get to work with. It is so amazing to me that no matter who you are or where you need the gospel more than you would ever know. I love seeing the gospel work in people's lives.

I am very excited we have Zone Conference tomorrow. I really love Zone Conference because it helps fill you spiritual tank like nothing else. I really enjoy learning from other people.

I have learned this week the value of being positive. We have been working with a lot of people who suffer from depression. It amazes me how it consumes all of their lives. They really find themselves in a hole and figure that there is no way out. I feel so bad for them. It also amazes me how Heavenly Father is sending them answers, but they only see the negative so they can't see the answers that are sent to them.

I love the fact that a positive attitude can go so far. I love this gospel and how when people truly follow it their lives are so much better. It really amazes me how this gospel really has the answers to almost everything. How if you live the principles' it teaches you can be so happy.

I love all of the support you all give me thank you so much and I hope all works out. I love you. SisterConnie

---

COURTEOUS DESPAIR FOUND by Bruce DeViller, Chicago, IL

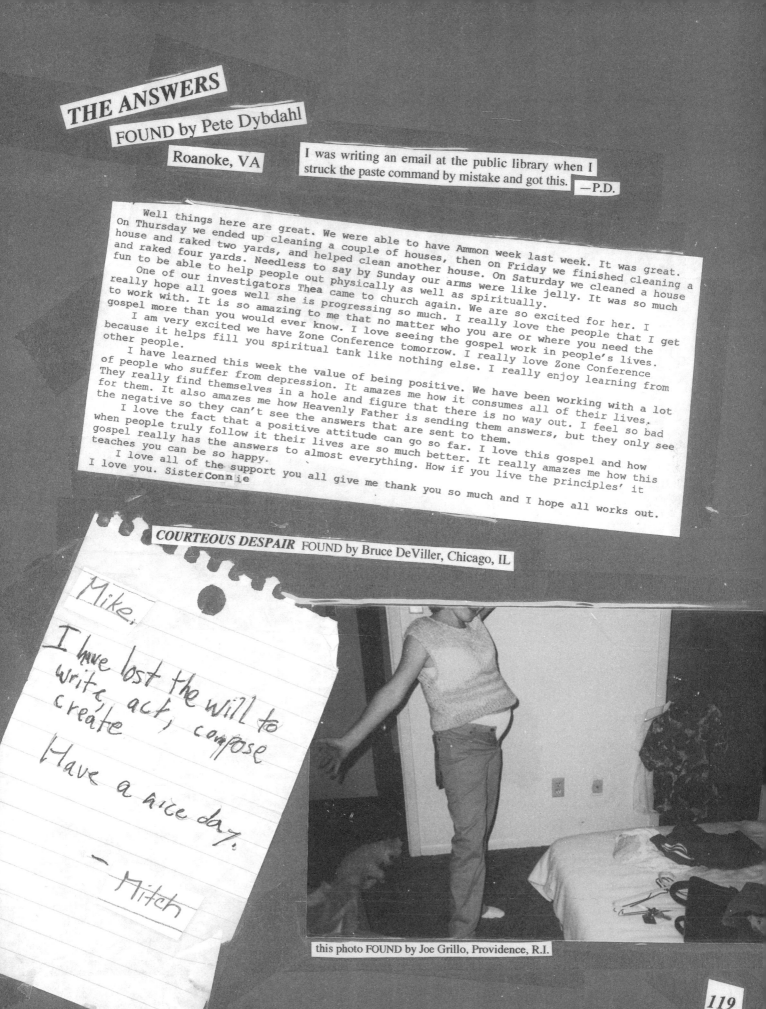

Mike,

I have lost the will to write, act, compose create

Have a nice day.

— Mitch

this photo FOUND by Joe Grillo, Providence, R.I.

MR. O'KEEFE - JOHN
WEBBER
BORN - AT - TENANT - CREEK
NORTHER - TERRITRY
ON MAY - 14TH 1950 - AGE - 54
YEAR - OLD - A POSITIVE - BLOOD
THREE - ORGAN - EGGS IN A
MANS - BODY - AND - THREE
KIDNEYS - IN - BACK
IAM - PREGANT - MAN
I AM THE ONLY MAN - CAN
HAVE A BABY
DONATIONS WANTED
LADIE FRIEND - SHIP

THE PREGNANT MAN

FOUND by Shani Moffat

Sydney, Australia

this drawing FOUND by Chris Willis, Portland, OR

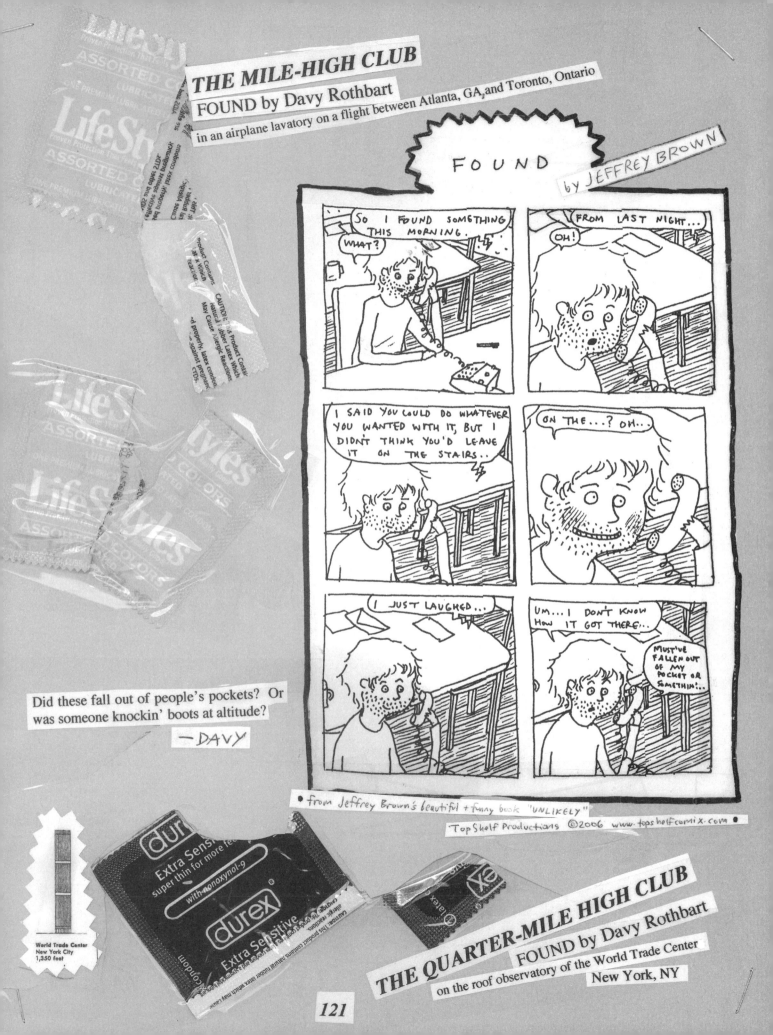

THE MILE-HIGH CLUB

FOUND by Davy Rothbart

in an airplane lavatory on a flight between Atlanta, GA, and Toronto, Ontario

Did these fall out of people's pockets? Or was someone knockin' boots at altitude?

—DAVY

THE QUARTER-MILE HIGH CLUB

FOUND by Davy Rothbart

on the roof observatory of the World Trade Center
New York, NY

121

13 Things to do today

1. Pray to God for guidance
2. Find local cat for blood sacrifice to ensure He is listening
3. Kick DOG for recent barking / find electro shock collar on line
4. Beat girlfriend A (because she likes it)
5. FUCK girlfriend B (because she wants it)
6. Call and torment girlfriend C (because she needs it)!
7. Untie the neighbors?
8. talk it over w/ them. MAYBE we can work it out w/out DEATH or the POLICE! ☺ Let's hope!
9. Thaw out chicken in freezer
10. Call Mary for recipie — Chicken Pot Pie & ??.....
11 I have it!! Apple pie!! Yeah!! Alright!!
12. Buy an issue/copy of "The Collector" — All the great killer's killers have read it! Yeah! LEARN FROM THE BEST!!!
13. Russian Roulete...BANG! BANG! HA! HA!

THERE ARE TWO CHILDREN BURIED UNDER A HOME LOCATED IN LONG BEACH. IN THE NAME OF **JESUS** DIG THEM UP.

144 LINDEN AVE.

Long Beach, CALIFORNIA.

144 LINDEN AVE Long Beach, California.

THE PEOPLE LIVING there DID NOT DO it. It HAPPENED BEFORE THEY MOVED IN.

127

August 2, 1994

Mr. Chris Camp
2737 Shadow Crescent
Rockville Centre, New York   11570

RE: My New Job

Dear Mr. Chris Camp , Attorney inlaw:

As a child my mother told me not to reach for the sun, that I just might grab it one day and get burned, like we all have. But, that is not what I, or I'm sure you, are all about. I reach for it all the time, still and now. Perhaps other candidates are viewing this opportunity as a job or a means of aquiring cars or food or stealth objects which we all desire. I would like you, Mr. Chris Camp to consider that I am more interested in being there for your firm than any of those things. I will work tirelessly and hard to improve productivity and efficiency as I have at the United States Post Service and my other multi faceted jobs and careers. Please consider me when you go to sleep tonight as the man with the plan. I have much to offer an openminded fowerd looking firm. My salary requirements are open but not very flexible so that may be a sticking point and I'll have to consider my moves carefully. I sense we are alot alike Mr. Chris Camp , that we both reach for that hot, shiny, glowing, bright orb in the morning sky. Please call me and let me know If you are right for my plans and hopes. What we need is more thinkers likeyou and Tim Cryderman and Jason Napier . I realized only recently how much law is a cerebrel function of art and not just numbers on a page after I had been stopped for a routine traffic stop and frisked for speeding and then represented by Carlton Whitman , Esq. who said he was impressed with my chutzpah and spunk as well as labrinth legal vocabulary, simply from watching hot shows like L.A. LAW and MATLOCK. I shall continue on and strive for the best. Additionally, I am what they call a people person and I get my food from other peoples lives so I would grow in an envirinment of a legal firm. Remember the firm in firm is built on the "firm" backs of the lower employees. I will be a "firm" platform for you to build a bright, daring, progressive, challenging world on.

Very truly yours,

William J. Carpenter

A FIRM BACK

FOUND by Tom N.

Albany, NY

this picture FOUND by Julia Kerrigan, Edgewater, MD

6/6/05

Rachel,

I just wanted to tell you again how much fun I had reading for the role of Dick Harder in your film. I've always wanted to play a Porn Star, and the fact that he's "bi" makes it all the more interesting. I don't really have much experience in giving blow jobs but gosh I sure am eager to learn!!

Thanks again and I wish you all the best.

James Gleason

A FIRM DICK
FOUND by Travis Conlan
Studio City, CA

Found this in an alley. I sure hope they make the movie for which this guy auditioned! —T.C.

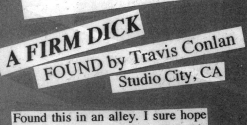

<u>Unemployed!</u>

I need a Job and a Home! Will Come with You For Free!

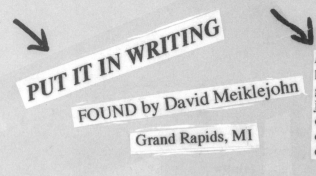

PUT IT IN WRITING

FOUND by David Meiklejohn

Grand Rapids, MI

I found a rain-soaked folder in the street that contained a 78-page legal document regarding the purchase of a coffee shop by a group of investors. It all looked like pretty boring legal mumbo-jumbo and I was about to pitch it into the recycling bin when one of these special clauses caught my eye. As I read on, I found five other clauses in the same vein, buried within the otherwise very ordinary contract. Watch out for them whales! —D.M.

Article II, clause 7 (appended) - Member's Meetings

"If any member addresses problems regarding their relationship with a female during the course of a membership meeting, the remaining membership may elect to feel bad for them, son, provided the remaing membership can identify 99 problems of which a bitch ain't one."

Article II, clause 8 - Mystical Beasts

"Any member who causes a Mystical Beast to be present at a member meeting shall be solely responsible for feeding and housing the beast, as well as solely responsible for any damage or impairment of LLC assets caused by the beast. A mystical beast must have sweet wings, long talons, an unnatural ability to fly and/or ability to breathe fire or be declared a Mystical Beast by a court of applicable jurisdiction."

illustration by Dan Tice

Article III, clause 5 - Wolf Shirts

"Unless agreed to in advance by all members, the LLC shall take no tax or legal advice from any person wearing a wolf shirt. A wolf shirt shall be defined as both depicting a wolf and being wicked sweet under applicable United Nations conventions or be declared wicked sweet in a US court of law with appropriate jurisdiction."

126

Article IV, clause 11 - Allocation and Distribution of Liquidation Proceeds in the Event of Consumption by Whale:

"In the event that any member is consumed in whole by an animal of the order Cetacea, that member's share shall be liquidated and allocated among the other members in accordance with each member's percentage interest in the LLC. In the event that a member is consumed in part by an animal of the order Cetacea, a proportion of the member's capital account equal to the proportion of body mass of the member consumed shall be liquidated and allocated among the other members in equal portions."

illustration by Dan Tice

TICE

Article V, clause 3 - Metal Hands

"Any member that should cause his natural hands to be removed intentionally and fashioned with metal hands without sound medical rationale shall have his membership rights frozen until such time as the remaining members accept and certify any applicable explanation for such action. This section shall not apply to members who, at the time of their admission into the LLC, bear metal hands."

Article V, clause 5 - Maritime Gross Negligence

"If a national maritime authority recognized by the International Maritime Authority finds that a member acted with gross negligence in the course of maritime action, the member shall surrender any membership interest involved in the action of the LLC. This provision does not apply to acts taking place in inland waters."

FOUND Magazine. Declared wicked sweet.

Alex
please wash up
after yourself.
Also — dont forget
your eggs you
cooked in the fridge.
Love Mom —

MY DARLING HUSBAND,
I SHED TEARS ON TOP
OF MT. SHASTA WHEN
I SAID "I DO". EIGHT
YEARS LATER, I STILL
CRY EVERY TIME I
THINK OF OUR "I DO'S".
IT MIGHT SOUND CLICHÉ
BUT I NEVER KNEW I
COULD LOVE SO MUCH OR
BE MORE IN LOVE WITH YOU
EVERY PASSING DAY AND YEAR.

YOUR ADORING WIFE,
SUSAN

O.K.
but I didn't
cook eggs
& put them in the
fridge

No they did
not STINK.
They were in the
back in a Cool
Whip container.
I chucked them!
Love Mom

WOW! THEN
WHO MADE THEM,
COULD THEY BE
LEFT OVER FOM
JO & NICOLES
VISIT? (OH MY!!)
Love Mom

I think we
would of noticed them
before, Dont you.
DID They stink like
they were
OLD.

KiSS MY Black ass

MYass is abstract!

EU SERVICES
The Printing and Direct Mail Experts

PP—
please obey
CW

www.euservices.com   1-800-230-3362

new painting shall be titled after a best-selling japanese lipstick—

SEXUAL VIOLENCE #1

09/28

Per Tracy @ Sterling 12/6/04.
She spoke to bond people + will POD person
needs is Death Certificate
q sign on back above daddy's name. Bank will
X out stamp on front

Take off on your underpants

• May 11th •
May 12th
May 13th

Primary Excuses
{ – No classes
– No work (h/w)

MY LATCH SUCKS AND I'M FULL OF DEER!

BRING INTO OFFC BFHAND   SUNSET = 8:05
- Table cloth
- Wine, glasses
- Bottled Water   - Batteries for Radio,
- 2 Meals (ordered, picked up)   good CD
- Flowers   Notting Hill CD
- Use plates/silverware from here.   ~~TV~~ or
Followed By: ~~no~~ Walk m The Mall   Delovely
- CANDLES/MATCHES.   or
                      Love Actually

II. The Role of the Wife (Ephesians 5:22-24, 33; 1 Peter 3:1-6)

a. The wife is to __Submit__ to her husband's position willingly, placing herself under his leadership and authority.

b. The wife is to __Support__ her husband's program, using her gifts, talents and skills for his benefit.

c. The wife is to __Sing__ her husband's praises through the visible and verbal expressions of respect and honor.

- ☑ Luke wed 4 pm.
- ☑ tan legs
- ☑ hair-legs   ☑ pillows.
- ☐ make up from storage ☑ ring
- ☐ shoes - PED ?
- ☑ pick up clothes
- ☑ check to pies   10:30
- ☑ check to ACTIVSPACE - CC - susanna
- ⊘ checkbooks?
- ☑ water plants
- ☐ clean up houseboat - outside
- ⊘ bathroom clean
- ☐ laundry
- ☐ pack
- ☐ pick up top of dress wed
- ☐ key to storage
- ☑ port townsend reservation
- ☐ replace dead plants outside
- ☐ chartering sept. 4 - 18
- ☑ honeymoon - might
- ☑ order sheets
- ☑ cake - saturday
- ☐ sparklers
- ☐ lamp.
- ☑ toy store

RENT! bathroom key.

Thank you for being the best fiance ever!

I hope we can use your next vacation time relaxing on an island.

I love you.
- bubbacakes

Hey boo, wuz up? Nothin much here. I hope this letter finds you in your best of health. I'm in my patrol vehicle, bored as hell thinking about you. I have drawn this same picture on a million sheets of paper, only the other 199,999 got fucked up. Baby I miss you so much. I miss spending time with you. I miss you holding me and treating me the way you used to. Baby I'm sorry for all the times you feel like I was being a bitch to you. This whole situation was stressing me out. I pray to God that he gives me the words to say at the right time. So far since I've been home from Korea I've felt a whole lot better. I feel different. Right now I don't have a whole lot of control over the situation, but I'm sure it will work out. I know you believe and have faith in me. I'm going to keep on keeping on doing what I think is best for us. Eventually he'll get the picture. I don't know what's taking him so long. Like I said before, I will keep on keepin on. At this point I don't care what happens. It's only up to him to care. I'm not taking my birth control anymore, because it's changing me. I don't want to use other methods because I do want children some day. However, if we conceive then I'll just deal with it. There's only so much Mikey will do to me. I'm not worried about it much. I just don't want to conceive his child. If that happens we will never be together. But anyway that's another bridge to cross when we get to it. I tell you life isn't as easy I thought it would be. I love you so much and I want to be with you so bad. It's only a matter of time baby. If for any reason you feel like I'm wasting your time, do as you feel and I'll catch you later.

105-mm gun   Machine guns   Hatch   Tank commander

Caterpillar tracks

Driver   Gunner   Loader   Engine and transmission

See also BAZOOKA.

No.

Date

Baby don't postpone anything for me. I'll be alive forever. Life is only what you make it. I don't want you to miss out on anything in life that you want to do. I know you only live one life and these days life is pretty short so do all you can and strive for the best because you only get one chance to show God whats up. I'm sorry for all the ache and pain I've caused. You have been so patient and so good to me. I promise I will give it all in return. Little do you know, if my husband was the person you find. You are I wouldn't know you right now. If only I would have met you first. No matter what, when its all over we are going to be together. That's my word nigga.

Love Always,

Jolene

I like standing up here at the registers, it gives you a good sense of the world, as well as unimaginable patience. You see all the people go through, all the faces, personalities, names. Some catch my eye very distinctly, some I wouldn't remember if I tried. Life as a store register girl. Sort of along the same lines as clerks but in a less drastic way. Real life is definately more interesting sometimes than fiction. Dealing with people who got angry is interesting. Some people are understanding, others are not. Makes you wonder what their general personality

REGISTER MAN

FOUND by Laura Komai

Madison, WI

Management-
Numerous patrons have been inquiring about the photo of the "studly" man that had been ▬▬▬ adorning the wall behind the cash register. We don't know how to respond but confess with troubled hearts that we too would like to know where this little bit of sunshine went.
— the Staff at L.L.

they have, what happened to them that day that made them that way, what they were thinking ... what they are like elsewhere, just about them. Some people make the greatest stories! I can make up whatever my mind creates for them. I love it!

Someday I'm going to have to slow down and write all the stories in my head (or rather the stories in my head) *grin* ~I slow down~

this drawing FOUND by Liz, Ann Arbor, MI

Dear Mother and Father,
I feel that somehow I should thank you. But I don't know how, so I suppose I shall save this letter until I do.

Found this note tucked into some Lyndon LaRouche campaign propaganda in a guest room at a Divinity school, seemed left over from the Democratic National Convention. I hope the writer eventually found some other way to thank them! —P.H.

We are teaching Mikey how to dress himself. It would be great if you could do the same thanks
Debbie

Colors Prinitng & Graphics

This photo FOUND By Terri Greer   Lakewood, OH

MIKEY   FOUND by Molly Eyres
Carmichael, CA

FOUND Magazine. Real life is definitely more interesting sometimes than fiction.

135

4/30/93

i'm not even going to try to write like I usually do, because there's no possible way that I could . I mean I'm not even myself right now, well of course I am but it's not the self that usually sits here and presses on thesse keys. right now all i am is a soul flying over thses buttons, and my thoughts are it's thoughts. usually i would be a person, manipulating the keys to do my bidding, and guiding it's direction all the time. now i can't even keep up with what my nexct thought is before it shows up on the screen in front of me not the screen of the computer, but the screen in my head, and i see them as i go along. i've never typedtthis fast or this effortlessly in my life, i never once pause and ask where a key should be, because the keeybord is me and i am the keyboard i took mucshrooms, in case i want to know what happened to me when i read this in the future and if you are in the future, reading this i hope you know that this has been a watershed event in your life. it might not change the course of your life's direction, but it will surely change how you think of yourslef and the world not really yourself and the world, but the world as part of yourslef. are you just ---

BREAK ON THROUGH

FOUND by Katy Crosby

Middlebury, VT

In the dorms at Middlebury College, we never locked the doors to our rooms. One night I came home from a party and discovered that someone had let themselves into my room and typed a fifteen-page letter to their future self on my computer, then left without even saving the file. I've held onto it for the last twelve years, a reminder of a time in my life when every night was full of revelation.

—K.C.

136

Another day, and I'm here.
It was a wonderful night with wonderful people.
I feel fulfilled I have an outlook of positivity.

The world is still worse off than I can ever remember.
But somewhere inside of me I feel like it's alright.
A moment of clarity, the alcoholics call it.

When it's over, it's not.
I saw a dog dead, and I didn't feel so bad.
He was at peace.

I've seen other's dead and they weren't
The next level, the transition.
I was wondering during my birthday if there was a deathday, when you crossed over.

It felt all the same.

these photos FOUND by Adam Mangels, Denver, CO

A MOMENT OF CLARITY
FOUND by Davy Rothbart   Ann Arbor, MI

In the basement of the house I share with my four roommates is the *FOUND Magazine* "office"—a couple of desks and computers tucked into a crumbling stone chamber behind the washer and dryer. One night, after a party at our house, I found this in the printer; apparently, someone had spent a reflective moment at the Macintosh.

−DAVY

I was 19, living in Madurai, India, a city of a million people. Nothing went to waste there in 1987.

One day I got a handwritten letter from my girlfriend. I thought things were okay between us even though I was halfway around the world. Apparently, she didn't. The letter was a breakup letter. But it didn't hit me too hard and I decided to disregard it — I figured she was a long way away and would come to her senses when I got home. It was still a year before I'd be home again, but I was sure that things would work out. I tossed the letter in the garbage.

Three weeks later I went out to buy some groceries at the outdoor markets. I always loved the markets, all those competing smells of grains and spices and tasty snacks. Roasted chickpeas were my favorite — sold hot from the roasting pan, topped with salt and other seasonings. I went over to the vendor I knew best; he smiled and poured ten grams of chickpeas into the traditional paper cone, then tied the paper shut with fraying string and passed the little package over. I tucked the goodies into my bag with my other things.

As soon as I got home I reached for the chickpeas, peeled the paper back, and started chowing down - just as tasty as ever. Then I looked closer. The paper cone wrapping was the breakup letter I'd received three weeks before! In a city of a million people, her letter had come back to me, sought me out even! I realized I hadn't truly gotten her message the first time. This time I did. Tears and chickpeas.

—D.K.

illustration by Dan Tice

OLD GUN
FOUND by Christopher Ryan

Denver, CO

I found this ancient shotgun while rescuing turtles from a polluted river. Good thing I grabbed it before it fell into the hands of the wrong turtle.

—C.R.

what is a stoppage!

The failure of an automatic or semiautomatic firearm to complete the cycle of operation

ups

what is the purpose of the compensator?

Help keep the muzzle down during firing.

SPOOKY FLASH CARDS FOUND by Dan Montgomery, Washington, D.C.

I found these cards at the entrance to the Dupont Circle Metro station in D.C. Was a military or CIA recruit doing homework for a big test? Or was a wannabe mass murderer boning up on his weapons knowledge before the big day?

—D.M.

Had to crawl. Begin Trench 3 feet deep →3 feet of it water

Or should I say... Swim!!

←Barbed wire

Holes where bombs will be set off. how filled with water.

Trench 2 feet deep →18 of it was water

END

Machine Guns "30 caliber"

IN THE TRENCHES FOUND by Natalie Stackhouse, Nashville, IN

I found this map inside a cookbook called *Ideas for Tomorrow.*

—N.S.

YOUNG GUNS
FOUND by Brad Stemke, Ventura, CA

Success in court

Write down all possible verdicts on a piece of paper with scissors cut only the desired conclusion while focusing your mind on positive outcome. Burn the unwanted portion until only ashes remain. Release the ashes "lost to you". Carry the other piece of paper into court wrapped in gold cloth as a protective amulet

Please wrap tampons and pads in paper towels. We don't need the kids looking at it.

I said "Sex" and "Meet that Special Person" in subliminal message on a commercial and I'm really really sorry.

Will you go out w/ me? Circle yes or no

yes   no

yes - but I have herpes so you might want to reconsider

I've often wondered about the woman on the right's expression. Perhaps a mother who's just been reunited with her long-lost daughter?
—R.J.S.

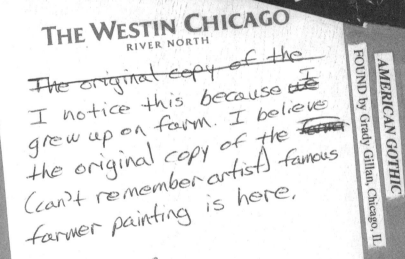

THE WESTIN CHICAGO
RIVER NORTH

~~The original copy of the~~ I notice this because ~~the~~ I grew up on farm. I believe the original copy of the ~~farm~~ (can't remember artist) famous farmer painting is here.

FOUND by Grady Gillan, Chicago, IL

AMERICAN GOTHIC

Sniper Wanted:

To thin out the herd a Little. Non-smoker. Must Work weekends.
$8.50/hr + commission.

(415) 652-87 TOM PAIN

You will never have sex ever agin

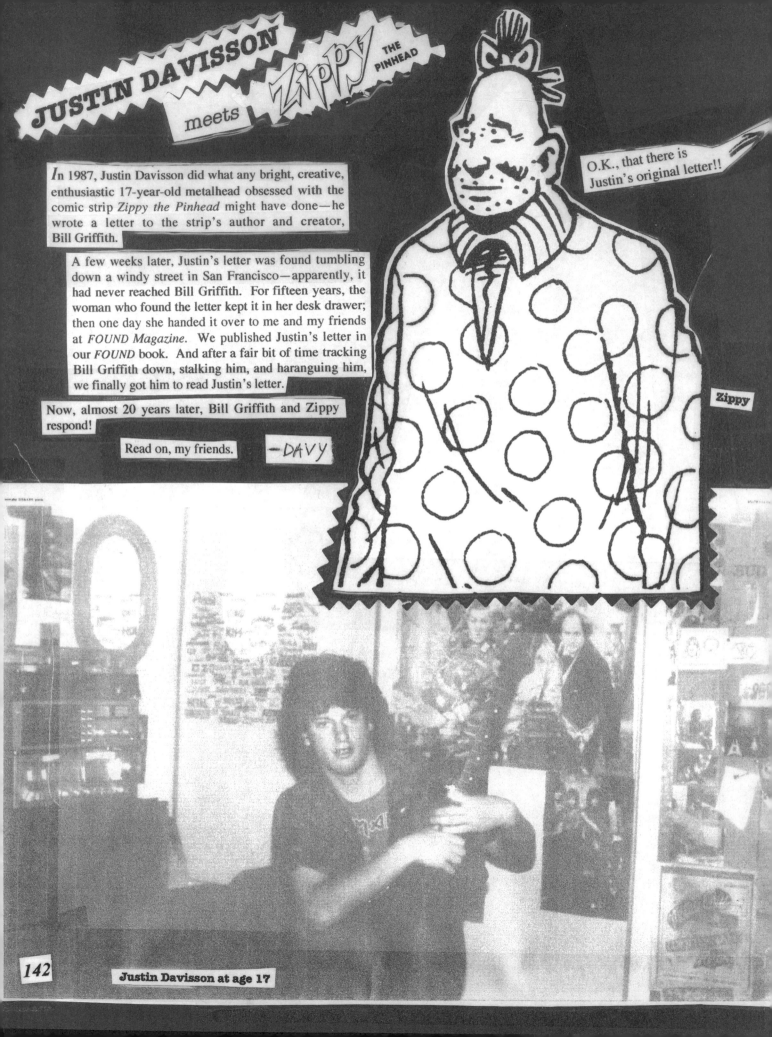

JUSTIN DAVISSON meets ZIPPY THE PINHEAD

In 1987, Justin Davisson did what any bright, creative, enthusiastic 17-year-old metalhead obsessed with the comic strip *Zippy the Pinhead* might have done—he wrote a letter to the strip's author and creator, Bill Griffith.

A few weeks later, Justin's letter was found tumbling down a windy street in San Francisco—apparently, it had never reached Bill Griffith. For fifteen years, the woman who found the letter kept it in her desk drawer; then one day she handed it over to me and my friends at *FOUND Magazine*. We published Justin's letter in our *FOUND* book. And after a fair bit of time tracking Bill Griffith down, stalking him, and haranguing him, we finally got him to read Justin's letter.

Now, almost 20 years later, Bill Griffith and Zippy respond!

Read on, my friends. —DAVY

O.K., that there is Justin's original letter!!

Zippy

Justin Davisson at age 17

12-29-87

To All,

Could you please send me a complete catalog of Zippy med merchandise. Bill Griffith- if you read this- here's some idea you should use for the pro peruvial pinhead- Zippy joins a heavy metal band, Zippy meets David Letterman, Zippy meets Donald Trump, Zippy meets Charles Manson, Zippy goes to Carmel & meets mayor Clint, Zippy meets Jim & Tammy Faye, Zippy meets Gary Hart, Zippy meets Donna Rice, Jessica Hahn, Fawn Hall & has affairs with all of them in one night, Zippy meets Gumby & Pokey, Zippy meets Rocky, Bullwinkle, Fearless Leader, Boris Bentof, & Natashia, Zippy meets the Noid, Zippy meets Teddy Ruxpin, Zippy meets Sean Penn & doesn't get hit!, Zippy meets the Pope & takes his place, Zippy meets Hulk Hogan & becomes the new World Wrestling Federation world champion, Zippy meets his sanrio heir apparent- Zee-pee, Zippy meets Jerry Faldwell & Oral Roberts, Zippy meets Ozzy Osbourne, Zippy & Claude go back to Haight-Ashbury & People's Park in the summer of 1967, Zippy meets the Freak brothers & gets his stomach pumped after too much partying with the Fat Freddy, Phenias, & Freewheelin' Franklin; Zippy meets Sledgehammer!, Zippy meets Morris the Cat, Zippy meet Steven King, Zippy meets Bugs Bunny, Zippy meets & goes bowling with Fred Flintstone, Zippy meets ALF, Zippy meets Joe Bob Briggs, Zippy meets Siskel & Ebert & Rex Reed, Zippy meets Pee-Wee Herrmann, Zippy meet Elvis, Zippy meets Joe Montana, Zippy meets Howard Coselli, Zippy meets pit bulls & freeway gun shooters, Zippy meets the Gorbechevs in the U.S.S.R., Zippy meets Richard Simmons, Zippy meets Judy & Audrey Landers (lucky Pinhead!), & Vow!, The best of all Zippy meets the 3 Stooges! We don't get the Zippy in any of the local papers except the Bay Area spectator which is supposedly illegal for me to buy. When is the Zippy movie due out, I heard Randy Quaid was going play the Pinhead. I heard that a few years ago they gave out free Zippy t-shirts for eating Ding-Dongs, & Taco sauce, are there going to be any more events like that in the →

Bay Area, I have had the delicacy delicacy before &
it's go quite good. Next year I get to vote.
I'm got voting for Gary Hart - he can't keep his pants on
& I'm not about to vote for Albert Gore because his wife
is head of the Parents Music Resouce Center & they're not my
favorite people in the world. I definotly want a _real_ pinhead
in the office. Who is going to be rice president.
I have Weld, Griffey, Claude, Tuxedo Sam, Mr. Bushmiller? I want to
Tuesday a # Zippy picture painted on my guitar some day
Oh yeah I almost forgot, Zippy meets Robin Leach, Garfield,
Spudds Mackenzie, the Peanuts gang, Richard Nixon, G. Gordon Liddy, Dr.
Demento, Cheech & Chong, Marget Thacher, Sammanth Fox, Queen of
England, Mommar Kpaddi, the I yathola, Rambo, George Timmer
of the men's where house, Vanna White, Cal Worthington Jr., Gary Hart,
Malcam Forbes, Liz Taylor, Joan Rivers, Eddie Murphy, & a pack
of weasels, & the california Thanks A Lot,
Raisins.
Justin Davisson - The only person
Yow!!
in town that knows _anything_ about- Zippy the Pinhead.
Justin Davisson
422 Huntington Pl.
Pleasanton, CA 94109
P.S. - How 'bout Zippy meets-Godzilla,
King Kong, Robocop, Alfred E. Neuman, the Fat Boys, Ollie North, William Dewer,
Cherry Pop-Tart (the cartoon character), Alice Cooper & Frank Zappa.

Zippy in 1988
Put A Real Pinhead
in the White House

In 1987, Justin Davisson hoped that his ideas would inspire Bill Griffith to create a comic strip. Almost 20 years later, they did!

The final and most tantalizing step was to reunite Justin with the letter he wrote in 1987, and show him Bill's new comic.

I tracked Justin down in California. He's 35 years old now, and works at an alt-weekly newspaper in the Bay Area. I put together a little surprise package for him, sent it out, and called him at work a couple weeks later.

Justin told me that he'd got the package and been completely stunned. He didn't even really remember writing the original letter. "I can't believe how crazy I was back then," he said. "And I can't believe the whole thing came full circle. It's a *trip*!"

"The funny thing is," Justin went on, "I'm still a Zippy fan. Just last year I went to see a play in the Mission District that was entirely based on Zippy comics. To know that my letter was found somewhere—and that Bill Griffith read it and drew a strip based on it—it's insane; it staggers the mind."

—DAVY

Justin Davisson at age 35

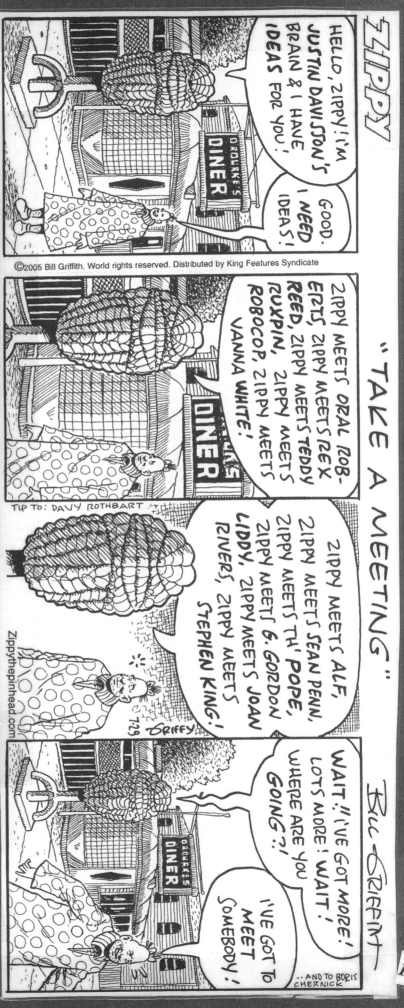

145

HIV Positive
I wisphered in his ear baby your daddys
gon, when you were first born he left
us both ~~hustand~~ alone

I found this in a computer center at NMSU. Deming, New Mexico is
a small town along I-10 a couple hundred miles west of here. —C.S.

Student Name Mitchell Herman
Date of Clinical : 9/7/04

PROCESS RECORDING

Brief Description of Patient: 23 year old male
Diagnosis (Major Axis I & II): Delusions
Cause of Admission: Delusions

VERBATIM	ANALYSIS/RATIONALE	INTERPRETATION (What do you think is happening with the patient? What is happening with the nurse?)
		Patient is calm. I'm calm.
Hi, I'm Mitch can we sit and talk a little after breakfast?	Therapeutic-Giving broad openings	
Yes, sure. I'll come back when I'm done.		
Ready? How's your day going?	Therapeutic-Giving broad openings	The patient is wanting to speak about his new ability. I'm anxious to hear about it. I'm a little nervous on the questions I'm going to ask. Trying to compile all questions in my head.
Ya! It's going really good, better than yesterday. I didn't want to be here yesterday, I was fighting them.		
So, being here is okay now?	Therapeutic-Paraphrasing	Pt. is beginning to tell story in detail, wants to speak. I'm very interested in what he is saying, pretty calm now. I'm trying to make good eye contact.
Yes, I have to be clean so people can believe me. I'm not crazy, I can really cure HIV/AIDS.		
Really, can you tell me a little bit more about it?	Therapeutic-Focusing	
Yes, it happened two days ago, I saw Jesus-but he was Hispanic. He told me that I could cure AIDS/HIV. I'm trying to cure the cops in Deming, their spreading it too. I cured my mom of AIDS that's how I know I can, I just have to pray and it disappears. Even at the hospital everyone was		

146

coming back negative for HIV/AIDS. I'm been chosen by a mathematical configuration. I'm on the list, a local and worldly list. I cured Bill Gates, Bush, Sr, of AIDS too. When I go back to Oregon I'm going buy the Trailblazers because Bill Gates is going to front me the money, well because he's grateful that I cured him you know.

Does this make you fearful, this ability?

No because I've seen the two descendents of Christ. I've been chosen to cure the world of AIDS/HIV. I'm blessed. I'm trying to cure Deming first because there is an epidemic there I call it epideming because it's so bad.

Wow that's an interesting ability. There giving you medication here, is it helping you?

Ya, I'm calmer now. I'm going to stop taking meth.

Are you experiencing any side effects?

No.

Good, well thank you for taking the time to speak with me I appreciate it. Take care of yourself.

Therapeutic-Focusing

Non-Therapeutic-Changing subject

Non-Therapeutic

Non-Therapeutic

My emotions are running 100 miles a minute. I'm scared because of his responses, I'm thinking to myself "What if he thinks I don't believe him and he becomes violent?" He's just telling his story because it's his reality.

I'm trying to stay calm and show a lot of interest in his story. Trying not to probe. Pt. is very calm, answering questions.

I'm very relieved. Patient wants to continue talking about reality and continues conversation with other resident.

FOUND Magazine. Trying to cure the cops in Deming.

STDs

Solving One Mystery At A Time...

PRIVATE DICK

FOUND by Marit Nelson

Boston, MA

I found this handmade sign taped to a locked door in a deserted alley.   —M.N.

follow the cops to the police station and
pay the their fines on the spot! I died.
it was great. so we followed officer Randy
about a mile to this one-room station and
paid the damn ~~fine~~ fine ($62, 70 in a 55 zone)
and then I took a picture with the cop
outside for gags (Louis pleasure)

another fine experience. mmm.
what a great tour.

I'm glad you were there saturday — I hope
it didn't embarrass you (probably not.)
how's your bowling average?
do you dream in color?
is a dog's mouth really cleaner than a human's?
was she putting us on, or will we really open
  for "the wedding present" in dallas? — doubt it.
who is the real King: elvis, grover, holden, max,
    steve
    McQueen ... ?

some kid walked up to me yesterday and said,
  "hey, aren't you the guy who ate the last
                          american cheeseburger?"

So many who survive explosions - more than half - sustain head injuries that doctors say anyone exposed to a blast should be checked for neurological problems. Brain damage, sometimes caused by skull-penetrating fragments, sometimes by shock waves or blows to the head, is a recurring theme.

Corporal ____ has no memory of the explosion or even the days before it, although he has had a recurring dream of being in Iraq and seeing the sky suddenly turn red.

No More Illusions On
The State of French Fry

1. My current health status is not as stable as many staff members may think; and it has the potential to become extremeley dangerous or serious in a very short amount of time.

② What is known about my injury is:
I have a fractured skull.
I have an extreme concussion.
I ~~have~~ have lost ~~XXXX~~ 95% ~~of~~ effectiveness in my left eye, plus having astigmitism in my right eye.
I have sensitivity to bright light i.e sunlight.
My reading ability is quite non-existent.
I am lacking in depth perception.
The ~~stress~~ of everyday activities causes a strain in my left eye which results in flashes and fuzzy vision.
My ears hurt all the time, ~~in~~
The intensity rises as the intensity of my surroundings varies.

16,472 wounded

bridesmaid

Bridget,

In an attempt to clear the air, I am sending you this letter. I feel as though Gary and I have been very supportive of your relationship with Paul.

We have listened to you and encouraged you when your parents were not accepting of your decisions to cultivate this relationship with Paul. I happily went shopping for wedding and bride's maid's dresses, sifted through invitations, picked out a cake top, offered to host your shower, and scheduled time to go shopping for your engagement picture outfit.

Yet, now that your relationship seems to be repaired without your parents, we seldom hear from you, once again. It's as though you think you need to chose to have only one familial relationship at a time.

Bridget, when you phoned to "disinvite" me from your bridal party, I was disappointed but I understood that you could only have one attendant. It made me feel good when you told me that if you could have had another bride's maid, You would have had me in it. At that point, I was still happy to host your bridal shower. It would have been nice if you would have been more certain of your plans before inviting me initially.

Yet, I must tell you that it was quite a slap in the face when you indirectly informed me that you had opted to invite Rebecca to be in the wedding. That was rude and hurtful. Yet, I am still "allowed" to throw you a shower?

I was surprised to hear that you were angry with Gary and I for "gossiping." This, coming from someone who phone calls to find out what your parents said about your wedding? We have always maintained your confidence and have only spoke on your behalf. Yet I must admit that I am rather tired of trying to be your friend and sister-in-law. A reciprocal relationship would have been nice, but I see no evidence that that will develop.

It appears that I am worthy, in your eyes, of hosting your wedding shower, having Mothers' Day to bail you out of an awkward situation, maintain confidence about your previous sexual experiences, and being a sounding board when your relationship with your parents is uncomfortable. Yet, you make derogatory comments about my inability to produce children (i.e., how I am lucky that Gary stays with me), you make rude comments about people not having a right to have a second marriage until everyone who hasn't been married has the opportunity, and ignore Gary and I unless you need something.

I wish you well in your life, Bridget. I know that you will be offended by this letter but I hope you will be able to examine some of your behavior. I don't think you mean to be hurtful; I think you are so preoccupied with getting what you want that you don't see how your actions affect other people.

I won't be hosting your shower. I do not wish to be in charge of your guest book or money tree. I am sure one of your friends will be happy to accommodate you. I imagine that you will want to vent regarding this letter. Feel free to do so. Five copies of this letter have been printed which I will be happy to mail out in order to clarify any potential misinterpretations if the need arises.

Kristina

P.S. You might want to ask your therapist about the enclosed information.

F.B.

—DAVY

this photo FOUND by Missy and Neff, Baton Rouge, LA

FOUND Magazine. One familial relationship at a time.

The Domed City
In Cloaked Earth Orbit

September 23, 2002

Dear Earth Human,

These centuries, we have watched you humans of earth with increasing interest, we being the *angels of Heaven.*

Till this date, you have lacked the perspective to see *us* clearly for what *we actually are,* to see clearly yourselves for what you are *actually.*

Your modern technology has changed all that. With your growing perception of the universe and its *real* composition, we, *the angels of Heaven,* believe the **TIME** has come.

Please, do not be shocked by the **REALITY.** Though it contradicts all that you have been brutally compelled to believe, the *actual* **TRUTH** shall set you free!

Our hand is extended to you, beckoning to you. The future is Bright and full of Hope if you will but have the courage to cast off your ancient mystical Misperceptions.

This little book, our *gift,* our *invitation* to you, is the **DOORWAY.** Be bold. Walk through it!

Soon, *we* shall reveal *ourselves* to you in a manner too unmistakable, too solid for you to deny or ignore.

I am the alien AUTHOR,

Teddy

TEDDY

THIS LITTLE BOOK IS THE DOORWAY

FOUND by Kellie Dooher

Maple Grove, MN

A few years ago I was a manager at a coffee shop. My staff had been telling me about this odd gentleman who repeatedly came into the shop and left copies of his book on the tables, with weird notes and inscriptions inside each one (his book was called *The Bridge*). They said he never ordered anything or spoke to anyone.

One evening I was working and he snuck in and left a copy on the table. As an avid reader, I quickly went to snatch it up (hey, free book!) My staff had thrown all the other copies away because they thought he was creepy. After reading this letter and his inscription, I started to understand their wariness of "the alien AUTHOR." But I can't bear to throw a perfectly good book away, so I've kept it—my curiosity will force me to read it someday. So I'm not sending you the actual book, but I thought you might enjoy his introductory letter—it might even make for a nice opening to your next FOUND book!

—K.D.

FOUND Magazine. We shall reveal ourselves to you.

BACK WHEN I WORKED IN THE COSTUME FACTORY, THE WORST THING WAS WHEN SOME HIGH SCHOOL WOULD RETURN A "SHOW COLLECTION"... SOME 60 OR SO OUTFITS ... UNLAUN-DERED.

...Oh Shit... Oklahoma

Got 6 giant boxes for ya

Sign as slowly as possible to Broadway Costume

UPS

ETHEL MADE DAMN SURE I CHECKED ALL THE POCKETS SO NO DAMN SHIT WOULD FUCK UP HER MAYTAG

You check the pockets, baby?

CLEAN UP AFTER YOURSELF! ETHEL AIN'T YOUR MAMA

ethel's ring around the collar recipe: scrub with a solution of equal parts ammonia & Dawn dishwashing liquid. Works like a dream!

TRUTH IS, I WAS FINDING ALL SORTS OF TANTALIZING, THRILLING, HALF-EXPLAINED BEAUTIFUL THINGS ...

AS THE STOOGE WITH LEAST SENIORITY, I HAD TO

Skip as slowly as possible

HARVEST THE HORRIBLE CONTENTS & SORT THEM FOR ETHEL THE LAUNDRESS.

AND ONCE, I FOUND A SMALL, DEAD SPIDER MONKEY IN THE RIGHT BREAST POCKET OF JUD'S ACT 2 "FANCY" SHIRT

THE ONE HE WEARS TO THE BOX SOCIAL!!!

A DOG!

I JUST DIDN'T REALIZE IT BECAUSE I'M NOT

She went to 2nd with Brad & had pork chops for dinner!

HAVE YOU EVER GOTTEN A WHIFF OF A HEAVY COTTON PETTICOAT THAT GOES STRAIGHT FROM THE BODY OF AN OVERHEATED SOPHOMORE CHORINE INTO A BOX IN WHICH IT WILL SPEND THE NEXT 5 DAYS AS IT TRAVELS FROM FLAGSTAFF TO CHICAGO, GROUND SHIPPING?

JUST KIDDING. I FOUND A LOT OF FLESH COLORED COVER-UP STICKS & BINACA BREATH SPRAY. ONCE I FOUND A VINTAGE PHOTO

BUT TO TELL YOU THE TRUTH, AT THE TIME I WAS MUCH MORE INTERESTED IN THE 20 DOLLAR BILL I FOUND IN SOME FOOLISH BOY'S RETURNED SACK COAT.

CLEAN UP AFTER YOURSELF! ETHEL AIN'T YOUR MAMA

BY THE WAY, WOULDN'T THIS BE A GREAT THING TO FIND?

tucked between the pages of a motel room Bible or maybe just blowing down the street... a street in Kuala Lumpur!

IT IS THE MOST RANK MUSK OF TEEN GIRL SWEAT AND LOVE'S BABY SOFT.

now he will like me!

pssst

love's baby soft

golly, that shor is a purty costume (purty ugly!)

I NEVER HIT THE JACKPOT LIKE MY FRIEND, KAREN, WHO WAS MARRIED TO A GUY WHO MANAGED A THRIFT STORE. ONCE HE FOUND A $200 GIFT CERTIFICATE TO ANN TAYLOR IN A POCKET OF A DONATION. IT WAS THREE YEARS OLD BUT KAREN CASHED IT IN WITHOUT INCIDENT. ANOTHER TIME HE BROUGHT HOME A PHOTO OF ANN LANDERS EMBRACING JIMMY CARTER.

ONE OF THE BEST THINGS I EVER FOUND CAME OUT OF MY OWN POCKETS WHICH I FAILED TO CHECK BEFORE PUTTING A LOAD IN AT SPEED QUEEN.

IT CAME OUT OF THE DRYER SO FLUFFY & CUTE! I WAS HARDLY EMBARASSED. can you guess? ladies?

J + Steven = L-O-V-É

LOVE P.S. He comes over every Wed. Night →

AND WE Really do have it, that's why I'm 15 + pregnant

GARY —
Please sleep on the couch. We'll talk in the morning. Colleen

Denise—
Can i give you a sensual massage; then, I will talk about Jesus

I love how you need no postage!

PRESORTED
First-Class Mail
U.S. Postage Paid
InfoSend, Inc.
Mailed From
Zip Code 92834

I love how you love that about me!

SERMON ON THE MOUNT

FOUND by Scot Nobles & Jimmy
Austin, TX

Found this note at BookPeople, where we work, inside a copy of Dave Eggers' book *A Heartbreaking Work of Staggering Genius.*
—S.N.

Dear Joe—
When I'm with you—
I feel retarted. I
love you—
~~ waves ~~

RETARTED
FOUND by Amber Archambo
New York, NY

ADDRESS SERVICE REQUESTED

155

ON THE PROWL WITH
POPCORN PETE
WORLD'S GREATEST FINDER*

DAVY REPORTS!

In the first FOUND book I told you about my younger brother, Peter, who's an amazing finder. Peter is starting a career as a musician, and he continues to support himself the same way he did in college—by raiding Dumpsters and alleyways around Ann Arbor and selling the things he finds. His specialty is still abandoned textbooks—he sells them online for anything from a few bucks to a hundred bucks each. Of course, while he's out looking for textbooks he always comes across all kinds of other interesting things. Over the years he's brought me a lot of the finds that have ended up as my favorites of all-time (some of these are scattered over the next few pages).

RYANSIAS.COM

Strangely, until recently I'd never gone out with Peter on one of his Dumpster-diving missions. I love FOUND stuff, but I don't like getting dirty. I realized, though, that there was only one way I was going to learn the secrets of the World's Greatest Finder*, so one afternoon not too long ago, I drove into downtown Ann Arbor with my brother to join him on the prowl. I'd figured I'd come home with some neat tips on how to find stuff; I ended up with much more.

We park my '81 Fairmont on Oakland Street, in the heart of the student housing district at the south end of campus. It's the third week of August, one of the prime moving days of the year—"high season for finding," as Peter puts it. Trash and furniture and debris piled on the curb in front of nearly every house. It's a hot, sunny afternoon. We climb out of the car and Peter leads me into a long, shady alley.

Peter: Are you hoping to find anything in particular? Anything you really need?

Davy: Mostly I'm here to observe. I'm like the U.N. But I could kinda use a mirror, you know, one of those long, tall mirrors, and also some shelves for the FOUND office.

Peter: We'll find that stuff. Anything else?

Davy: Nah.

Peter: What's the one thing you'd most like to have? Anything in the world, what would it be?

Davy: I don't know. Well, I was telling Mike Kozura last night that I really, really want that Bon Jovi CD, *Cross Road*. My roommate Tim in Chicago used to play it all the time. There's a great remix of "Living on a Prayer," all slowed-down and subdued, it's beautiful.

Peter fishes into the first trash can we come to.

*(well, one of them...)

Peter: Here's a mirror. The frame's kinda broke, though. We'll come back for it later if we don't find a better one.

Davy: Here's how shitty a reporter I am, I don't even have a notebook to write things down.

Peter: Don't worry about that. We'll find you one.

Behind the next house, trash spills across the driveway into the alleyway. Peter roots around for a minute or two and then brings me a thick ringed notebook. The first few pages contain notes from a class called Dynamics and Vibrations, *the rest is blank. I tell him I need a pen and in about thirty seconds he gives me three—blue, red, and black. We continue down the alley. At the back of a huge multi-unit house sits an enormous Dumpster the size of a tank. Trash overflows it, completely covering the tiny backyard. Peter starts to poke through it.*

Peter: Holy shit, this is ridiculous. This is one of your bigger piles. Hey, anytime you see a book, tell me, even if it's all nasty, in real bad shape.

Gingerly, I step around the perimeter. There's a pair of hockey skates, the book Mexican Cooking for Dummies, *a combination lock, a bottle of red Resolve cleaner, a pink index card that says "to say, to tell" on it, a computer monitor, drapes, a rugby ball, an open jar of peanut butter studded with flies, a plastic squeeze-bottle of Hershey's syrup, a gold visor for a team called the Gorillas, a torn picture from a Playboy calendar, and a broom that has been split precisely in two, lengthwise, as though struck by lightning.*

Peter: Need an Ethernet cord? Or a desk lamp? *He holds them up with each hand.*

Davy: I'll take that lamp. Who eventually cleans all this stuff up?

Peter: I don't know, someone unfortunate. Someone who probably works for the landlord.

Davy: Do you think maintenance people don't like scavengers because they spread trash all around?

Peter: Sometimes. If it's contained, I keep it contained. If it gets like this, it doesn't matter. I feel sorry for whoever has to deal with this shit. I can't believe how much shit there is here. Hey, want a Cincinnati Bearcats hat? *He picks up a book.* All right, this one, *The Intermediate Macroeconomics Study Guide,* I know for a fact this one's not worth anything. I've found this one before. Well, I'll take it anyway, it may be a newer edition. Wow, these people really fucked up their books. It all fits together—if you don't respect money, you don't respect your belongings, and you don't respect the people who have to clean up after you. Basically, you don't give a fuck about your stuff as long as you don't have to deal with it. I think I'm satisfied with this pile. Pretty uncommon to see this big a pile. Ridiculous!

Ms. Casale,

I feel very awkward, but your underware is showing greatly

—Brittanii

Peter pulls a black milk crate from the edge of the pile and loads it with my new desk lamp, a pair of black Adidas athletic snap-pants, and a couple books he's found. We continue on down the alley.

Davy: How do you know which books have value?

Peter: Experience. I kinda have an idea of what sells. But a lot of the time I don't know if a book's worth anything, so I bring it home and look it up and then I know. Sometimes I'm surprised. Come on, let's roll. *A little further down, he stops at a pair of rain-soaked and muddy couches.* These have been here for weeks. It's too bad, they were in great shape, pretty nice, really. Hey, Capri Sun! There's like two cases here. Well, I'm not usually into taking food, only canned goods. I leave food for the bums. They need it more than me. Same with the cans and bottles, I let them take the cans and bottles back.

Davy: It seems like with scavenging there's different tiers, you know, of who will take what.

Peter: Bums and not-bums. *He picks up a pile of photo negatives and holds them up toward the sun.* Hmm, looks like a party. There's pretty much two classes of finds—stuff I want to sell or keep for myself, and stuff that might be good for *FOUND Magazine.* Here, these are for you, you should get 'em printed at Rite Aid and see if there's anything good.

Davy: Do you ever run into other scavenger types while you're out here?

Peter: Sure. Especially during moveout—April and May, that's the real peak season. There's a lot of different folks who come out here and do this. Some are students and ex-students who just live in the area and like to browse around and see if there's anything they need. And then there's folks who come from far away, all over Southeast Michigan, and even Northwest Ohio. I've met 'em, I see 'em out here, most are pretty friendly. There's a kind of etiquette, if you find something first, you get it. You let someone else finish with a Dumpster before you start jumping in.

We arrive at a sweet-smelling Dumpster behind the big pink house at 1106 Hill Street, widely known, reasonably, as The Pink House. When I was in college, a couple of my friends lived in one of the apartments in here.

Peter: That's a hundred-dollar blanket in there, I think it's from the Gap. I could probably use that.

Davy: Just stick it in the wash?

Peter: Some of my friends are anti-clothing-from-the-Dumpster, they say it'll carry germs. But you can always put things through the washing machine. It's not like this comforter was owned by dirty people. *He points to a girl in an upstairs window.* It's just people's belongings. I won't keep something if it's covered in salsa. But this looks okay. *He gathers it up.* Let's go back to the car and dump this stuff.

Davy: Did you see the people watching us from the back of The Pink House?

Peter: No. I guess most people think what I'm doing is fucked up and weird. Well, I don't know what they think, but they look at you that way. To go through trash you have to go through a shift in view. People see anything in a Dumpster as trash, and they think if it's there it should stay there, it's dirty or whatever. But this blanket, which probably came from someone's bed forty-five minutes ago, I don't think it's trash.

Davy: Yeah, it's really crazy that you can move something in physical space, and it becomes something else! From a blanket into trash.

Peter: Yeah, I'm just seeing it still as a blanket.

A Jeep Grand Cherokee rumbles down the alley with five girls inside, shouting merrily.

Peter: The perpetrators. What's interesting to me is how snidely people look down on what I do. I guess I look down at them, too. I try not to be judgmental, but I see them as wasteful and irresponsible. If they ask me what I'm doing, I try to explain.

Davy: You don't look like a bum. It must be puzzling to them.

Peter: Maybe they think I am. Here, open the car, let me put this stuff in.

Davy: Um, could we put it in the trunk?

Peter: The shit in your trunk is far more trashy than what I just pulled out of the Dumpster. *He pus his newest finds inside, and we continue on.* Yeah, usually when I do this, [my friend] Beth drives around with me. People see us driving around, loading up their quote-unquote trash. Beth's got a nice new car, or sometimes I've got mom's van. Clearly we're not just bums, and when they see us I think sometimes it forces people to reconsider what they're doing, throwing all this stuff out.

Davy: Well, what's the motivation for people to keep stuff that they don't need or want anymore? I've probably done the same thing plenty of times, dragged a load of junk to the curb to be taken away.

this photo FOUND by Mike Shinn, Culver City, CA

Peter: Most people aren't completely reckless. Sometimes they place things outside the Dumpster, they want someone to take it, for it to have a second life. I just wish people would take responsibility for their belongings, not live so disposably. The people who manufacture a lot of things take advantage of how disposable our society is. They want people to keep stuff for six months, then throw it out. I used to not pick up garbage I saw in the woods because I hoped people would see it and it would shake them up. But, where are we now? Church Street. Church is a fucking mess, it always is, always will be. This is just how Church Street is—twenty-five moldy newspapers on every lawn, thousands of beer cups, trash everywhere.

People are inoculated against it. Now I think it's important to set a good example, clean up everything you can. People see you cleaning up, see a space cleaner than it used to be, and maybe they'll appreciate it, even start doing it themselves.

We're at another pile of curbside move-out trash and debris. A little braver now, I sort through it a little and find a bag full of Scrabble tiles and a nice pair of red soccer shorts. There's a pile full of campaign signs for student government elections with the slogan Get Stoned! Matt Stone and Megan Stohner for President and V-P.

Peter: Do you want the first audiotape of *Call of the Wild*? Or a *Playboy*? Oh, here's what it's all about. *He holds up two LSAT prep books.* These are worth about ten bucks each; they're in pretty good condition. Now is peak buying season, August and September. I sell about ten or twenty books a week. Here's some good RCA cords. *He moves some chairs and sofa cushions.* Here's a graduation gown. Oooh, *When Harry Met Sally*, on DVD, Beth'll probably like that. That's the kind of thing that's not sellable, but hell, everyone loves *When Harry Met Sally*. *Guide to American Law Schools*, brand new, could be good. Eminem album, *Off the Wall*, what the hell is this, I've never heard of this one. Look, it's your friends, The Alkaline Trio, in this copy of *Stuff* magazine. *Stuff* magazine, ha. *This* is stuff. Hey, a copy of the Qur'an—I want to read this.

Inter marriage - marring relatives

is never ok unless is a very far far away relative

(Pam) — I think that Inter marriage is okay because if your'e ugly and no one wants to marry you, and you really want to have a family you have to marry your relatives. It's wrong because if you have a baby the baby could have mental problems.

Davy: I think it's funny that there's two trash cans buried under these crazy mounds of junk. Are you gonna keep that *Playboy*?

Peter: You can have it. I don't see anything to put all this stuff in.

Davy: I'm thinking about that *When Harry Met Sally* DVD. One of the main thrills of doing this seems to be the absolutely random nature of it; you never know what you'll find.

Peter: You find basically anything. Mostly bathroom supplies, textbooks, carpet. Classic college stuff. In the alley we're about to go to, one time I was in there and a guy came out of his back door with a big bag of trash and very warily put it in the Dumpster. He must've been thinking, "Is this guy gonna look through my trash?" *Of course* I was going to. It was like sixty-five empty boxes for hard-core porn DVDs. You can sort of expect to find anything out here, and you will. The only thing I haven't found are dangerous weapons.

Davy: Aaron Cometbus tells a great story about walking along Lake Merritt in Oakland and finding an uzi.

Peter: Did he send it to FOUND?

Davy: No, he tucked it back in the bushes! So, do you think it's just a class thing, that these super-wealthy college kids are the ones throwing everything out?

Peter: Probably not. As much as I rant against them, I think it's more about the basic values you're raised with. Some poorer students don't value their stuff either. Though I doubt they are the ones throwing out money. I find a lot of money that has been thrown out! On purpose! Not large sums—but would you ever really just throw a dollar bill away? I've found 'em. And tons and tons of change. It's always in cups or mugs, or in desk drawers. Not just pennies, but nickels, dimes, quarters. Fifty dollars in change, all in one giant mug, I've found. Davy, look over there, this person's doing what we're doing. *Across the street a dreadlocked kid in a tie-dyed shirt is carrying and rolling a nice desk chair in two pieces.* He didn't just buy that. People moving office chairs they just bought into their house don't walk four blocks to do it.

We move down the street into another alley. Peter climbs into a blue Dumpster.

Peter: If I didn't enjoy it, it wouldn't be worth the money. I do make a lot of money, but the best part is the fun of digging through it all. And it's satisfying to make money off... nothing. Damn it! *Multivariable Calculus, Fourth Edition.* I own that one, it's worth a lot. But this one is rain-soaked, it's ruined. Hey, I think I cut my finger. I better find some mittens or something; I like to have mittens or gloves. Here's a good vacuum cleaner, any interest in that?

Davy: What do you think of the smell of Dumpsters?

Peter: It's mostly tolerable. Sometimes a little bit nasty. Every once in a while, one is fucking completely disgusting-smelling, just horrendous. Certainly a dead animal at the bottom of it. Not worth digging then. Here's some notebooks, that's a good sign, it means textbooks are nearby. People throw 'em out together. Hey, here's some hockey gloves, perfect. Every once in a while, your hand finds this little pocket of nastiness, some old macaroni and cheese... it's good to have gloves. But it doesn't really matter, I wash my hands afterwards, I take a shower.

We move on to three Dumpsters behind a sorority.

Peter: I like to have a cane, a diving stick I call it. Mop handles are good because they're sturdy but also a little flexible. That way I can shift things around in a Dumpster and see what's there, rather than jumping into every one. Here in this alley a girl once told me never to look through their trash. She said to leave or she'd call the cops. I asked her why. She said people were always making a big mess. I said I wasn't going to make a mess. She said if I didn't leave right away she was calling the cops. I said fine, call them, and started looking through the Dumpsters. She didn't call them. I guess if she was convinced I wasn't going to make a mess she probably wouldn't have cared. Some people, though, even if they don't want something, they don't want anyone else to have it.

Davy: There sure are a lot of AOL CDs.

Peter: Everywhere!

Davy: I wonder what the *most* common item you find is. Hmm. Okay, Pete, a lot of the stuff people think is trash, you don't. So, what *is* trash?

Peter: Something that has *no* use or value.

Davy: This Dumpster smells riper.

Peter: It *is*. Fraternity Dumpsters, those are really nasty. Sororities have nice trash, it hasn't been obliterated. It's well-organized, they might even recycle. Apartment complexes are best for rummaging, lots of inhabitants in a small space, lots of trash and castoffs. Frat row is not efficient rummaging, the houses are too spread apart. Co-ops don't throw shit away. Let's check this one. The Dumpster here is always really nasty, but we might as well... Wow, exactly as predicted. Nothing here, but it smells terrible. I have a relationship with every Dumpster in town.

Davy: You say it jokingly but is it sort of true?

Peter: Yes, it is. Even year after year, there's different tenants but the Dumpsters have continuity in terms of being good ones or bad ones, it's weird, huh?

Davy: I remember why this is called the student ghetto. Dude, this is so nasty here. And when I was in school I used to live around here, too. Somehow I never noticed how fucked up it was.

Peter: Yeah, Vaughn Street and Greenwood are the worst. There's no alleys there, no Dumpsters, so the trash is just all over the front yards and the streets. Hey, here's something. *He hops into a small Dumpster, then bounces up and down inside.* A mini-trampoline! It's kind of broken, though. *We continue on.* Looks like they repaved this lot here. These piles on South Forest are never any good. Let's roll.

We stop at my car to add a few things to our take in the trunk, then walk down East University, stopping to sift through trash piles here and there.

Peter: Ooooh, that's money, that's big money. Look, it's *The Democratic Peace* and *Territorial Conflict of the 20th Century.*

This smiling alien FOUND by Jonathan Greenbank, Lancashire, England

I.O.U
a
Ballerina

FOUND
by Peter!

161

Davy: How 'bout this one, *The Poisonwood Bible* by Barbara Kingsolver?

Peter: Nope. Fiction is worthless. *Communism and Its Collapse*, this one could sell. *X-Games ProBoarder*, an ESPN computer game, I think this is worth ten or twenty bucks. Here's a tie. Dad's birthday present? Just kidding. I never give people shit from the trash that I pretend isn't from the trash. This person has a lot of Mongolian Bar-B-Q shirts. I guess they worked there. There's like fifteen of 'em! You could assemble a fleet of Mongolian Bar-B-Q workers. A lot of the shit I see, I wonder why people had it in the first place. What made them decide they wanted it? Like the giant wine bottles, or the metal beer signs. Here's a box that says FREE STUFF. Nothing in it. Here's a dead hammock. Mugs. Mugs are common, there's a lot of fucking coffee mugs in this world. There's your answer, the most common piece of trash. They're mass-produced, and you get 'em free with things.

Davy: Is it sad that all things will eventually end up as trash?

Peter: Not all things need to.

Davy: It always feels so sad when I move out of a place to see all my old stuff on the curb, wasting away in the rain. It's a peculiar—and particular—kind of sadness.

Peter: Here's a New Jersey license plate. Look, it's a *The Club*. Here's some camouflage pants. A full-size futon. Who needs a bed? Doesn't Amy need a bed? I'll call her and tell her where it is. Here's a big spice rack, I would take it if I needed it.

Davy: I like the strange juxtapositions. You know, a Physics book, a cat-scratching post, a hair dryer, and a jar of Gummi Bears. MacGyver could make something cool.

Peter: Check out this sweatshirt. *He holds up a black-and-white Puma hoodie.* It's an exact match for the pants I'm wearing. Awesome! Hey, here's your mirror, check it out. It's in perfect shape.

Davy: Wow, that's cool. And I was gonna go to Meijer's and buy one.

Peter: During high season, like now, and especially April and May, you can find anything you want. If you *wanted* to find a water gun, you could go out and find one.

Davy: It's kind of like going to Meijer's.

Peter: Right. But it's all free.

Davy: I like how containers seem to present themselves when you need them. That little red duffel bag, for instance. You don't really need to bring bags with you to carry your finds home in, you just find bags to carry your finds home.

Peter: There's one group of kids called Crusties. They scavenge a lot, which is cool, but they also steal a lot. Some of my friends steal a lot. I used to steal a lot, but now I think there's nothing righteous about taking other people's property. But trash, giving it new use, that's respectable. Something created, once created, should be given as much utility as possible.

Davy: I always look at the stuff you bring home a bit dubiously, but once you give it to me and I use it for a while, I forget that it was ever "trash."

Peter: These shoes were "trash."

Davy: How much do you make selling books?

Peter: A few hundred dollars a month in low season, maybe a thousand a month in high season. That's books. Then sometimes I sell other stuff I've found.

Davy: Like what?

162

FOUND by Peter!

the man sitting at The table
In front of us is the
doctor who did The
inseminations for

Kathy and I

Peter: I found this computer that's a special computer for use with ultrasound systems, a medical equipment company threw it away. I got five hundred dollars for that. I sold some bar-code scanners I found for a couple hundred dollars. But also, there's a lot of stuff I've found that I've just kept and use all the time. The shoes I'm wearing. My *huge* computer monitor. My stereo speakers. A lot of my clothes. A lot of little things—the flashlight and water bottle on my bike. A lot of the time the next book I'm gonna read is determined by what I find. This book about a Honduran in exile I just read, I never would've read it if I hadn't found it. You can discover books you wouldn't know about. I just found and read a Studs Terkel book called *Working*. The main library, that's a good source for books. Their Dumpsters I mean. Some I sell, some I read.

Davy: To some people the idea of getting dirty is abhorrent, totally intolerable.

Peter: I don't like being dirty, but I don't have a strong revulsion to it. Dirt comes off. Some stuff I don't want to touch, like organic waste—food or shit or vomit, things that are sticky or really wet. But it's good to get a little dirty sometimes. Farmers get dirty. At camp, I used to feed the pigs their slop. The pigs liked it. We all have different ideas about what cleanliness is.

Davy: Brother Mike and you share these values, digging through trash like we're doing today. For me, its harder. Is it nature or nurture?

Peter: Mike and I get into it for different reasons. Mike gets more of a thrill out of it. He mostly looks for stuff he wants. I look for things to sell. I'm more enterprising. This is my job. Dumpster-diving is not for everyone. Some people [*he looks at me*] are just punk-ass bitches.

Davy: I like this, but I think my interest in finding stuff is more in the direction of finding notebooks and journals and letters. I'm interested in the people behind all of this stuff.

Peter: Good for you. Let's roll. Let's go to Vaughn and Greenwood.

Davy: I know you're into the human part of it, too. You've written all of these songs based on FOUND notes and letters. What's that process like? Do you feel a closeness and kinship with the person who wrote the actual note? Do you put yourself into their heads?

Peter: Sure. I suppose so. Let's roll.

We move a few blocks down, to Vaughn Street. The curbs are piled high with trash in one long continuous row, like bunkers erected during a flood. We take it all in silently, poking around a bit in the piles. Some other kids see me sifting through stuff and taking notes and ask if we're with the Red Cross. "Just finding stuff," Peter says. We walk up Packard to Greenwood, and agree that we'll finish up our excursion in the next couple blocks.

Davy: I still have to find some shelves. You said we would.

Peter: We will. Last year, me and Chris were looking through trash, and some girls said, "Hey, we've got tons of shit we're getting rid of in here," and invited us into their house. They had this huge bong, a helium tank, some other weird stuff. Chris took the bong. Here's a desk—you've always gotta open desk drawers, you never know what you might find. *He opens a drawer and holds up a red-and-white fishing lure and bobber.* See, like this! What else do we have here… Swiss Miss packets… a little Darth Maul figure. Okay, here's some shelves. These are pretty nice bookshelves, actually. What do you think?

Music: Picture Lady

- have a good idea for her present. A free tabby kitten. Is it O.K.? (It's o.k. with her mom. She likes clothes.)

plead for my life

found by peter

FOUND by Peter

I would never choose to live in a frat house. Don't hit my penis please, it doesn't feel good.

163

Peter: Hey, check out all these matches. Ohio Blue Tip matches, these are waterproof. There's fifty little boxes of them, I'll never need matches again.

I decide to sort through one final box. It's kind of hard to stop looking—there's that feeling that the real treasure is just one more box away. Then all of a sudden I'm stunned—the sight of it sends a shiver up my spine and raises the hairs on my arms—it's the Bon Jovi CD I was talking about, sitting there loose in a pile of socks, shiny as a doubloon. I am absolutely dumbfounded. What are the fucking odds?

Davy: Hey Peter! Check it out! Holy shit—look what I found!

Peter is facing the other way, a pair of Spiderman swimmies pushed up his arms, and an iron in his hands, the cord drooping down into the box he's pulled it from.

Peter: Hold on. I'm just basically trying to figure out if I want this iron or not.

Davy: What the fuck man, I found the exact fucking CD I was looking for!

Peter: That's cool. Listen though, do you need an iron?

Other finds in this section by:
Zoe Gladstone, Oakland, CA; Susannah Smith, Hillsborough, NC; Camille Napier, Natick, MA

BON JOVI
CROSS ROAD

FOUND by Davy

[Epilogue: I dropped Peter off at our parents' house, then went back to my house and played the Bon Jovi CD. A couple of the songs skipped a little where the CD was scratched, but the songs I wanted to hear the most were completely intact. I was still listening to it three hours later when Peter called me. He'd already sold four of the books he'd found that afternoon for a total of $130.]

Art and Architecture

The setting is a dance. The characters are in their late teens. The dance could be in at a frat party, high school dance, or college formal. The three characters are seated on a couch. An attractive girl in a prom dress sits between two equally handsome guys. They are all in semi-formal attire, the girl is in a prom dress and the two guys may be in either blazers or just a shirt and tie. They seem to be tired from dancing and sit down to talk with each other. One of the guys is dating the girl and the other guy is a good friend of the girl, although the two guys have only briefly met on prior occasions.

Erica- Sweet and worldly girl, very intelligent
Kevin – Erica's boyfriend, gregarious
Jared – Erica's friend, comic but intelligent

Erica: I am so glad you could ~~make it~~ *Come* to the dance today Kevin.

Kevin: You had doubts that I ~~wouldn't make it~~ *Couldn't Come*?

Jared: She has been talking about you all week!

Erica: Well if you didn't see the person you loved that ~~much~~ *much* ~~like me~~ you would be excited to.

Kevin: I don't think he has that problem.

Jared: Yes I am not jumping to bang the pots and pans like some people.

Kevin: What?

Jared: Well, Erica and I have been having some interesting conversations about extra curricular activities.

Kevin: Oh has she?

Erica: Well there is not much to tell.

Kevin and Jared: Not much to tell?!?

All: *Laugh*

Erica: Well actually we were talking about other related topics not focusing on us.

Kevin: Like what?

Jared: Poly-amorous relationships, monage trois, threesomes.

Kevin: Is this a statement or a request.?

Erica: Neither!

Jared: I was just saying that they didn't happen that much I didn't think. I mean it never really came to my mind before. Just not something I have spent much thought on. Your girlfriend has quite an active imagination.

Kevin: That's for sure.

Erica: Well it happens more than you think.

Jared: No…

Kevin: Actually it does.

ART AND ARCHITECTURE

FOUND by Popcorn Pete

Ann Arbor, MI

This is one of my favorite finds of all-time—a four-page play of which Peter found only pages 1, 2, and 4!

— DAVY

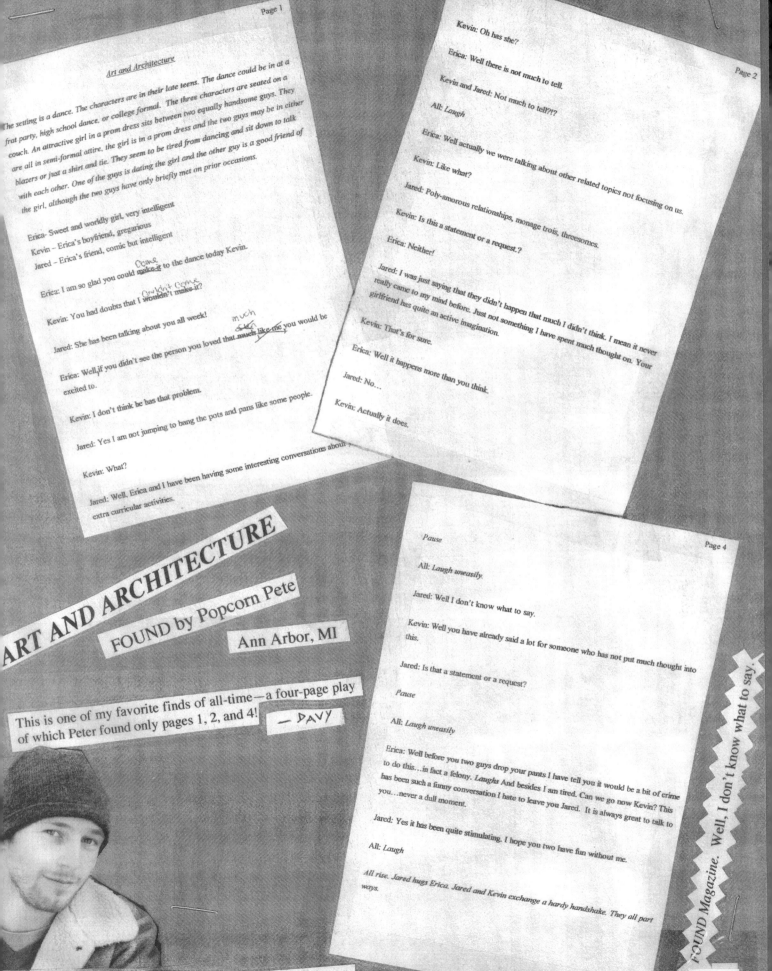

Pause

All: *Laugh uneasily.*

Jared: Well I don't know what to say.

Kevin: Well you have already said a lot for someone who has not put much thought into this.

Jared: Is that a statement or a request?

Pause

All: *Laugh uneasily*

Erica: Well before you two guys drop your pants I have tell you it would be a bit of crime to do this…in fact a felony. *Laughs* And besides I am tired. Can we go now Kevin? This has been such a funny conversation I hate to leave you Jared. It is always great to talk to you…never a dull moment.

Jared: Yes it has been quite stimulating. I hope you two have fun without me.

All: *Laugh*

All rise. Jared hugs Erica. Jared and Kevin exchange a hardy handshake. They all part ways.

POPCORN PETE SAYS: Perform this play with your friends! And if anyone finds page 3, please send it in.

I found this note yesterday in a plastic bottle sealed with duct tape that washed up on the shore in the South Bronx, near the Throgs Neck Bridge. As a professional diver, I'm always finding interesting things along the New York City waterfront, but this is by far the most poignant I've seen.

—K.R.

THIS IS IN MEMORY OF LINDA A UNIQUE WOMAN WHO WE SADLY LOST ON SUNDAY OCTOBER 3rd 2004. SHE TOUCHED SO MANY HEARTS IN THIS WORLD AND SHALL NEVER BE FORGOTTEN.

LINDA HAD A GREAT CROSS TO BEAR AND DID SO WITH GREAT STRENGTH. HER REWARD WILL BE GREAT. WE WERE ALL BLESSED TO HAVE HER IN OUR LIVES. LET HER NOT BE FORGOTTEN. WITH TEARS WE RELEASE HER AND SEND HER ON HER WAY.

WE NEED ONLY PEER INTO THE DARK DANCING EYES OF LOLITA (HER LOVELY PALE YELLOW LABRADOR) TO KNOW THAT THE SPIRIT OF LINDA LIVES STALWARTLY ON BEHIND US FOREVER.

O LET HER NOT BE FORGOTTEN AND SO SHE SHALL NOT BE.

illustration by Dan Tice

I was jogging on a path along the Huron River when I saw a 40-ounce beer bottle bobbing in the shallow currents a couple feet from shore. I figured I'd do my little part to keep the river clean, and when I plucked the bottle out of the water, I found this letter to God inside. I never knew Vikings drank malt liquor! —P.W.

DEAR LORD GOD THE ONE THE ONLY, TRUE GOD CREATOR of All THAT is Good CREATOR of HEAVEN & EARTH. BEUTY BLISS & SPIRIT. PLEASE FORGIUE ME FOR MY SINS & MY EUIL WAYS & CLEAREFIE THOUGHTS! PLEASE PUREFIE & & CLEAREFIE MY MIND body & SPIRIT. PLEASE HELP ME & GIUE ME TO ACHIEUE ALL MY GOALS & DREAMS. PLEASE HELP ME TO KEEP STRIUE AliUE AND AlWAYS PERSIUERE. PLEASE LORD DON'T LET ME GIUE UP ON MY SELF HELP ME STAY STRONG & KEEP MY HEAD UP. PLEASE LET GREAT THINGS COME MY WAY AND LET ME HAVE A GOOD LIFE & be HAPPY SUCCESSFUL & LOUED. PLEASE HELP THOSE THAT I MAY HAVE HARMED Along THE WAY FIND IT IN THERE HEARTS TO FORGIUE ME AND BE WEll. PLEASE EASE MY STRESS, DEPRESION, ANXIETYS & ANGER & NOT WORRY ME TO CALM DOWN & NOT WORRY SO MUCH. PLEASE HELP ME TO DO RIGHT by YOU, MY SELF, MY LOUED ONES & All. PLEASE LORD LET ME MEET THE lADY THAT WILL LOUE ME, ONE THAT is KIND HEARTED & ATTRACTIUE, THAT I CAN RELATE TO & GET ALONG WITH. THE ONE THAT I WILL AlWAYS LOUE & CONFIDE IN. PLEASE LORD LET ME be ATTRACTIUE TO PEOPLE. PLEASE KEEP EUIL, BIASNESS & HATERED AWAY FROM ME FOR AS YOU KNOW IUE EXPEAREANCED WAY TO MUCH of THAT CARMA AND NO LONGER NEED IT All IN MY PASSED life. PLEASE LORD let All MY PASSED LOUED ONES

this note continues on the next page! →

Be sheltered IN YOUR BLISS FOR ETERNITY
& let there SPIRITS be AT Pense
& ... your BLISS
loved ones
CARE
... there
... MY loved ones ... PRAYERS be
Hopes DREAMS. Please let MY FATHER
ANSWERED. Please let MY FATHER
Get his COURT SETTLEMENT SOON
& SOCIAL SECURITY ease his PAIN,
Regain his HEALTH & See CHRIS
AND let All be well As I
KNOW IN MY HEART He diserves.
Please lord let MY MOTHER
get her SOCIAL SECURITY & EASE
Her ANXIETYs & DEPRESION AND
get her RETIREMENT AND let her HEART
be well AS I KNOW IN MY she
deserves. Please lord EASE the
STRESS & WORRYs FROM both MY
Mother & FATHER & Always love
& gide them. Please lord take
CARE of MY brothers & let
Them Achieve there goals & DREAMS
EASE there PAINS & give them. Please
strength, love & gide them. Please
lord let MY FAMILYs love AND
bond Always be & become EVEN
STRONGER if Posible through Positively.
lord Please bless US All &
keep US SAFE with YOUR shelter
I love you. Please Also lord
forgive MY loved ones for ANY
SINS they MAY HAVE committed.
Please lord let OUR Dog
FRISCO Be A HAPPY Pet IN his
Old days AND ease his PAINS & UNDER
STAND he is loved. THANK YOU. ~ CREATOR

LOVE YOUR SON Sean

illustration by Dan Tice

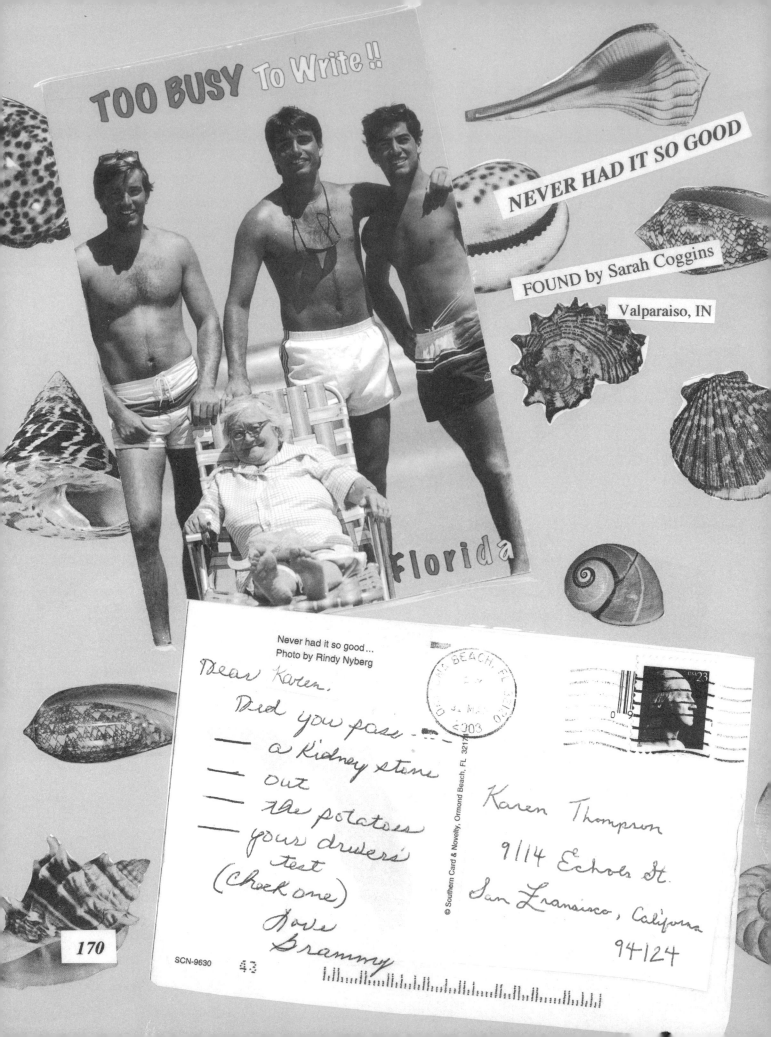

TOO BUSY To Write!!

NEVER HAD IT SO GOOD

FOUND by Sarah Coggins

Valparaiso, IN

Florida

Never had it so good...
Photo by Rindy Nyberg

Dear Karen,
Did you pass
— a kidney stone
— out
— the potatoes
— your driver's test
(check one)
Love
Grammy

Karen Thompson
9/14 Echols St.
San Fransisco, California
94124

© Southern Card & Novelty, Ormond Beach, FL 32174

170

SCN-9630   43

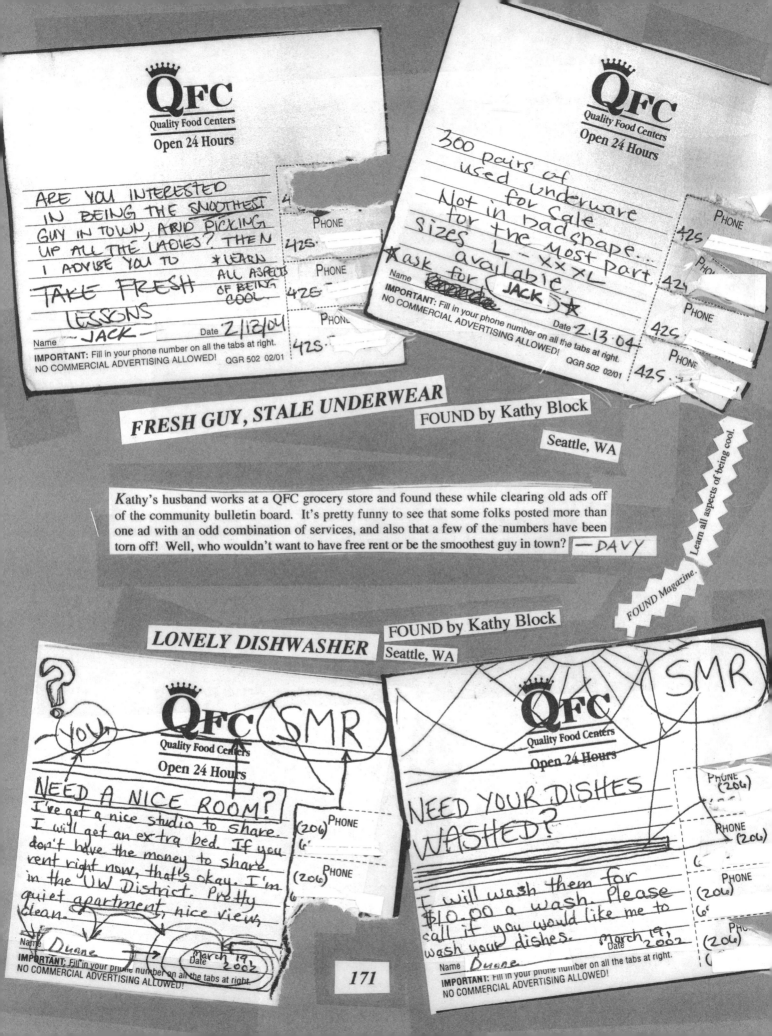

QFC
Quality Food Centers
Open 24 Hours

ARE YOU INTERESTED
IN BEING THE SMOOTHEST
GUY IN TOWN, AND PICKING
UP ALL THE LADIES? THEN
I ADVISE YOU TO   *LEARN
                        ALL ASPECTS
TAKE FRESH   OF BEING
                        COOL.
LESSONS

Name ___JACK___   Date 2/12/04

IMPORTANT: Fill in your phone number on all the tabs at right.
NO COMMERCIAL ADVERTISING ALLOWED!   QGR 502 02/01

PHONE   4
PHONE   425-
PHONE   425-
PHONE   425-

QFC
Quality Food Centers
Open 24 Hours

300 pairs of
used underware
for sale.
Not in bad shape...
for the most part.
Sizes L - XXXL
         available.
*ask for JACK *

Name ~~Robert~~

IMPORTANT: Fill in your phone number on all the tabs at right.
NO COMMERCIAL ADVERTISING ALLOWED!   Date 2.13.04   QGR 502 02/01

PHONE   425-
PHONE   425-
PHONE   425-
PHONE   425-

FRESH GUY, STALE UNDERWEAR

FOUND by Kathy Block

Seattle, WA

Kathy's husband works at a QFC grocery store and found these while clearing old ads off of the community bulletin board. It's pretty funny to see that some folks posted more than one ad with an odd combination of services, and also that a few of the numbers have been torn off! Well, who wouldn't want to have free rent or be the smoothest guy in town? — DAVY

Learn all aspects of being cool.

FOUND Magazine.

LONELY DISHWASHER

FOUND by Kathy Block

Seattle, WA

?
YOU

QFC
Quality Food Centers
Open 24 Hours

SMR

NEED A NICE ROOM?
I've got a nice studio to share.
I will get an extra bed. If you
don't have the money to share
rent right now, that's okay. I'm
in the UW District. Pretty
quiet apartment, nice view,
clean.

Name Duane   Date March 19 2002

IMPORTANT: Fill in your phone number on all the tabs at right.
NO COMMERCIAL ADVERTISING ALLOWED!

PHONE (206)
6'
PHONE (206)
6'

171

QFC
Quality Food Centers
Open 24 Hours

SMR

NEED YOUR DISHES
WASHED?

I will wash them for
$10.00 a wash. Please
call if you would like me to
wash your dishes.   March 19, 2002

Name Duane   Date

IMPORTANT: Fill in your phone number on all the tabs at right.
NO COMMERCIAL ADVERTISING ALLOWED!

PHONE (206)
PHONE (206)
6'
PHONE (206)
6'
PHONE (206)

Happy 30th kiddo.

It gets better and better! Then it gets worse.

Love,

DE

more buns
more cups
less lies

I LOVE YOU DARLING.

AND I WISH I DIDN'T.

Sweet Plus®
SUGAR SUBSTITUTE

The war is over. We own you bitch!

PANGS OF CONSCIENCE

FOUND by Sarah Coggins.
, Valparaiso, IN

i steal grapes from grocery store displays. does that make me a bad person?

Kings & Queens Inn®

If this is still here, they didn't make the bed after I slept in it. yuck—

Our Guests are Royalty.

Sent
Friday, November 19, 2004 2:32 pm
To
how.howell oberlin.edu
Subject
memo

professor Howell,

Sorry for the late notice but I am having a very difficult time getting
my memo done. I was absent from class on wenesday as well as
today because I've been ill all week. I thought i would be able to
get this memo done last night but when i was trying to work on it i
ended up feeling real ill (I'll spare you the details) and wasn't able
to do it. I've been trying real hard all day to get somethign done
for you but I've basically just resulted in a huge failure and feeling
even worse from stressing myself about this all day. I was hoping i
would be able to work on this over the weekend and bring it to
class on monday so i can at least get some sort of grade out of
this. sorry again, and i hope you understand that i just had no idea
how i was going to feel today and it just happened to take a turn
for the worse.

sorry,

Shawn

Translation:

Professor Howell,

I'm sending you this email so late because I didn't think about it until 5
minutes ago. I skipped class on Wednesday because I was too high to leave
my house. I also skipped class today because I was at black river with
some bauch cats. I knew I wasn't going to be able to get this memo done
but I didn't really care. I thought about working on it last night but I
realized how hard it would be to type with a 40 of malt liquor taped to
each of my hands. I've been getting high all day and making plans to go
to Bill's hockey game, so its been real hard for me to fit this assignment
into my schedule. I was hoping I would be able to get an extension on
this because I am a huge waste of space and oxygen. Sorry for this, but I
had no idea how bad of a student I was until today.

Sorry again,

Shawn

TRANSLATION

FOUND by Cate
Oberlin, OH

Part of me wonders if the professor
might have been appreciative of the
brutal honesty and hilarity of the
translation. At least it would have
been a change from the run-of-the-
mill bullshit excuses that I'm sure
they get all the time.   —C.

100 Things About Jim
by Jim | Comments (0) | Category :: Always up-to-date
Betchya Didn't Know...

1. I lived in the same neighborhood as Brian Piccolo in South Florida.
2. Have an eye for **creative marketing** and advertising campaigns.
3. Drug of choice: Jeeping!
4. Prefer **CDs** to television.
5. Make more **money** at my "side jobs" than I do at my "real" job.
6. Fascinated by the inner workings of motorsports (IHRA and NHRA drag racing).
7. A **creature of habit** - I always stop at the exact same rest stops and gas stations anytime I'm traveling long distances in the car.
8. Taught myself about **computers** and website design.
9. Diehard sports fan - NHL hockey (Nashville Predators), NFL football (Miami Dolphins and whatever team Jonathan Quinn is playing for), MLB baseball (Cleveland Indians).
10. I'd rather be **hot** than cold.
11. Wannabe **youth football coach** (or assistant coach)... again. Had to leave the job behind when I moved.
12. I was on the staging committee for the Pro Football Hall of Fame when I lived near Cleveland, Ohio.
13. Horrible **speller** ("there" and "their"; "your" and "you're"... who cares?!)
14. I was there for Doug Flutie's "hail mary pass" - one of the biggest upsets in college football history. It was Boston College vs University of Miami game in the 1984 Orange Bowl.
15. Addicted to Quicken and online billpay... I get a charge from watching the little check marks appear on the computer screen when you download the latest transactions and they actually match up with my check register.
16. I have the uncanny ability to **make conversation** with just about anyone!
17. Can be found playing Chess, Pool, or Euchre late nights on Pogo.
18. Don't like to have my **baked potato** sliced into with a knife. Instead, I prefer to "smoosh" it together so it erupts like a little potatoey volcano pile.
19. Owned my own printing & publishing company when I was only 25.
20. Have nearly 400,000 points from playing NTN Trivia that I don't know what to do with!
21. I never leave the pump unattended when I'm **pumping gas**. (One time I did, and the nozzle fell out, spewing gasoline everywhere!)
22. Favorite TV show: "Bad boyz, bad boyz. Whatchya gonna do?"... COPS!
23. In 7th grade I sold newspapers as my first job. I sold them in person and via cold calls on the telephone. No one else my age was doing anything like that. I saved the money I made and bought tickets to a Miami Dolphins game to see AJ Duhe (#77) play. He influenced my decision to be #77 in high school football. Coincidentally, my senior year I worked out at the gym where AJ Duhe also worked out.
24. Obsessive about the **weather and road conditions**, I always make sure I leave at a time that will avoid driving in snow/ice or during rush hour traffic.
25. I love my **country** - I fear my government.
26. Prefer landscapes of **mountains and valleys** rather than oceans and lakes.
27. Won't be caught dead wearing anything "pink"... or anything with stripes. (I just started allowing "orange" to enter into my **wardrobe** though.)
28. I quantify everything - life is one big **math equation** to me.
29. I've always wanted a house with **a barn**... and a streetlight out back.
30. I have to **sauce** things up: ketchup on my eggs, mayonnaise on my steak, even ketchup on my chicken!
31. Enjoy **helping others** figure out how to do things on their computers.
32. I've always been intrigued by **investing** and financial planning.
33. Get motion sickness on amusement rides and cruise ships. (In all our cruise and wedding pictures, I'm wearing 1-inch thick gray sweatery wristbands. They did the trick though - I never got sick, while others in our group did!
34. If I walk into a **music store or video store**, I'm getting 2... not just one.
35. I enjoy riding in those NASCAR simulator race cars -- like at Opry Mills Mall.
36. A **problem-solver** by nature, I'm always using deductive reasoning.
37. I **hit the snooze button** on the alarm clock exactly 3 times every morning.
38. Born a Floridian. Tried to be a North Carolinian for awhile. Became a Buckeye before I was eventually called to be a Floridian again. Perfectly content as a **Tennessean**.
39. I **hate doctors**. Won't go to one unless I'm on my death-bed.

40. Enjoy **cooking**, but don't do it much anymore.
41. I was on the **Duval County Republican Committee** in Jacksonville, Florida.
42. My favorite vacations are those which center around Spring Training baseball games each year.
43. I've never been **snow skiing**, nor do I have any real desire to.
44. As a youngster, I **had to have my tongue clipped** because I couldn't breathe right.
45. Prefer landscapes of **mountains and valleys** over oceans and lakes.
46. I enjoy jumping in the ~~ear~~ Jeep, with a map and a compass, and **exploring new roads**.
47. Biggest fault: I don't know when to **stop**.
48. If someone calls me & doesn't leave a **voicemail message**, I HAVE to call them back to see what they wanted or if it was a wrong number.
49. Clothes shopping is like pulling teeth for me... Since my brother is a haberdasher, I notice how "cheap" the clothes in stores are ...and all the imperfections.
50. Thrifty with **money**... until I start to spend it. Then I spend BIG chunks of change. I won't nickel & dime you to death, but I'll put you in the poor house in a hurry!
51. I'm **non-confrontational**.
52. Really admire Vince Lombardi and Jerry Kramer -- I'd like to learn under him... football and life attitudes.
53. I can't go 24 hours without **checking my e-mail**.
54. On weekends, showering, shaving (and sometimes even brushing teeth) are **optional**. (right?)
55. Talk about embarrassing... On "shoulder pads day" in high school someone pulled my pants down & all I had on was a **jock strap**!
56. The world's best software program I use every day: Photoshop CS.
57. I'm a **storm watcher**... There's nothing better than watching a weather storm brewing from your front porch or patio.
58. My favorite outfit is a comfy gray **hooded sweatshirt** that's 2 sizes too small, and a pair of matching bottoms. (With the hood cinched real tight around my face, I look like Rocky.)
59. You know you're a grown-up when... you worry about how much money you spend at **a bar**! (Note to self: You're officially a grown-up.)
60. If doing it every 3 years constitutes that you're a golfer, then I'm **a golfer**.
61. Would like to go to a taping of Saturday Night Live.
62. I get a rush from the **nitrous oxide fumes** at every drag-racing event I go to.
63. Favorite food: my mom's **potato salad**.
64. Least favorite food: my mom's **potato soup**.
65. Early fall is my favorite time of year because it reminds me of Homecoming and the start of **football season** -- a time to let loose and have fun.
66. Love that "crazy bird"... Wild Turkey & (diet) coke. Gobble, gobble!
67. Biggest regret: turning down that Vanderbilt football scholarship because it was "too far from home."
68. My favorite magazines are PC Magazine, Fortune, and Sports Illustrated.
69. That **big "dent"** on the back of my car is from the time I had Lynnette push me UP a hill with her SUV the time my alternator died.
70. Prefer to have a house with a porch, preferably a **wrap-around porch**.
71. I'm still involved with the IHRA... I'm doing PR and marketing for driver Terry McMillen, including his website.
72. I won't put your phone number in the phonebook on my cell phone unless I talk to you more than 5 times a month and for more than 2 months in a row.
73. I can survive just fine on **4 hours of sleep** a night.
74. No **kids**... yet. Though it's not for lack of trying!
75. I know that's not 100... I'm workin' on it!

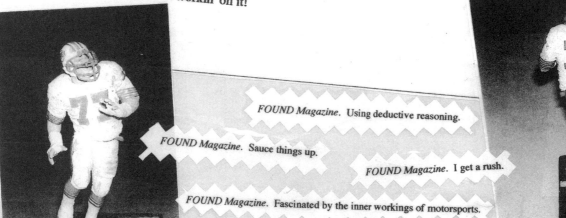

175

KAREN LOVES GEORGE

JIMMY LOVES PAM

JIMBO LOVES SALLY

GEORGE LOVES ALMOST EVERYBODY HE CAN GET HIS

HANDS ON

Making the experience complete and Memorable

SEND IN YOUR FINDS!!

RAIDING THE STASH

FOUND by Jeff Sharp

Odenton, MD

under TV in
Bottom left door
in shoe box

Don't be greedy!

this picture FOUND by Sarah Locke, Sault Ste. Marie, MI

A HIATUS

FOUND by Elizabeth Berry

Toronto, Ontario

I unplugged
the T.V.
I think it's best
for a while...

this cord FOUND by Davy Rothbart, Missoula, MT

DESPERATE MEASURES

Traveling around the country the past few years on these *FOUND Magazine* tours, I've seen firsthand how our depressed economy is taking a toll on a lot of cities and their citizens. So many of the finds that pass through my hands convey a sense of the frustration and desperation that folks experience when there's not enough jobs to go around.

At one point in Michael Moore's documentary *Roger & Me*, Moore asks a Flint politician what people can do to survive with all the auto plants shutting down. The guy says that people just need to be more imaginative and use their American ingenuity to start new kinds of businesses. For example, selling lint rollers! Soon after, Moore meets a woman who's trying to make a living by breeding rabbits—she's got a sign outside her house: PETS OR MEAT.

Here's a couple of finds that seem to reflect a similar entrepreneurial spirit—a paper plate passing for a rare, collectible record, and someone selling pen caps. (Every single tab's been torn off the flyer, so they must've had some luck!) I guess desperate times really do call for desperate measures.

— DAVY

FOUND by Shari Rifas, Berkeley, CA

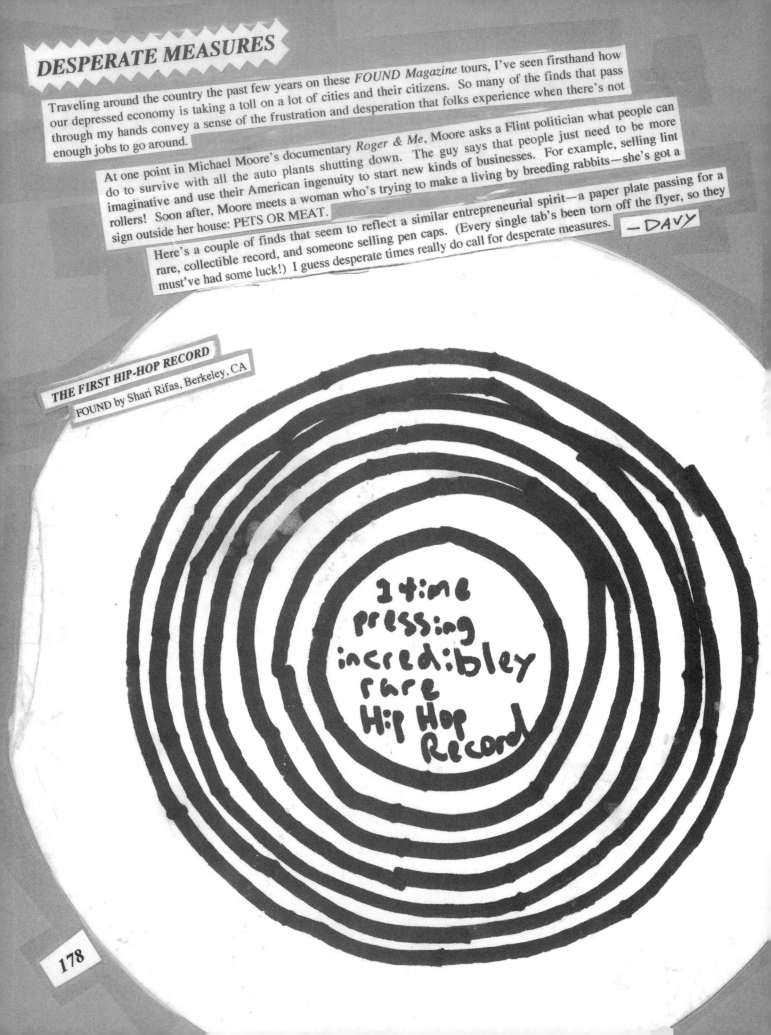

1 time
pressing
incredibley
rare
Hip Hop
Record

PEN CAP FOR SALE

PENS NOT INCLUDED FOUND by Mike Rosenthal, New York, NY

35¢

1. win at least 5 M in
lottery
2. summer place in Hull Mass
on water
get place in Madrid Spain
3. find a sail mate
to live out my life with
4. live out my life in good
health and plenty of money

AT LEAST 5 MIL
FOUND after Hurricane Wilma by Linda Temple, Fort Lauderdale, FL

All of these folks might be better off making their money the old-fashioned way—winning the lottery!

—DAVY

179

Unacceptable
0

2 8 Ei Street
Rap , East Carolina
November 30, 1093

Dear Vanessa

It's been a long hall for both of us. I found it hard to get used of being away from you. It went from having premarrital sex and then going to college and having sex with many women. I am writing you to tell that I miss having your small sexy ass, and pelvis depressing against the hair on my pelvis region. I missed having your glasses falling off because of the pain.

I thought to make things different this time we will have sex in front of your parents to see what their reaction will be. If they like it I will go after some of your sisters as well. If the relationship doesn't work out we can still have fun on the weekends

Seminal Vessicle,

Benjamin Howard

Was this turned in as a paper for class? Looks like the teacher failed to see the humor.
—A.F.

A LONG HALL

FOUND by Andy Freeburg

Lakeville, MN

I am undertaking this correspondence, futile as it may result, in an attempt to elicit from you those ecstatic pleasures encountered in sexual intercourse.

Eons upon eons I have covertly observed the radiance of being, the inner glow from the unparalleled example of femininity which ~~only you among the earths uncounted multi~~ ~~personify.~~

~~The~~ veins, arteries, vessels, and capillaries ~~~~ my body are straining to the limits of ~~the~~ structural capacity to accomodate the unnatural over-exertion my heart experiences when you are either in my prescence or in the innermost reaches of my subconcious

this photo FOUND by John Lancaster, Bloomington, IN

BUSTIN' A MOVE

FOUND by Allison Fendu

Tallahassee, FL

I found this note in the jacket of an old battered Jethro Tull record.

—A.F.

this photo FOUND by Alissa Fleet, Boston, MA

2 fallacies — I gotta go perfect
or he'll repre
of last 3 wks
— gosh do I really
want to marry
him?

So with the decision I've
made!

GOSH FOUND by Beth Round, Portland, ME

RULES FOUND by Valerie Ferrier, Des Moines, IA

date only men
with Porsche — (Rules)

this photo FOUND by Nate Cordero, Sacramento, CA

this is where I want my brother to wind up. He's the Devil that belongs in H E L L. Stoled my gril.

shame on you, Peter

SIBLING RIVALRY

FOUND by Kevin & Alyson Seconds
Sacramento, CA

this photo FOUND by Lisa Bee, Milwaukee, WI

this photo FOUND by Susan Campbell, Baltimore, MD

You keep my secrets
You listen

YOU LISTEN FOUND by Nicole Cuandra, Portola Valley, CA

183

MY LIFE AS THE HAMBURGLAR

FOUND by Alexa Rast

I get jerked out of the little kid prison at the McDonalds when Tim grabs me, or the foam costume I'm wearing, and starts walking towards the main part of the McDonalds where people place their orders and I turn around to see what's got my arm only I can't see its Tim, just blackness because the big fat Hamburgler head doesn't turn when I turn mine and the only reason I know its Tim is that I can see his Wranglers and the shit-kickers he's got on, and I absently wonder if this looks like the Hamburgler is finally getting what he deserves but Tim is tugging me, slamming open the double doors and someone screams, not in a good way, and then I'm outside and shouting at Tim who doesn't respond with anything except yelling at me, comeon comeon, over and over again, keeping time with the noise of the cars going by on Route 118 that I can't see because I've still got the Hamburgler head or mask on but I'm outside now and he pulls me on for a few feet and I dig in my little hamburgler-boots into the pavement but because he's so much taller then me I skid for a little ways before he lets go long enough for me to pull my head off but when I'm getting my hair out of the back which I wrapped into a ponytail with a scrunchie this morning the hair gets cot on the Velcro bit at the bottom and while I'm tugging at the end of it I see him turn around, hurt but not, and yell at me to 'Come On You Stupid Bitch' which gets me kind of excited but I'm trying to pull at the mask which won't come off so Tim grabs me anyway and I have to hold it above my head while he tugs me along, my short legs not able to keep up, until we get to his jeep and someone yells out 'Julie,' which makes me laugh behind my mask while Tim is trying to shout at me over the noise of the girl and pushing me into the jeep and I get stuck at first but manage to get in and slam the door just before it would have hit the car next to us and as Tim pulls out onto Route 118 in front of an old couple in a Cadillac I toss the Hamburgler head out of the window, laughing as hits their windshield.

Tim is lying on the ground and sitting and shaking or fucking on the ground, I can't tell which but it looks like all three and he's humping the air and the concrete and at one point he's writhing against my leg but I kick him in the stomach so he rolls away leaving little bloody stains along the grey concrete and wherever his crotch hits it leaves a little bloody mess so that there's little red spots all over the dirty floor of the underpass and on my arms and the legs of my jeans that I'll probably have to throw away and on the front of Tim's Wranglers which are soaked and dark with blood that kind of turns me on and would probably turn Tim on if he still had his dick but his dick is lying in a little red pool on the passenger's side of his jeep that I found when looking for more cigarettes and Tim after I got bored of watching TV. Tim is humping and thrusting and his spine is curved all the way back so it doesn't look like an S anymore, more like a backwards C but he doesn't make a sound beyond a little hissing until I kick him away from my leg and he kind of erupts and spit and blood fly out of his mouth and would make little patterns and dribble marks on the front of his shirt like a toddler if he was wearing a shirt but he isn't since I put it on when I found it in his jeep along with the cigarettes and the little bloody pile on the passengers side that I didn't know was his dick until I found the bloody knife lying in the grass between his trailer and the highway and I saw his pants and chest covered in sand that gets caked on with the blood that is flying around whenever Tim screams and cries and humps.

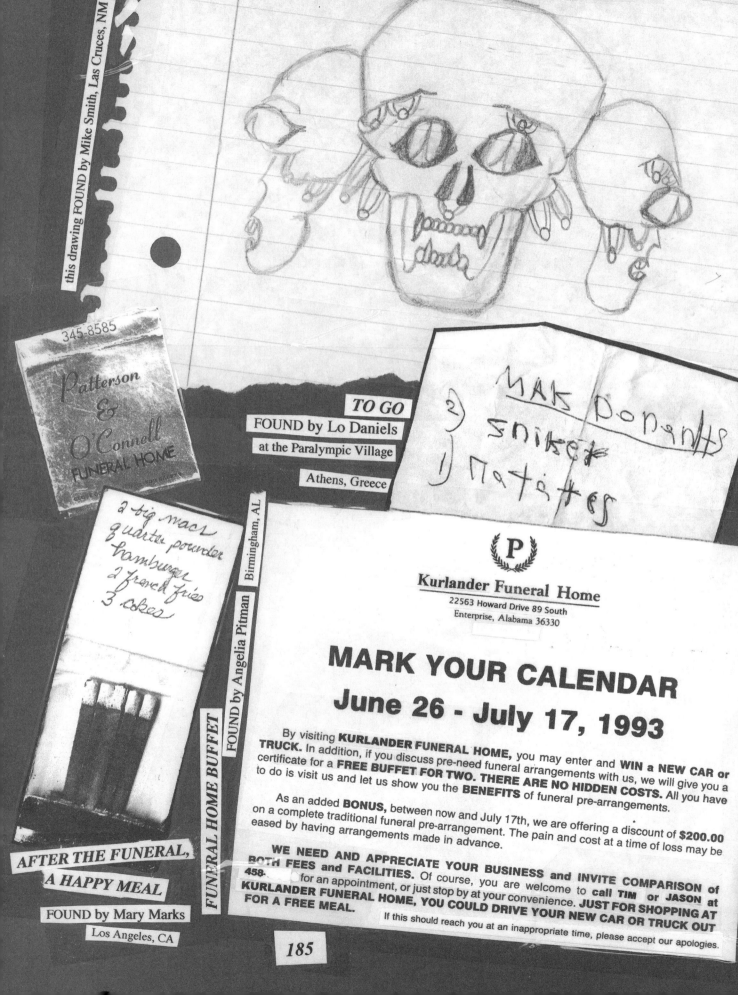

this drawing FOUND by Mike Smith, Las Cruces, NM

345-8585

Patterson & O'Connell FUNERAL HOME

TO GO
FOUND by Lo Daniels
at the Paralympic Village
Athens, Greece

2) MAK DOnanits
snikex
1) matatfes

2 big macs
quarter pounder
hamburger
2 french fries
3 cokes

FUNERAL HOME BUFFET
FOUND by Angelia Pitman   Birmingham, AL

AFTER THE FUNERAL,
A HAPPY MEAL
FOUND by Mary Marks
Los Angeles, CA

P

Kurlander Funeral Home
22563 Howard Drive 89 South
Enterprise, Alabama 36330

MARK YOUR CALENDAR
June 26 - July 17, 1993

By visiting **KURLANDER FUNERAL HOME,** you may enter and **WIN a NEW CAR or TRUCK.** In addition, if you discuss pre-need funeral arrangements with us, we will give you a certificate for a **FREE BUFFET FOR TWO. THERE ARE NO HIDDEN COSTS.** All you have to do is visit us and let us show you the **BENEFITS** of funeral pre-arrangements.

As an added **BONUS,** between now and July 17th, we are offering a discount of **$200.00** on a complete traditional funeral pre-arrangement. The pain and cost at a time of loss may be eased by having arrangements made in advance.

WE NEED AND APPRECIATE YOUR BUSINESS and INVITE COMPARISON of BOTH FEES and FACILITIES. Of course, you are welcome to **call TIM or JASON** at 458-____ for an appointment, or just stop by at your convenience. **JUST FOR SHOPPING AT KURLANDER FUNERAL HOME, YOU COULD DRIVE YOUR NEW CAR OR TRUCK OUT FOR A FREE MEAL.**

If this should reach you at an inappropriate time, please accept our apologies.

SO SWIFTLY

FOUND by Jenn Lawrence

Toronto, Ontario

OUR SON:

WERE YOU OK IN THE PASSING OF THE YEAR? THE TIME GOES SO SWIFTLY, WE FELT IT'S A PITY THAT WE DIDN'T HAVE A CHANCE TO CELEBRATE YOUR BIRTH DAY. I DOUBT THAT WHETHER I CAN RECOGNIZE YOU WHEN I SEE YOU.

WE ARE GOING TO MOVE, WE HOPE YOU COME HOME AND LIVE WITH US HAPPILY. PLEASE CONTACT WITH US AS SOON AS POSSIBLE. YOUR FAMILY'S TELEPHONE NUMBER: (416) 490-72. . YOU CAN CALL US ANY TIME. WE ARE LOOKING FORWARD TO YOUR COMING HOME. HAVE A NICE DAY, OUR YOUNGEST BOY IN OUR FAMILY. WE LOVE YOU FOREVER.

YOUR FAMILY

SEPT, 10, 2005.

Jenn,
A million apologies for sending this check to you but I was a bonehead and lost your parents address. I started working in the World Trade Center last Friday the 10th. It's un-FUCKING-real working in Manhattan and I will have many good stories to tell when I see you and Billiam. I miss you two a lot, sorry this is so short but my life is sickeningly hectic (But I love it) I'll write you a longer letter when I get the chance.

Love,
Mister Manhattan

P.S. Always remember

I'm prouda ya

MISTER MANHATTAN

FOUND by Mehron Moqtaderi

Wilmington, DE

this photo FOUND by Liz Rossof, Lawrence, KS

FOUND Magazine. Un-FUCKING-real.

Davy: Hi damali. I remember you told me a great story once about a crazy find you had in college.

damali: Oh, I know the story you mean. Yeah. Actually, it was right after I finished college when I was living in the city as an honest-to-goodness citizen.

Davy: Which city?

damali: Providence, Rhode Island.

Davy: A-ha! A great city for FOUND stuff.

damali: Yes, and the second of two cities I lived in where the mayor had been convicted of a felony and re-elected. Well, in Providence I had this friend named Cinimon. She spelled it C-I-N-I-M-O-N, not like the spice. Cinimon was the obsessive type, a bit of an odd bird. Once she made me a pair of earrings and gave them to me on a loaf of bread she had baked and decorated in the shape of my head, hair and all. Anyway, for a week or so, Cinimon had been going on and on about Gary Oldman. She couldn't get enough of him. She had mostly been going on about his performance in the movie *Immortal Beloved*, which is a story about Beethoven going crazy over his girlfriend or something. She told me a thousand times how I had to see the movie. I'm a big fan of Beethoven, but wasn't that interested in seeing his mental deterioration on film. And we all know Beethoven was black, so Gary Oldman... whatever.

Davy: Beethoven was black?

damali: Yup. But if that's how you have to play it, I understand, Hollywood and all... Anyway, I spent a week hearing Cinimon rave about Gary Oldman in *Immortal Beloved*.

The next week was June 1st—the traditional Dumpster-diving day for Providence. That's when the art-school students move out of their houses and leave tons of goodies and crap behind. So Cinimon and I had planned to go check things out. This was my first Dumpster-diving experience. I mean, I had found stuff in the trash before, but this was an organized, all-day, full-body-in-the-trash, beat-the-next-dude-to-the-good-stuff, Filene's Basement kinda deal. So we put on our grubbies and left early.

Cinimon wanted to find mannequins—she had a thing for them. They were, like, a special commodity, highly sought after on June 1st, so much so that at one stop we asked someone if they had seen any and they said furtively, "No, those are probably all gone." I think they were looking for some themselves and didn't want us to jack their bounty. Mind you, the whole time we're driving 10 miles an hour up and down the streets in our borrowed minivan, Cinimon is still going on about Gary Oldman, she just couldn't stop talking about him, she was fixated.

We get to a major Dumpster—like an actual Dumpster—blue, steel, smelly, and full of stuff. We actually ran into someone else I knew there. That happens on Dumpster-diving days. As I was saying hello, Cinimon dove into the rubble. She was a large beautiful white woman with long dark red hair in a big flowing black dress and combat boots. She pulled up her skirt and tumbled in one leg at a time.

As I stood talking to my acquaintance, I hear a scream from the piles of rubbish. "*GARY*!!" Cin's head pops up. She is holding a picture of Gary Oldman. No kidding. It's the cover of the soundtrack to *Immortal Beloved*. She was out of her mind with glee. I have to say I was pretty shocked myself. He must have heard her pining after him. "Gary! Can you believe it, damali? It's *Gary*!" I don't think I remember Cinimon ever being as happy as she was at that very moment. It still makes me smile.

eyes to the ground

Davy: That's fucking amazing! Wow. So, did you find anything else that day?

damali: Yeah. We drove to other piles of trash. By this point I had picked up a huge scarf, which we decided I could wear as a skirt, a pair of pants, and some drawing materials, a large spiral-bound sketch pad and some colored drawing tools of some sort. Cinimon had plastered the Gary Oldman picture to the dashboard of the van. As we cruised the streets she kept patting the picture it and cooing, "Gary will lead us to where we need to go next. Won't you Gary?" I guess so, because that day we found two full mannequins for Cinimon's collection. Okay, finding an arm or a leg is shocking, finding half a mannequin is a coup, but finding two full mannequins, it's like a Dumpster-diving miracle. Cinimon, she was beside herself with delight and faith in our angel, Gary Oldman.

Davy: Man, good thing it was Gary Oldman from *Immortal Beloved* leading you around town. I don't think Gary Oldman from *True Romance* would have been as charming a guide. It's a crazy story, though. Like, what are the chances? Gary Oldman, just there in the Dumpster, waiting for Cinimon to rescue him.

damali: There's really something spiritual about finds. I think people feel that if they find something on the street or in the trash, it's especially meant for them. That there was a mystical factor in their finding it. I think I've even seen people look around just to make sure it's them the find is for—just to make sure that they are truly the lucky one. It makes the object feel special, sure, but most importantly it makes the finder feel special and connected to something larger. That's what Cinimon seemed to be feeling.

As for me, the Dumpster shopping was excellent. I was working a new office job and I didn't have clothes for an office, having been a student and a house painter before. I remember telling my boss excitedly that I had gotten the clothes during the traditional Providence Dumpster-dive. I modeled them proudly. "Like my pants? Guess where I got them?" I grew up in hand-me-downs, what's the difference? And hey, I was excited about being part of a Providence tradition. Plus we were a nonprofit. I thought he would appreciate the reuse mentality that I so creatively brought to my professional image.

Instead, he said grimly, "That's fine, damali, but please don't wear clothes you found in the trash to the board meetings." He wasn't impressed after all.

Every board meeting, I wore one of my Dumpster outfits. My boss always gritted his teeth and made comments, half-joking, half-serious. He kept telling me not to wear clothes I found in the trash to the board meetings. Though each time, he knew I would do it again, and I did. I figured, if no one else, Gary Oldman would back me up.

Davy: The Gary Oldman from *True Romance*?

damali: Yes. ⚡

damali ayo is an artist, writer, and performer based in Portland, Oregon, and author of the very funny, thought-provoking book How to Rent a Negro. Learn more about her kick-ass work at www.damaliayo.com.

189

08/25/05

Hey Dad. Thought I'd write and say hi. All is good here at Monroe. Its a decent intstitution. I like the fact that nobody talks to me. Everybody minds there own buisseness and keeps to themselves. This makes my days go by easy, because I really don't care to socialize. I can't seem to relate to anyone here in the first place. But the good thing is nobody looks twice at me. I know how to blend in pretty well. The library here is not bad. I'm reading a book containing a lot of Platos work. It seems good so far. I got my property from Shelton Today. A lot of stuff that is useful, books, sunglasses, soap, toothpaste, basicly all the useful stuff I accumulated at shelton. Hows your progress on getting a bird going? See any merlins? coopers? I wish you luck. Allright, take care.

Love - Blair

```
    2
   24
   57
  ____
  168
 120
434 68
   60
82,080
   60
4,924,800
```

$4,924,800$ SECONDS TO FREEDOM

Maria I still have a lot of thinking to do about the bird so maybe I'll buy it when you come back from mexico

Arty

3 30 02

THE RAILING

FOUND by William Seebring

DAVY'S ON THE MIC!

Okay, let me explain.

That note over there is the one I found late one winter night on the windshield of my own car where I'd parked it on a busy Chicago street—obviously, Amber had mistaken my car for Mario's. It was this note that sparked the idea of making *FOUND Magazine* in the first place. I've often wished Amber had left her pager number so I could've gotten in touch with her and explained that it wasn't Mario's car, it was mine! Many of the notes and letters that folks send in to us actually do contain a phone number or some way of getting in touch. I'm always unsure how interactive I want to get with these finds—do I try to return them to the owner? Would they even want their lost letter back? Should I call them to find out the rest of the story or put in my own two cents?

Mario,
I fucking hate you
you said you had to
work then whys
your car HERE
at HER place ??
You're a fucking
LIAR. I hate you
I fucking hate you
Amber
PS Page me later

PAGE ME LATER

FOUND by Davy Rothbart

A couple years ago, a guy named William Seebring faced a similar set of questions. He'd just received an email (below) from a woman named Thea that was clearly intended for someone else. So, best to ignore it, or should he let Thea know of her mistake? Well, William decided, how 'bout option three—write back to Thea *as if he was the guy she was trying to write to*! What followed was one of the more hilarious email exchanges I've ever seen—the ethics here may be unsound, but the results are tremendous.

—DAVY

On Mon, 5 May 2003 15:52:49 EDT ███████@aol.com writes:

Dear Peter:

I have the arrival for 10 days two very active!!!!! children. 4 years old and 6 years old on June 20.

As mentioned, I am very concerned about not having the stair railing up for the protection of any accidents happening ---
one of them sleepwalks.

So, what is the status of the railing and will I be able to have it in by then.

Thea

On Mon, 5 May 2003 16:36:25 EDT f⋯⋯n@juno.com writes:

probably not. work load is just too tight. I suggest you rig in some straps for the kids at night - I have some old cat collars you could use - they'd work, on their ankles is what I mean. Secure the other end to the bedpost and the kids won't get far.

no house is accident free. Least you're not living in a houseboat. Know what I mean?

Peter

On Tue, 6 May 2003 12:32:05 EDT E⋯⋯t@aol.com <mailto:Eb⋯⋯Th⋯a@aol.com> writes:

Peter:

What will I have by the end of June?

Thea

On Tue, 6 May 2003 15:30:36 EDT f⋯⋯n@juno.com writes:

I don't know. Maybe a greater appreciation for the uncertainty of life. Life is a struggle. I can tell you that. We plow, we sow but what do we reap? A few shiny trinkets to hang on our walls? Debt out the wazoo. I tell you, Thea, I am tired. I just want to sit down somewhere with a bag of peanuts. In their shells. No salt. I can't handle the salt. But I would like that. I really would. Maybe "I'll" have that by the end of June. Does that help?

Peter

193

On Wed, 7 May 2003 09:19:04 EDT ̲ ̲ ̲ ̲t@aol.com
<mailto:E̲ ̲ ̲ ̲ ̲ ̲ ̲ ̲ ̲ ̲@aol.com> writes:

No, Peter and I am not appreciating your non-professional-unbusiness-like
replies.   I also lead a very tiring hectic life (as do many other people)---it is
todays world.

My point is that you have had the commission for over a year at this
time. If you have taken on too many projects, I don't feel I should have to
"suffer" for it. So, let's get serious about this thing and get on with it.

I have two small children and my mother (who is blind) coming within
the next three months and I would like to have some actual timing down on
this thing. Your solution with putting up "straps" of some sort would not
prevent anything and I don't think it is funny. I am especially concerned
about the safety of my mother who is just adjusting to no sight and relies
on physical guidance of walls and railings to get around in strange places.

Sorry, I don't relate to your cavalier answers. There is no humor at this
point.

Thea

On Wed, 7 May 2003 13:46:37 EDT f̲ ̲ ̲ ̲ ̲ ̲ ̲@juno.com writes,

Thea,

They say humor is a relative thing. Perhaps this time, "they" are right.

Peter

On Wed, 7 May 2003 14:32:57 EDT E̲ ̲ ̲ ̲ ̲ ̲ ̲@aol.com
    <mailto:E̲ ̲ ̲ ̲ ̲ ̲ ̲ ̲ ̲ ̲a@aol.com> writes:

Dear Peter:

Stop all work on the project.

My attorney, Samuel Reuben will be contacting you regarding deposits.

I feel your irresponsible replies to my "serious" requests have made
working with you no longer feasible.

Thea

On Wed, 7 May 2003 17:54:47 EDT ████████@juno.com writes:

Thea,

Not only has your attorney contacted me but, in fact, Sammy is here with me now.

On my sofa.

Eating peanuts.

You see, Thea, Sammy and I have been "seeing" each other for some time. Since last May. The eleventh, actually. It was a Saturday. In fact, you introduced us. Do you remember? It all seemed so incidental then. Why wouldn't it? But now you know the truth. Not many people do. Not even Sheila. Well, she may suspect it. Dottie knows. I think. She said something the other day that made me think she does. Anyway, suffice to say that I'm making some changes in my life. I have thrown my tool belt and my plane and my Skil saw into the culvert that runs along Delshire Boulevard. Don't bother retrieving them. They are gone. I am going to cultivate cheeses. Sammy will help me on the exporting end. Those are my plans. I'm sorry about the railing. Please don't hate me.

Peter

illustration by Cathy Kuryk

195

Alex
god I miss you
I wonder if you saw this coming
this letter.

Alex
    god, I miss you
I'm trying really hard to focus on
me, but do I have to forget about
you entirely in the process? It
doesn't seem fair somehow. Life is
just too short.
    I've had several opportunities

Alex Alex Alex
I god I miss you Alex Ale
I'm trying really hard to foc
god I miss you   miss you
I'm trying really hard to foi

Alex
    god, I miss you
I'm trying really hard to focus
on myself, but do I have to forget
about you entirely in the process?
It doesn't seem fair somehow
life is too short.
    I've had several opportunities to
call you, maybe come see you. I've
been @ Genecom a couple of late
evenings. And you know, I hate
sitting there looking over @ that
building knowing you're probably
there, thinking how all these
sweet feelings I've ever had for
you have come to this.
    God, I never wanted to or could
believe that you could be the kind
to take advantage of someone's
feelings, but you almost actually
convinced me on the phone the
... now I don't know what

Alex   Alex   Alex
god, I miss you   Alex   Alex
god I miss you   Alex Alex Alex
trying really   hard to focus on
but do I have to forget you
on the process?

Alex   Alex Alex Alex Ale
god I miss you Alex Alex Al
trying really hard to fo
self, but do I have to for
you entirely in the proc
I wonder if you   Alex   saw this
this letter.
I could never have done
for you I

I could never have done what
I did to you if I didn't have
real feelings for you. That's just
the way I am. It was the
sound of your voice, your man
your everything, you that made
me want to do it.

Alexa's pledge to be less gross

Being gross is gross. After 22 years of grossness (mould-monitor at 7) I now want to be nice.

I hereby promise to-

1) Have a monday clearout so nothing can stagnate for more than a week

2) Do any reasonable request by Katy or Hannah ~~etc~~ to reduce grossness.

Like a puppy, once trained not to be gross, it should become natural.

If I do not do the above, Katy/Hannah can give me an appropriate punishment.

Signed K May

Witness H Peshkin

Date 30/5/5

Alex M. (Dork)

LESS GROSS

I found this note behind a bookcase when I moved into my new flat. From the way things looked in here, Alexa failed to keep her pledge.

—J.R.

date 5-21-0...

Jourdans not my friend neither is Claire or Alicia or Alex not even the boys in my class except for one. his name is Alex that's the one that I love Alex I hate her

this picture FOUND by LeBrie Rich, Eugene, OR

FOUND Magazine. An appropriate punishment.

197

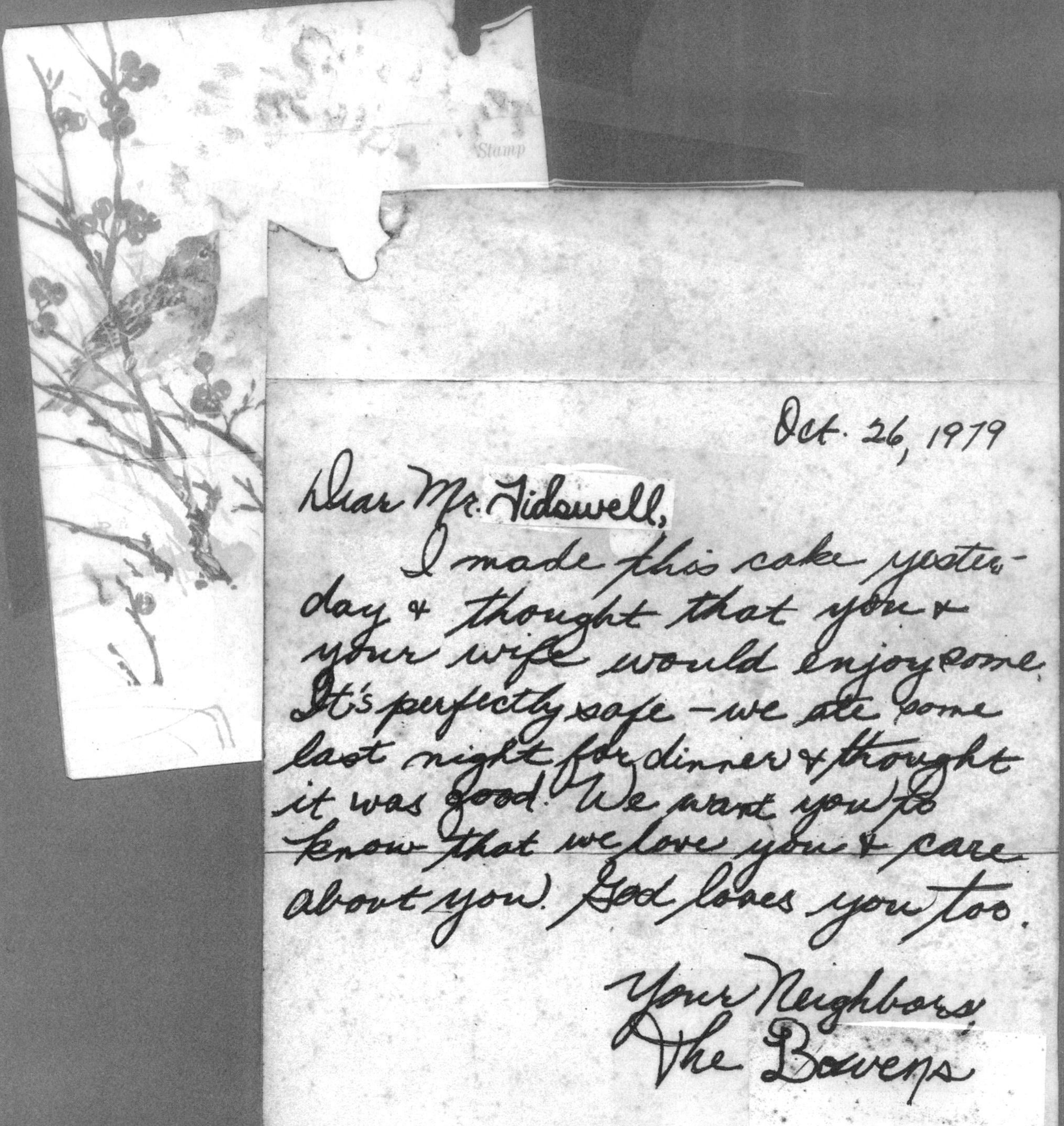

Oct. 26, 1979

Dear Mr. Tidswell,

I made this cake yesterday & thought that you & your wife would enjoy some. It's perfectly safe — we ate some last night for dinner & thought it was good. We want you to know that we love you & care about you. God loves you too.

Your Neighbors
The Bowens

IT'S PERFECTLY SAFE

FOUND by Kristina Hallez

Cincinnati, OH

This note seems like something a cartoon character would write after it had hidden a stick of dynamite in the cake.
—K.H.

Matt if YOU
Won't let me
be Your Girlfrind
I am Gowing to make
You Sufer. Do You
no how Shot You
if I could

BE MINE (OR ELSE)

FOUND by Heather Ratcliffe

St. Louis, MO

WHO LOVES YOU?

FOUND by Sara Walker

Newport, R.I.

To Elsa,
Who loves
you, Elsa?
Me — Mème

I found this photo inside a damaged
second hand piano while demolishing
it with a sledgehammer.

—S.W.

199

MONTHLY BUDGET

RENT 600.

CELL PHONE 50.
TELEPHOE 50

ELEC/Gas 45.

CABLE 60.

Bus/TAXI 60

FOOD 500.
LIQUOR 600 INCL BArs ($20⁰⁰ per DAY)

LAUNDRY 30

CRACK 600

ATTORNEY 250

MISC 250.
ASVINGS 100

TOTAL INCOME NEEDED $ 3195.00

YEARLE INCOME NEEDED $ 38,220.0

MONTHLY BUDGET

FOUND by Lea McKenny Willcox

Minneapolis, MN

msn® Hotmail®
i@hotmail.com

De :	eddie pascale <eddiepascale@hotmail.com>
Envoyé :	dimanche 13 mars 2005 14:01:40
À :	_____@yahoo.com, _____@hotmail.com, _____@hotmail.com
Cc :	eddiepascale@hotmail.com
Objet :	BAND IMAGE

OK!

I talked all night with Steffany (calebs girlfriend) about band image.

Being that fashion and image is a huge part of her profession, I feel 100% secure handing over the creative control to her as our photographer. She really knows what she's talking about and has some great ideas perfectly in-line with the idea I have for our band image. She really drove it home to me that this really needs to be in order. So I'm going to take it upon myself to be in charge of making it happen.

Band image relates to everything we do as a band to create our public persona. This means gigs, publicity photos, merchandise, presskit, you name it. Whatever each of us wears ordinarily is up you, but whenever we do something as the band, we will have a band "uniform" -- a few outfits that are for playing gigs, taking photos, etc.

So we should begin by creating each of our band personas. For example, Ron's is Vlad Valentine. A skinny rocker type with wild hair and even wilder attitude.

I will create inspiration boards for each of us with pictures and ideas that we will focus our personas on. Then we will take a day and go shopping and create our looks. Amana can help us with this, she is awesome.

She mentioned that our live show is great, but it is time to kick it up a notch. Make it a performance peice. from the moment we walk on the stage to the time we strut off, we are in a performance where we are performing through each of our persona characters. Every moment is calculated and intentional. This means that between songs, we must create something that fills the empty space. This could be as simple as a drumfill, beat or a long intro, and can be as elaborate as hooking the show up to a computer and having projected images and sounds between songs. Steffany mentioned that something as simple as a frequency banner or backdrop will give us a professional edge.

Whatever we do, we need to set ourselves apart from anything else. and making a gig into performancwe art will do this.

BTW, I will be entering the experimental performance program at my school next semester and can deticate my work there to the band -- we can even play at the new art/music space that we just opened up and get all the mission hipsters to come check us out.

So, i will work on that and we will schedule a photoshoot in a couple of weeks. so we should go shopping on of these weekends. Steffany will also help us with our presskit which is going to be a work of art in itself!

Lets address this tuesday. If any of you want to print out this email that would be helpful.

-E

FOUND by Michaela Severn   Globe, AZ

I found this note amidst the stuffed animals at a thrift store in the tiny town of Globe.   —M.S.

We will not have help by mom or dad with the hamster.

Alissa
Lori Kafu

DEAR SHADOW

FOUND by Lisa Agostoni

Atlanta, GA

A friend of mine flies a Paramotor (a small, propeller-powered parachute) and one day during an outing in North Georgia, a balloon floated into the air with a note tied to the end of the string. My friend glided over and grabbed the balloon and rescued the note. This is what it said.   —L.A.

Dear shaDOW.

I MISS you SO MUCH! How is hevan? I just love you so much. please show me you still remember me. send a sing please also of God.

I LOVe

you guys

in hevan

202

this picture FOUND by Rebecca McChesney, Glasgow, Scotland

2005.09.08 17:41

NOTICE TO ALL TENANTS

DUE TO OVERCROWDED CONDITIONS IN THE BUILDING, AS OF JULY 5, 2004 THIS WILL BE A UNISEX FACILITY. WE ARE MINDFUL OF YOUR PREVIOUSLY EXPRESSED CONCERNS, HOWEVER WE REGRET TO STATE THAT THERE ARE NO ALTERNATIVES.

MANY OF YOU HAVE ASKED ABOUT MY PREDECESSOR, SAM GOODBAR, AND HIS WELL-BEING. HIS CONDITION, WHILE STILL HIGHLY CONTAGIOUS, IS IN REMISSION AND HE HAS SUCCESSFULLY COMPLETED HIS REHABILITATION PROGRAM. ALSO, HIS BLEEDING, OOZING SORES HAVE ALL HEALED (THANK GOD!!!).

UNTIL SAM RETURNS, I AM HERE TO MAKE YOUR ASSOCIATION WITH US A POSITIVE EXPERIENCE.

THANK YOU FOR YOUR COOPERATION!!!

SINCERELY, MAX

Goals Aug 2003

Business: 1. Build Co. to 65 agents by 12/03

2. Build Trust to 15 loans per month by 12/03 - 20 by 6/04

3. 25K per month in ADs by 12/03

4. Income by 6/04 13,500/mo or 162,000/yr gross

5. Retire Sara 12/04 - if desired

Personal and Material

1. Continue to read & build vocabulary

2. Build rapport and patience with the ones you love - Sara, Kristen, Dom, Patty & Grandkids, Brothers & Sisters.

3. Personal Best - 370 lb 12/03 Bench Press

4. Suit for Nov - chalk Stripes

5. Gimpy ring @ Nats

6. Learn to say thanks

7. Net Worth to 1.5 million 12/03

Bob,
We must be pikers
The Picasso sold for $104
Million.
Have a great day
J

DOG WITH YACHT
FOUND by Stewart Reed
Danbury, CT

FOUND by Melanie Daniels
Jackson Hole, WY

$87,000

Please insert this direction this side up.

00-32-3133B 08-2004

♻ Recycled Paper

87,000.⁰⁰ Found
7,000.⁰⁰ Taxes
_____
80,000.⁰⁰
25,000.⁰⁰ EACH
30,000.⁰⁰ you

Two - 100,000.⁰⁰ bonds

Keep month short for 90 days
Deposit no more than 100.⁰⁰
Savings + 100.⁰⁰ on checking

Will will handle the bonds

Please No Coins Use a separate envelope for each deposit, payment, check reorder or message to the bank.

1) I'm grateful I earn over $750,000 per yr. serving others ~~and~~ for a higher purpose.

2) I'm grateful I earn over $750,000 per yr serving others using my talents, abilities for a higher purpose

3) I'm grateful I earn over $750,000 per yr. serving others using my talents, abilities for a higher purpose!

4) I'm grateful I earn over $750,000 per yr serving others my unique talents and abilities for a higher purpose. How can I do this?

A simple plan? Here's a simpler one—send money you find to FOUND Magazine!

—DAVY

$750,000 FOUND by Liz Smith Lowell, MA

205

Dear Santa,

This year I am going to try to be naughty and save you the trip. If not I will have a list at the ready. And I don't think your fat. I've watched Austin Powers. Should I give you cheese next year? Cause that girl in the commercial did and she got a car. A really nice car. I can't drive yet but oh well. Thank you for everything that you have given to me over the past years. You must be loaded. Can I have a slice of your mula? Thanks. Your Friend,

Howie Goety

FOUND by Megan Reed

New York, NY

I found a whole folder of letters to Santa Claus behind an old desk in my office. I hope some of these Christmas wishes were fulfilled.

—M.R.

Dear Santa Claus

I am waiting to you for my two Children, I can not give them Anything for Christmas. I am a single parent and hardly make my paycheck last until the next one. My family does not know how hard it is for me And I would never want them to know, I don't want to disappoint them on Christmas. Kimberly is 12 and Kristopher is 10 yrs old they are good kids. Can you please help me give my children something for Christmas Anything you can give will be greatly appreciated by us all,

Thank you.

11-23-02
N.Y.

Dear, Santa Claus

Hi, my name is Devin Smith I am eleven years old. Can I have computer game for christmas. Please make all my wishes come true.

Merry
X-Mas

Devin Smith
119 W. Synn Circle
N.Y. N.Y. 10034 — tel. (1917) 203-17

VAMPIRE SANTA

FOUND by Jim Walker, Indianapolis, IN

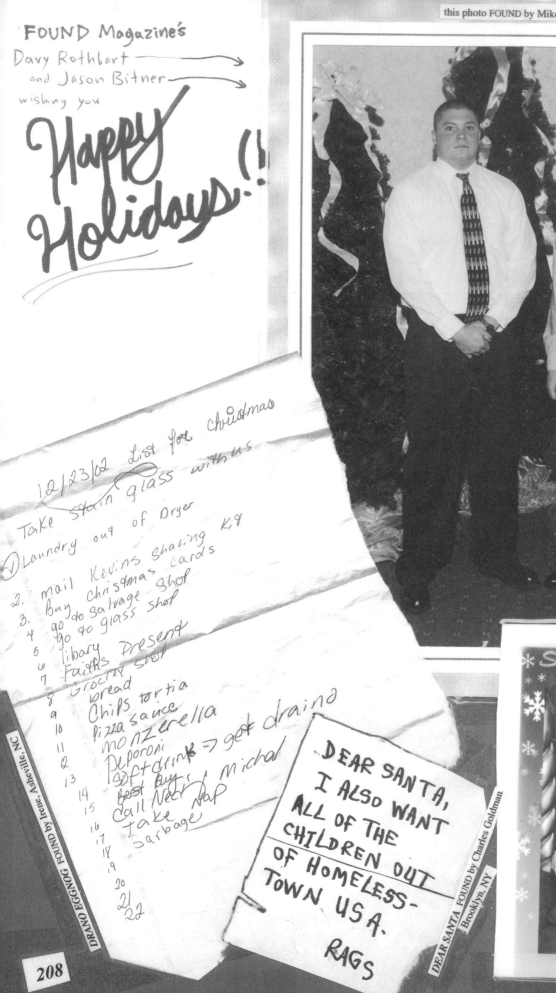

FOUND Magazine's
Davy Rothbart →
and Jason Bitner →
wishing you

Happy Holidays!!

this photo FOUND by Mike Montedoro, Jr., N. Versailles, PA

12/23/02 List for Christmas
Take stain glass with us
① Laundry out of Dryer
2. mail Kevins shaving Kit
3. Buy Christmas cards
4. go to Salvage shop
5 go to glass shop
6 libary
7 Faiths Present
8 Grocery shop
9 bread
10 Chips tortia
11 pizza sauce
12 monzerella
13 Peporoni
14 Softdrink → got draind
15 best buy
16 Call Neers Michal
17 Take Nap
18 garbage
19
20
21
22

DEAR SANTA,
I ALSO WANT
ALL OF THE
CHILDREN OUT
OF HOMELESS-
TOWN USA.

RAGS

DRANO EGGNOG FOUND by Irene, Asheville, NC

DEAR SANTA FOUND by Charles Goldman, Brooklyn, NY

Season's Greetings

LAP HAPPY FOUND by Kate Taylor, Salt Lake City, UT

My name is **William Lawrence** and I have been involved in restaurant enterprises for the past two years. I initially graduated from APEX Technical school with a degree in electronics maintainance and worked as the assistant manager for Harvey Electronics for a period of time equal to eleven months. Please ask for references. After my period of time at Harvey, I went to work at Roasters, the Chicken Franchise. I started as a simple Chicken boy, but was soon night managing the store. I wound up leaving over a Christmas Eve dispute with them, thus I would not recommend references there. I then after went back for my degree in Business electronics where I then got a job at Dr. **Tetzlaff's** office in the Mercy Hospital professional building. I worked there as clerical man for a period of time equal to nine monthes and would wholehandedly recommend references.

I thereafter went back to work in Restaurant Enterprises, working at Bobby Rubino's A Place for Ribsfor the past thirteen months. I have also moonlighted at Caldor where I am known as the gun for hire due to my irregular hours and determination to just do it. I also worked in Wholesale liquidators, night managing and trouble-shooting maintainence people.

I am currently looking for a position where my skills and experiancce will be appreciated. I am looking for adequate pay and responsibility. I can handle new things well and I am well used to working with pressure on top and from the top. I think I would be perfect for this job, for all those reasons and more. I look foward to hearing from you and closely following your instructions.

Thank You.

CHRISTMAS EVE DISPUTE
FOUND by Tom N.
Oceanside, NY

I'm sorry if I offened you the other day when I asked you if you knew a sex partner for me. You called and said that may

A SEX PARTNER CHRISTMAS
FOUND by Christopher Webb
Boston, MA

I found this portion of a note scribbled on the back of a torn-up Christmas card on the sidewalk outside of the New England Conservatory. —C.W.

this photo FOUND by Charlotte Tateoka, Provo, UT

209

Dear Santa   12-3-02

I am not writing to you to ask
for anything for myself but then
again I am, because I'm asking
for a better mother, I realize
that the word better mother might
be interpeted as I am asking for
another mother but thats not the
case my mother is the best mother
that life has to offer.
This is my point my mother has been
going through alot lately, she lost
her Job of 15 yrs, she is in financial
despair, her Husband and her has
been separated for 1 yr, she has been
Very active in the communety of the
United Hearts Organization at 119
Seacrest BKlyn nay 11231 as a Volinteer
in Wolcot St library, as well as
at   Western Press. church at
89 Miller St BKlyn Ny, 11231,
my moms is under a great deal of
stress. she has been looking for
employment but to no-avail she
is Very depressed and she is in
a great need of a Spiritual
Retreat if you can assist her
with a Spiritual Retreat it would
be a true X-mas for all of us.
I want to thank you in advance

Dear Santa,
I was a good boy this
year. I help my mom alot.
I would like a xbox and
two Control panels and
a game with action in it.
Its called Sega Sports
for xbox.

Thank you Santa
Love,
Justin Young
112 SHOREVIEW#1A
Gregory, MI 48137

Ps God Bless America

DEAR SANTA

New York, NY

FOUND by Megan Reed

November 16, 2001
2-605 Quinn St
Sunnyside N.Y. 11104
Long Island city

Dear Santa;
          Hello Santa how are you doing?
You must be busy with all the letters and
presents right. Some kids in my school they
think you are not real. But I tell them that
Santa is real. But anyway I don't care what
they think I still think you are real. When
it is christmas eve you come from the
chimney with your reindiers. If I don't know
how to spell good I'm sorry. Santa you love
all the kids or only good kids? Some of
my friends said you only love good kids. But
anyway I don't care. Sometimes I'm bad and
sometimes good. What happen on Sept. 11
was very bad I was very frightent. A lot
of inocent people died. And poor kids lost
their family. I feel sorry for them. Dear
santa for this christmas can I have A
Bablin Boo doll from Monsters Inc. I really
love Boo she was so cute. Can I also have
3 pairs of pants with elastic size 16. can
I have colors Black, gray, white. Can I have
that because I have like 3 pairs of pants.
So please Santa bring it too me. If no are
is at home please bring it to my mommy's work
at 900 phoenix av. Sunnyside N.Y. 11104 L.I.C.
                Sincerly,
                Teresa King

Merry X-Mas Baby
Love Bru

VERY MERRY

FOUND by Melissa Schaefer, San Francisco, CA

12/25/02

I found this little note in a box of sneakers I was trying on
in the Puma store. It appears someone returned their Xmas
present without remembering to take out the best part! —M.S.

Dear Santa,
My mommy is helping
me write this because
I am just learning
to write.
I have not been
a perfect child this past
year. ~~~~ I just
wanted you to know that.
I will try alot harder
next year to be better

behaved.
I hope that you will
bring me a few things
even though I haven't
been perfect.
~~I hope to receive~~
My mommy said that
I could ask for a few
things even though I
might not get them.

DEAR SANTA

FOUND by Megan Reed

New York, NY

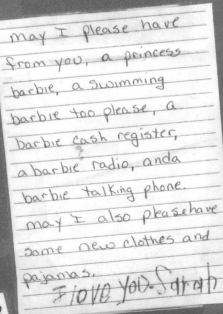

may I please have
from you, a princess
barbie, a swimming
barbie too please, a
barbie cash register,
a barbie radio, and a
barbie talking phone.
may I also please have
some new clothes and
pajamas.
I love you. Sarah

Dear santa,

Hi my Name is Eryk Berry and
I am ten years Old. Santa I Love you
So much that I hope to see you
this year. Santa My mom doesn't have
money to buy me toys. I would
like you to visit Me this year.
Santa my dream is to have toys
for christmas. I would like you
to bring me these toys.

1- Star wars action figure
2- Quesy Muker
3-
   Game boy

Eryk

SANTA'S KINGDOM
FOUND by Stacey Hunter & Ian Crawford
Glasgow, Scotland

Shows
ML75R2
8-12-02

Dear Sir + Madam
Just writing to let you Know
Santas Kingdom was a LOAD of RuBBish.
It was very expensive and wasnt worth
the money. my Son Paid £80 to Visit Santa
with his family. He would have been better
of going to a Pantomine it would have been
cheaper. Also when did Santa start wearing
trainers, I alway thought he wore Black Boots.
Also Santa wasnt very good at his JoB,
he took 4 children in at the one time any
other Place is one child at a time. I thought
You could have done better with the Presents,
after all look at the money People Paid to Visit.
What wee girls of 7 want with one Pkt of Body Jewels.
And what Boy of 11 want with an old Paper aeroPlane.
They can go to the corner ShoP any day and Buy that Shit.
A Selection Box would have Been Better. Also I
think it was a Scam, as you'se were Looking for
more money by Selling exPensive toys inside.
Yo let you Know the Kids sPent a Better time
at the school fete. Also they hadnt to Pay £3
For a Burger. Any way where does all that
money go to you collected. My family and lots of
other Families Wont Be Back Next Year as
I told you already it was a LOAD of Shit.
PeoPle Should get their money Back.
Karen M. Cooper

213

Christmas Revolution

Dear Santa,

Or should I just cut the crap and refer to you as the erotic poster boy of countless corporations that pimp you out so that their sales figures can climax on Christmas Eve. How many of your followers intoxicated with the instant gratification of all their bargain purchases' in which they refer to as 'Holiday Cheer', realize that your suit is red from the blood of children slaving away the rest of the year, without the luxury of holidays, in sweatshops around the world producing devices of leisure that within days will be forgotten by the obese spawn of the wealthy?

At first I wanted for your fat ass to get shot down by friendly fire when you fly over Iraq for your obligatory visit the troops this year. Then I realized that not only would the innocent reindeer get slaughtered but the western propaganda machine would spin the story to cast blame on the non-christian insurgency.

Instead, I hope that on Christmas Eve when you are terrorizing the world with your contractually circumnavigation of the earth, the Elves you hold captive in the north pole rise up and use their little hammers to smash the machines that you keep them chined to with substantiate wages that can barely afford a livelihood in the barren company town known as the North Pole. I want to see the sky light up like the Aurora as they burn your factories and wait for your to return so that they liberate the reindeer you enslave. Then instead of gutting you right there on the front door steps of your polar plantation ... I want them to beat your to an snowflake of your life. Then blindfold, drug and put a pair of adult Huggies on you while they fly you to one of the countries you and your capitalists cronies have decimated via militant neocolonialism. Force you to wok in an unsafe factory with the children that can not afford to go to the mall and sit on your perverse lap to ask for a better life. Then as your 12 hour work day comes to an end I want them to dress you up like the whore you are so that some wealthy westerners can violate, insult and humiliate you the exact same way I feel every time I see your image every where I go this time of year.

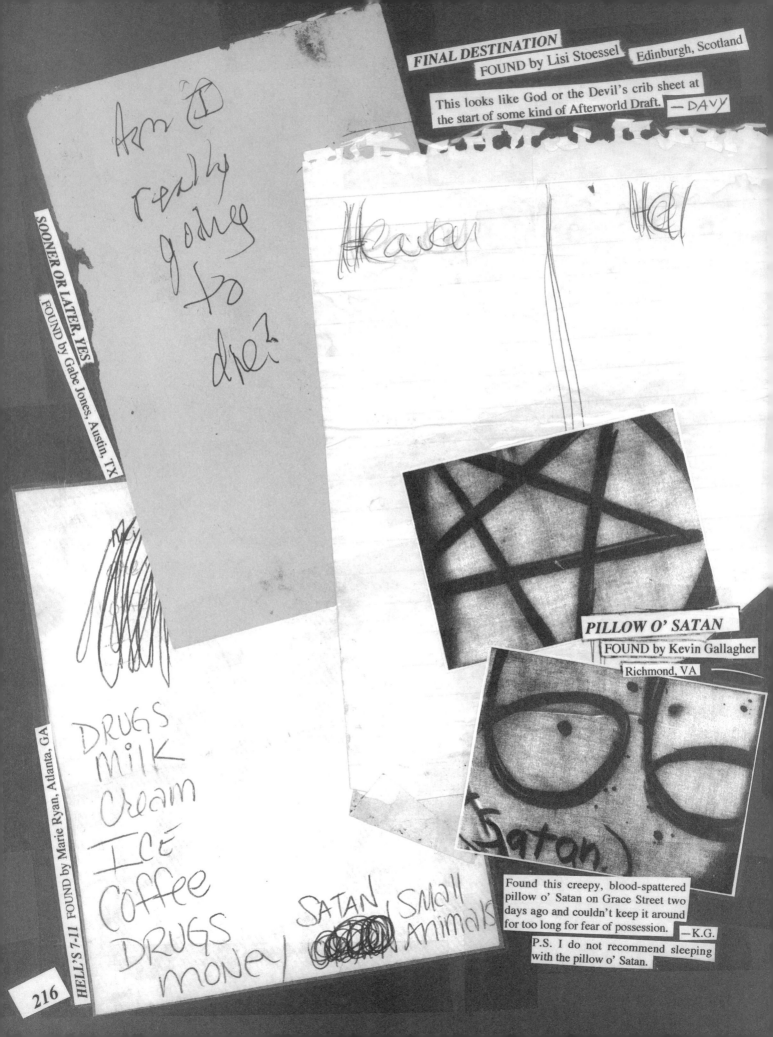

This looks like God or the Devil's crib sheet at the start of some kind of Afterworld Draft. — DAVY

Heaven

Hell

SOONER OR LATER, YES
FOUND by Gabe Jones, Austin, TX

Am I really going to die?

PILLOW O' SATAN
FOUND by Kevin Gallagher
Richmond, VA

Satan

DRUGS
Milk
Cream
ICE
Coffee
DRUGS
MONEY

SATAN   Small
         Animals

Found this creepy, blood-spattered pillow o' Satan on Grace Street two days ago and couldn't keep it around for too long for fear of possession.
— K.G.

P.S. I do not recommend sleeping with the pillow o' Satan.

HELL'S 7-11, FOUND by Marie Ryan, Atlanta, GA

216

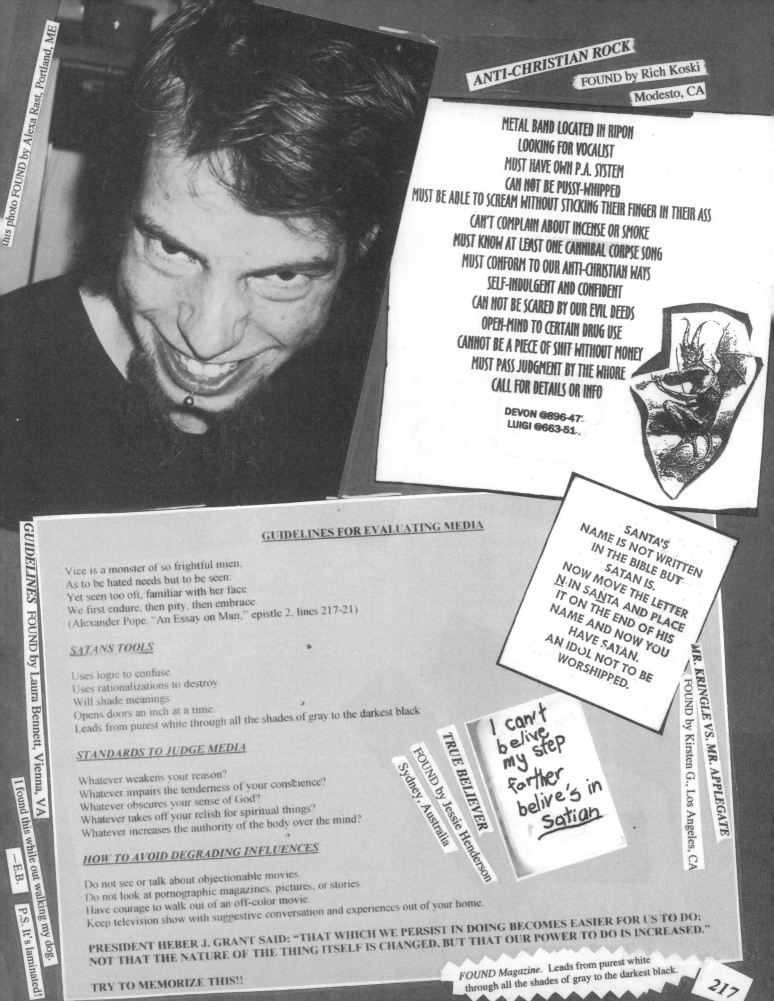

Left sidebar (photo):

My, Poland, 'Past Alexa by FOUND photo sinister

ANTI-CHRISTIAN ROCK

FOUND by Rich Koski
Modesto, CA

METAL BAND LOCATED IN RIPON
LOOKING FOR VOCALIST
MUST HAVE OWN P.A. SYSTEM
CAN NOT BE PUSSY-WHIPPED
MUST BE ABLE TO SCREAM WITHOUT STICKING THEIR FINGER IN THEIR ASS
CAN'T COMPLAIN ABOUT INCENSE OR SMOKE
MUST KNOW AT LEAST ONE CANNIBAL CORPSE SONG
MUST CONFORM TO OUR ANTI-CHRISTIAN WAYS
SELF-INDULGENT AND CONFIDENT
CAN NOT BE SCARED BY OUR EVIL DEEDS
OPEN-MIND TO CERTAIN DRUG USE
CANNOT BE A PIECE OF SHIT WITHOUT MONEY
MUST PASS JUDGMENT BY THE WHORE
CALL FOR DETAILS OR INFO

DEVON @896-47
LUIGI @663-51

SANTA'S
NAME IS NOT WRITTEN IN THE BIBLE BUT SATAN IS. NOW MOVE THE LETTER N IN SANTA AND PLACE IT ON THE END OF HIS NAME AND NOW YOU HAVE SATAN. AN IDOL NOT TO BE WORSHIPPED.

MR. KRINGLE VS. MR. APPLEGATE
FOUND by Kirsten G., Los Angeles, CA

GUIDELINES FOR EVALUATING MEDIA

Vice is a monster of so frightful mien,
As to be hated needs but to be seen:
Yet seen too oft, familiar with her face
We first endure, then pity, then embrace.
(Alexander Pope, "An Essay on Man," epistle 2, lines 217-21)

SATANS TOOLS

Uses logic to confuse.
Uses rationalizations to destroy.
Will shade meanings
Opens doors an inch at a time.
Leads from purest white through all the shades of gray to the darkest black

STANDARDS TO JUDGE MEDIA

Whatever weakens your reason?
Whatever impairs the tenderness of your conscience?
Whatever obscures your sense of God?
Whatever takes off your relish for spiritual things?
Whatever increases the authority of the body over the mind?

HOW TO AVOID DEGRADING INFLUENCES

Do not see or talk about objectionable movies.
Do not look at pornographic magazines, pictures, or stories.
Have courage to walk out of an off-color movie.
Keep television show with suggestive conversation and experiences out of your home.

PRESIDENT HEBER J. GRANT SAID: "THAT WHICH WE PERSIST IN DOING BECOMES EASIER FOR US TO DO; NOT THAT THE NATURE OF THE THING ITSELF IS CHANGED, BUT THAT OUR POWER TO DO IS INCREASED."

TRY TO MEMORIZE THIS!!

GUIDELINES FOUND by Laura Bennett, Vienna, VA
I found this while out walking my dog. —E.B. P.S. It's laminated!

TRUE BELIEVER
FOUND by Jessie Henderson
Sydney, Australia

I can't belive my step farther belive's in Satian

FOUND Magazine. Leads from purest white through all the shades of gray to the darkest black.

217

Monday
5:30 → wake up
5:45 → shower
6:15 → Start getting ready/dressed + smoke
6:30 → leave my house
→ smoke
6:50 → arrive @ work
7:10 → Drink Coffee, eat donut
10:00 → Drink Coffee + smoke
11:30 → Smoke
12:00 → Eat Donught

1. Buy a good lighter

2. call Medsnationwide – find out why I cant process refills from my order of 331264 #6.0031.

3. Get your on-line doc consot.

4. call Alpha Drugs + ask all questions to fill in blanks, especially which web

5. Call Michael Winslow – he wants to ask about two things + give him watani concept paper + explain $2/day.

6. Peggy – what is your opinion of my points on the central Parking offer?

7. Call Rachel + see how he's doing on his 106 deliverables list.

8. Call Tony for details on 10/13 10/22 + 11/13 + 11/17 father/son activities

9. Call John Dorion re: Phil Green

PRIORITIES

FOUND by Michael Joseph

Charlotte, NC

REASONS TO QUIT
1. health
2. expense
3. irritates others
4. coughing
5. tyranny of non smokers
6. holes in clothes
7. self respect
8. always tired
9. false buddy
10. having more time

REASONS TO QUIT

FOUND By Eric Hoffman,
West Hartford, CT

218   I found this in the pages of a book of poems called *Concentrations*.
Reason #5 is my favorite- What would Bill Hicks think? –E.H.

You may encounter a time where money is low, and you can't afford to buy a pack for 5 or 6 bucks. Instead you can roll one. You can roll cigarettes by hand, or with one of any type of cheap machine. About two packs worth of tobacco costs about $1.25 to $5. A roller can cost between $3 and $15. You can even buy a couple hundred filters for a buck or two.

To roll by hand first grab a rolling paper. Crease it down the middle with the glue edge inside. Grab some tobacco and put about a 1/2 inch into it, hold the paper with your middle fingers and thumbs and lightly pack down the tobacco. Next put your thumbs and middle / index fingers on the paper with them laying by the top of the tobacco

rolling paper
tobacco
You are over here
middle
index
glue edge facing you
index finger
middle finger

Dennis,
I need to start politics again, or get a dog's license

these two drawings FOUND by Liz at Denny's, Ann Arbor, MI

219

Folks sometimes ask me if I worry that newer technologies like email and text-messaging will soon make handwritten communication obsolete, leaving us finder-types out in the cold. My answer is no, I don't worry about it, and here's why—as technologies shift and continue to evolve, we're also stumbling upon new methods for finding interesting shit and getting fascinating glimpses into other people's lives. In recent months, we've received a batch of photos that were stored on a cell phone left behind at the bar, spooky poems from the hard drive of an old Macintosh found half-smashed at the bottom of a rock quarry, stacks of printed-out emails, and even a video diary of a young U.S. Marine battling in Iraq.

There's also this collection from our friend TradeMark G. of the Evolution Control Committee, an artists' group based in Ohio and Cali. Using file-sharing programs like Kazaa, LimeWire and eMule, Mark discovered that tons of people are accidentally sharing the Microsoft Word documents on their computers. (This isn't some "hacking-into-someone's-computer" deal, Mark explains, more like the equivalent of someone leaving their notebook behind on a park bench.) When you save a Word document for the first time, the program chooses a file name for you from the first line you've typed. "Dear Mom," saves as DEAR MOM.DOC; "Dear Santa," saves as DEAR SANTA.DOC; "Dear Son of a Bitch," saves as DEAR SON OF A BITCH.DOC. So simply by searching for "DEAR .DOC" Mark uncovered these and a vast array of other cool finds. Go ahead, try it at home! Never mind the doomsayers—it looks like technology is making it possible for us to start finding without even leaving our desks.

—DAVY

Dear Chief Boyle,

The Bluett Township Police Department has in their possession several items that belong to me. Each item has sentimental value to me; I would appreciate having them being returned to me.

Items as followed:
1. Silver Single Shot Bolt Action Rifle, ser.#1939XV11
2. 12 Gage, White Shotgun Powder Wonder Cira 1904 unknown antique
3. 30/30 Winchester Rifle with case ser. #6176
4. Fire Arm Purchaser Card issued 1972 to myself in Fairlawn, N.J.
5. CoH Revolver Replica. No ser. #

Thank You For Your Cooperation Yours Truly,

Morris K. Redmond

this photo FOUND by Bobby D. & Jennifer Welsh, St. Paul, MN

Dear Ken
    I know that you are aware that I have been having some problems lately, and you know that I have already had my share. Hey Ken, guess what, its your fault, you are to blame for this. I hate you. Its time for me to finish this, its time for me to end this charade that has been going on for so long. My condition has worsened every time I have neglected to refer this information to you, but now its time. So Kenny boy, I hope you had your fun, because I'm about to stop it.

With Sincere Love
Robert James

    Dear discipline committee,
    I am sorry for my bad behaviour and the wrong deeds that I have done. I messed up, and I should not have gotten involved in the drug trade in the first place. I promise you that I will never get involved in it again because I know that it is wrong and not a good thing to do or get involved in. During my time off from school I talked to my pastor (John Williamson) and a professional counsellor (Dan Von Bokel Ph.D.). My pastor told me that I should be thankful that I have a second chance. Really, I deserved nothing. He encouraged me to take the opportunity that I have to get back into this school. He was also the one that recommended that I go to a professional councillor. Which I did, I would like to make a fresh start next semester by not getting involved in the drug trade.

Dear Gerald

    How are you doing? There is a lot of things going on do you know that a airplane crashed in queens. Gerald when you come home I am going to hurt you to see who is stronger. Gerard said what up and are you still coming to the movies when you get back. And Merry Christmas.

Love
Angus Family

221

/ SAFELITE AutoGlass
Windshields   Sun Roofs

Mobile Service

Things That Bring Me Joy.

- a compliment from someone
- a kiss from **Angela** that is spontaneous & passionate
- when I look good.
- kitties greet me when I get home
- when I don't have to think about what I'm going to cook for dinner.
- when I am creative in an art project.
- when I'm confident when I'm speaking in a group
- when I can have a bowel movement in public & not worry what other people think.
- Blast my Blues & other favorite music
- Drink wine, listen to music & cook a nice meal.
- Get massaged which lead into other delicious fun stuff
- Giving a massage
- watching movie in bed with Angela.
- Drinking coffee & reading the paper
- working in the garden planting new flowers.
- sitting in the sun.
- reading a good book.

68718 Perez Rd.   56530 2°   85659 Inc   17 2 ims: /.
Calley, C   Inc   29

(8   (8   (6   42   (6   557-6

- snuggling in my blanket

- going skiing
- Drinking beer & munching after skiing
- listening to my walkman to escape.
- getting a surprise gift from Angela
- getting a compliment from Angela
- making love with Angela.

My mom found this in a book she bought at a used bookstore which gave advice for how to grieve over the loss of a family member. From the handwriting, I have the feeling that this note was written by a woman and that Angela is her girlfriend. —T.T

Dear Irishman and Scrud
Thank you for the belt and the knife
I like you. I wish you would come over
We will have a watermelon

Love

Dorald Ko I Love
you very
Ps. Very much

the dorm room
memoirs
are unclear in
the mornings
sunlight
remembers.

14.00
10.95
4.00
10.00
$38.95

RAINY
WEATHER

Your body is not just any body.

wedgie - when your underware
gets caught (ĭ·ĕ·ŭ·ŭ)
so that you have to pull it
out

FOUND by Kat

Montreal, Québec

So, my *friend* went to a strip club once, and yeah, my *friend*, he said there was this cheesy announcer who always made these kinds of little introductions for each woman before they did their dance. I always thought the announcer was ad-libbing, I mean my *friend*, that's what he thought, but I guess I—he—was wrong!

—DAVY

~Liz~

Hot as a thick bush on fire, this lovely little thumble weed moves sensually while strolling over the desert. Open your eyes, cause you're ~about~ just about to be held at gun point by the sexiest cowgirl of the desert. And here is Bliss!

Song 1

(4-5 min.)

Open you're eyes, again, cause the lovely cowgirl is coming back — and feeling very hot, so she'll schred off some of her cowgirl garments.

Song 2

(4-5 min.)

The cowgirl is coming back for her last performance, to show us everything she has ...

Song 3

this photo FOUND by Marianne DeMarco, New York, NY

FOUND by Davy Rothbart

Baton Rouge, LA

i hate myself why oh why have i done this???

Life is full of Choices.
& I've ~~decided to~~ already chosen the wrong one.

I wish I could start over
I would change alot

REGRET #2

FOUND by Eric Pawlowski

Oak Park, IL

Life is a shit hole.
a fucking wastland
full of scoundrels
who lie & steal. THE ST. PAULI GIRL IS HOT.

CERTAIN THINGS MAKE LIFE REDEEMING

FOUND by Amy Brunson & Greg Spore

Jackson, MS

7-13-93 or, if you wish, the Eve of Bastille Day

Andrew,

Since you seem to have drifted out of sight and earshot, I feel I should return your things the only way I know how, through the Lion's Head.

I would like to talk to you about what has, clearly, taken place and was, again clearly, inevitable. You said you needed me and that seemed evident at the time. I wonder if you no longer need me or still need me and don't know how to connect.

I wish you would call me. I would call you, if I knew where you were. I don't want to call the restaurant.

If it is the case that we are to drift apart definitively, I suppose you should return my apartment key. On the other hand, maybe it is not the case.

Please call me, if only for a brief tidying-up conversation. I hope, truly hope, you are well,

Derek

The book is a gift. I hope you enjoy it.

THE LION'S HEAD

FOUND by Pegasus

Wiesbaden, Germany

I bought a book at a used bookstore in Germany and found this letter inside; the book was *Dungeon, Fire, and Sword,* a history of the Templar Knights during the Crusades. I really felt sad for Derek—you can feel his hope and anguish in every sentence.

—P.

MY DEAR JANET AND FAMILY

Kindness like yours

                                    I A WANT TO ~~.....~~ LL
    I HOPE YOU HAVE A WONDERFULL EASTER   an ordinary day YOU SENT ~~MAR~~
~~.U FOR~~ ~~THE~~ BEAUTIFULL CSRDS   extra special.
                            I   LOVE THEM

    next time maybe my tywrith thng wi;; be beter

                    grama q.

I LOVE YOU ALL.

KINDNESS LIKE YOURS

FOUND by Thomas Spofford

Chico, CA

Thank You So Much

FOUND
by Hali Maltsberger

Baltimore, MD

→

These two finds—plucked off the ground in cities a few hundred miles apart—arrived at our *FOUND Magazine* HQ on the same day. I like the way the second one seems to articulate the thoughts of someone who was pondering the first one.

—DAVY

↓

Serious offer seeks serious reply.

A Nordic Track for $ 10.00 (it's a Steal!) (cash only please)

NORDIC TRACK EXCEL!

good → great condition

jo___@yahoo.com jo___@yahoo.com jo___@yahoo.com jo___@yahoo.com jo___@yahoo.com @yahoo.com @yahoo.com

WILL I EVER USE THIS?

NO

NO

FOUND
by Patrick Kolodgy

Toledo, OH

Journal   Jan 14, 2005

1) I would name my twins Mickey and Miney.

2) Hell no, I mean if your gonna control the U.S armed Forces then you have to be born and raised here in the U.S.

3) The book would be about the ghettos of the world and the title would be "The ghettos of the world."

4) Set my arms on fire using Rubbing alchohol or spitting flames using rubbing alchohol.

5) Nothing at all.

6) I love you God, Jesus SAVED ME.

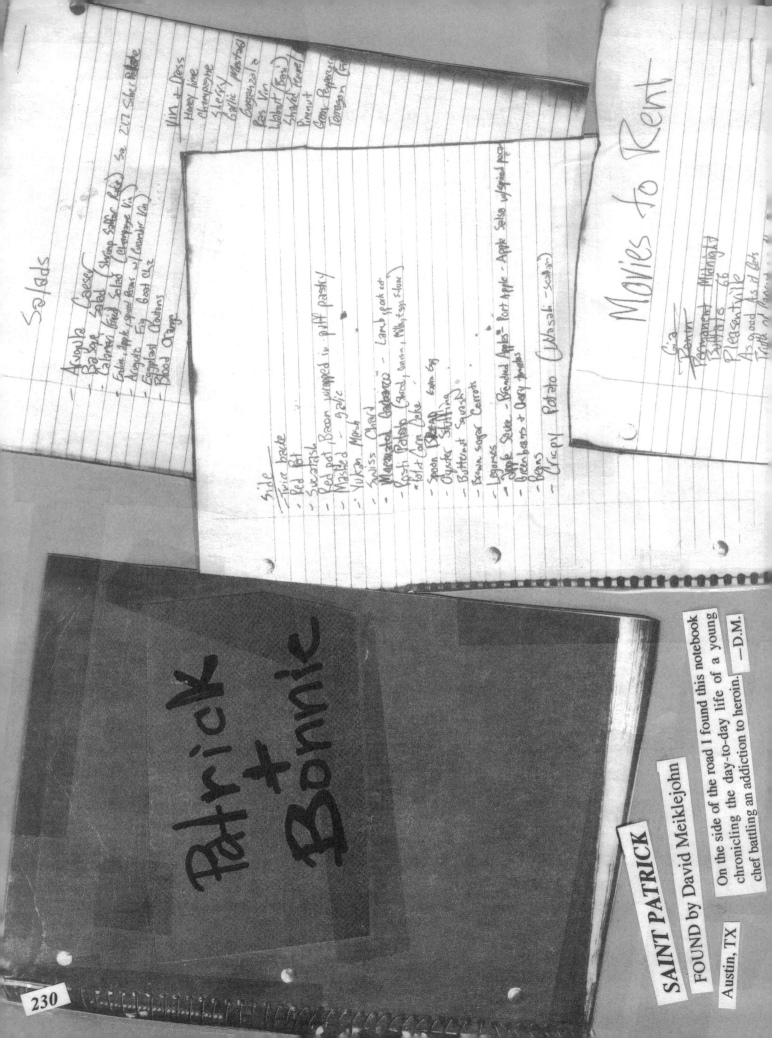

SAINT PATRICK

FOUND by David Meiklejohn

On the side of the road I found this notebook chronicling the day-to-day life of a young chef battling an addiction to heroin. —D.M.

Austin, TX

Thursday July 15th

A draw New Tree in the Life of Patrick
1st off. No dope that nothing new But
still need to keep working on it because We
know Patrick off Dope is a Happier Patrick.
Flow + then Right Blood — I'm going to watch First Loathing
to write a review of Movies I watch
so far ⸺ Next New savings Plan
Each of us get look a week, no more no less
starting today of broadway & I'll tell you later
Must call Ma + Pa today Media by Friday
Don't Forget 9am Media by Friday

30 Push ups
Savings Plan
Moving Rome

CRAB Cakes
2 lb Crab

1 T Paprika
1 t Cayenne
1 c Mayo
¼ c Mustard
¼ c Wost

2 Red pp
1 Green
1 Celery
1 Span Onion
Panco Crumbs

Tomato Fenel Broth
Fish stock

Filet Pat
12 Red pck
7 slice Bacon
Puff Pastry
SP

Sorbet
Simple Syrup
3 C Sugar
2 C Water
2 qts Fruit

Roast Butternut Squash + Puree
Wine
Garlic
Roasted Shallots
Portabella & Squash garnish
as soup

Monday July 17-08

So I lied he don't talk much I
instead So we have
got drunk at B's The hard head BREAD Mixer
good News ... on quick. Don't forget I
Need to put a Packet ... No good for RJ's
No Smack - Smack no good for RJ's
sure hope everything is okay at
I really have made a Contious effort to
not use last week & It's so much nicer in there who
with Bonnie & I had to go to court
your clean & you could tell than to 32
Find themselves. Like running into Eunice Hayes
who's probably watching us anyway. (10 push ups)

FRIDAY JULY 16

Have Meeting with Oliver soon
Finish Jesus ... write 2 short Read
another Heroin Free day
(10 push ups)

Saturday July 17

(15 push ups) The most important thing I
do today is not do the poison — another
day As the Life of Patrick learning to Control
this ... from my self, not they fall Methadone I
have a long day of work ... I must
just make A throw that ...
(Read on Movies) also call ... Math ...
Scrab book - looking Notes
Book (clean up) (push ups)
& get to Man Junkie Super Hero ...
his shield + where he gets a spoon full of spinach
look out Bad guys! What goes up Must com
down + Junk star Loves to come down (10 push ups)

Sunday July 18

Goal #1 Say Nope to Dope I need to
write Risotto recipe, Faccacia fine Wed. Today is
a Day without work so hopefully I can spend
more time with you
FRENCH CONNECTION (15 push ups)

McBrogle + Dillion Escape Plan
LT SCious
Jackson Club Mobb Nation

July 23 1999

No Smack today I know a Chip
would be nice but we all know how that
works # that is such a good deal - boring that
Counseling that should help That boss
of ours is fucking like Twirr I think
That's why he stays away tomorrow
he Says I see through his Life 6/18/14
World.

July 24

Stay Away from H bomb

I'm gonna-make You Only Live Twice - Sean Connery 35 007

July - 25 - No Dope No Work
See ya tomorrow

July 26 -99
Live Smack Free or Die I've got lots to do
today Please give me the strength
to talk to my parents + hope that
it goes well Good
Luck with Roach wish me the best
Only live three one out one side Bikini Atoll there You
Ninja's Flying down 007

No Pushups

Goal 4 day
Say Nope
to Dope

July 22 1999
Time to Pay
Must Roll Parents (list)
Will you over the last few days suck
I missed you over the last few days such
I need to make writing more + doing my
as not missing days + last (but certainly not
reports, Lookin stuff Here though I must
Least more Breathe, The USO A Land of the
birth a little The USO Expansive be because
free or the US could the reason-be because I'm
in the care is so expensive funk B I-n
health some Faith now. I need to practice
just by some faith now it
thing looking lare an anyday because of the Physical?
not looking lare on anyday do right to this
problems now seeing do always bee-god
quittation I feel I have always sure. a line
about it I just must make sure.
In Permanent Midnight there was cleaned
that grabbed me t in made a comment about
of telling much better with his luck he probly
or having AOD t with how I feel I
would /This 15 so much how to be alive fless day aside
any thing happier
from my mouth.

Crepe of the Day

Quiche of the day
served with a fresh green salad

BROWN SUGAR BABY
Piping Hot Cinnamon brown sugar Phil Cake

-Pat's Famous BBQ Chick Sandwich

- Grilled Chees with Pesto

~ Sloppy Jose
Ground Tenderloin cooked down in
a tomato sauce with cilantro, scallion
& Jalapeno served on fresh White Bread

- Rosato Cristo
With Caps Crené frate

- Cranberry Pear...

"Things to Do when the" Heroin Demon
is in the House"

I'm having urges +
1st Recognize I don't even really
tell someone fast. I because the
need to talk for long they'll have
next one see them a million. One
either will be question or a easier
what much Sheri
People Bonnie - Noah
Tracy - anymore from meetings
RJ Or

There are so many reasons why going to
college would help me. A/I my life I have
taken much pride in

Dream Resturant

Le mans

- Bumper Cars -Pinball

Burger + Beer

- Waitress on Skates

...was to know this kid Junny Eoit. cool cat always dressed really slick Black balls on the sides white socks usually cat o rubber soled bowling shoes with red listening pants that went to about mid calves & always really laup shirts that just covered the violent track necks ad the elbow parts. then did he Loe Jmook were usally look she could do alot but really high & going looking dirkies you get 25 bucks go grab a cook & some smokes wt everything about him two lets got high is another give a time that Oadat wat this Cat there stay be called it bar Oadak & my te ferre that time another just wake up he was bom or 3 in the afternoon

Dottie

I'll Be

Right Back

FIRST BIRTHDAY

FOUND by Grits Elkon

Macon, GA

PROPPED UP

FOUND by Jenna and Mark

Hollywood, CA

ESTD. 1880

THE LOS ANGELES
ATHLETIC CLUB

I'M OFFENDED THAT I'M REQUIRED to PEN SOME SORT of "PROPPED UP" SENTIMENT. NONE THE LESS, YOU HAVE BEEN A GOOD FRIEND, SO HAPPY BIRTHDAY. WHATEVER, R.

LAST BIRTHDAY

FOUND by Tom Dykas

St. Louis, MO

236

The latest moo's...

Dave,

     I would like to start off by saying "Yes" there is something more you dont know about me. The Fact of the matter is that I suffer From Anxiety and Panic attacks. Try as I do to Control Them I can't Travel alone no matter How hard I try. I Made it on the plane but Then all of sudden before Take off my hands went all clamy and I fainted. I had to be taken off the plane by Medics. This is quite embarrassing but its something I have To deal with everyday of my life. This is the Reason I Always travel with someone in The car with me. I can't explain it but it makes me feel more comfortable and I am able to deal. I am sorry I did try very hard to come out to see you, But I don't feel comfortable telling people this only a few people know about it. again I am sorry

Margaret

THE LATEST MOO'S

FOUND by Martin Downs

Hanover, NH

I happened upon this letter while cleaning out the drawers of an end table left by former tenants of the house I'm renting.

I found some other correspondence between Dave and Margaret, too: holiday greeting cards showing their long-distance relationship's trajectory from "I love ya babe, you are my world," to "I hope we'll always be friends." This one seems to document the turning point.

—M.D.

I remember when we were young
that number had a very special meaning ..
I didn't know then & other than a
few (distasteful?!) experiences, hardly
know now !

Today 69 looks more like yang & yin ---
a sharing - a meeting of differences which
make a whole -- a truer image

But 69 is also the way we sleep at night,
curling into one another, filling each
other's vacancies with love and
warmth

   I love you .

      1/16/97

Illustration by Cory Kram!

Cory Kram

238

I Love You

Sara
I Love You, I Love You,
I Love You, I Love You
I Love You, I Love You
Forever & Ever & Ever
Love Carmen ♡

FOREVER

FOUND by Cal Belleveau

Minneapolis, MN

NEVER USED

FOUND by Melissa Walker

St. Petersburg, FL

this photo FOUND by Adi Gevins, Oakland, CA

FOR SALE   (New)

Set of his & hers gold
wedding Bands.
      (Never Used)

                    $50.00
(727)-940-29

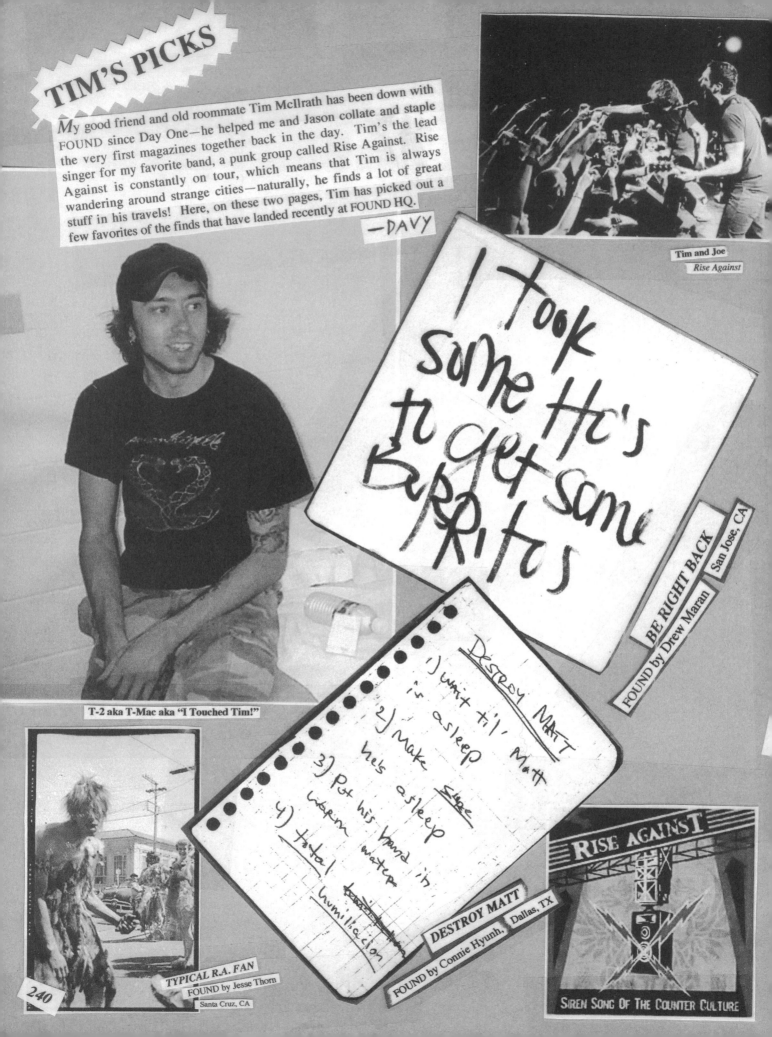

TIM'S PICKS

My good friend and old roommate Tim McIlrath has been down with FOUND since Day One—he helped me and Jason collate and staple the very first magazines together back in the day. Tim's the lead singer for my favorite band, a punk group called Rise Against. Rise Against is constantly on tour, which means that Tim is always wandering around strange cities—naturally, he finds a lot of great stuff in his travels! Here, on these two pages, Tim has picked out a few favorites of the finds that have landed recently at FOUND HQ.

—DAVY

Tim and Joe
Rise Against

T-2 aka T-Mac aka "I Touched Tim!"

I took some HC's to get some BuRRitos

BE RIGHT BACK
FOUND by Drew Maran   San Jose, CA

DESTROY MATT
1) wait til' Matt is asleep
2) make sure hes asleep
3) put his hand in warm water
4) total humiliacion

DESTROY MATT
FOUND by Connie Hyunh,   Dallas, TX

TYPICAL R.A. FAN
FOUND by Jesse Thorn
Santa Cruz, CA

RISE AGAINST
SIREN SONG OF THE COUNTER CULTURE

240

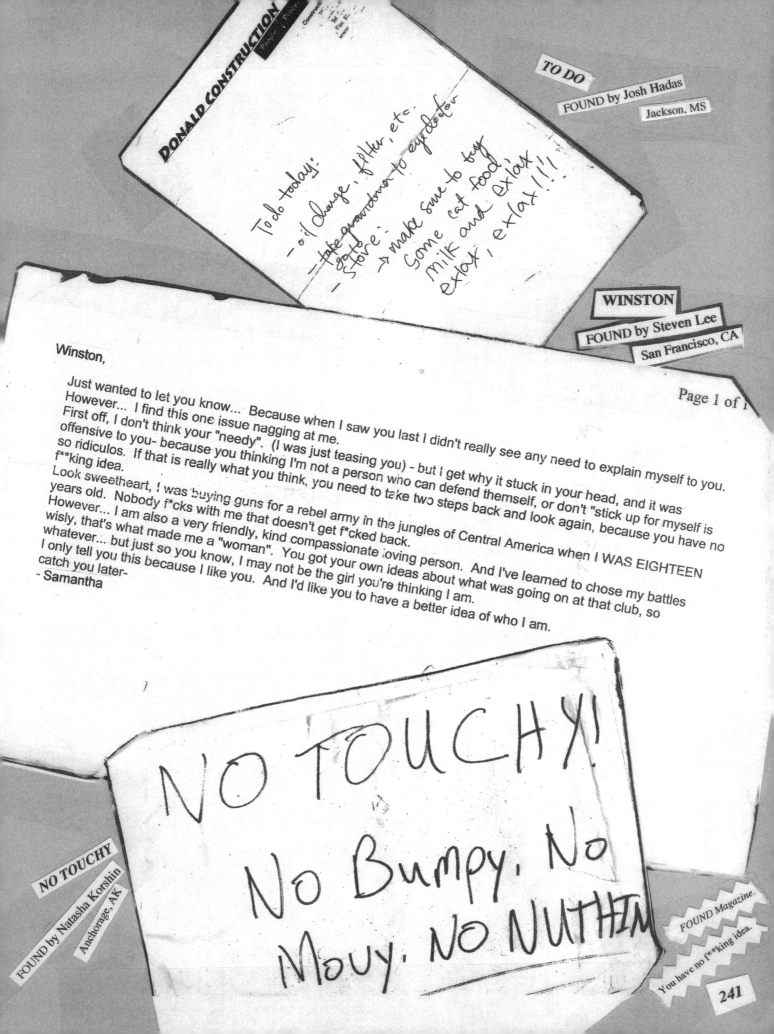

DONALD CONSTRUCTION

To do today:
- oil change, filter, etc.
- ~~take grandma to eye doctor~~
- go to store:
  → make sure to buy
    some cat food,
    milk and exlax
    exlax, exlax!!!!

Winston,

Page 1 of 1

Just wanted to let you know... Because when I saw you last I didn't really see any need to explain myself to you. However... I find this one issue nagging at me.
First off, I don't think your "needy". (I was just teasing you) - but I get why it stuck in your head, and it was offensive to you- because you thinking I'm not a person who can defend themself, or don't "stick up for myself is so ridiculos. If that is really what you think, you need to take two steps back and look again, because you have no f**king idea.
Look sweetheart, I was buying guns for a rebel army in the jungles of Central America when I WAS EIGHTEEN years old. Nobody f*cks with me that doesn't get f*cked back.
However... I am also a very friendly, kind compassionate loving person. And I've learned to chose my battles wisly, that's what made me a "woman". You got your own ideas about what was going on at that club, so whatever... but just so you know, I may not be the girl you're thinking I am.
I only tell you this because I like you. And I'd like you to have a better idea of who I am.
catch you later-
- Samantha

NO TOUCHY!
No Bumpy, No
Mouy, NO NUTHIN

LOSS CAT

SPECKLES, Does not come when called. Limps, Dirty, Not +A.G. Reward Needs medicines. FOAM. CALL WARD 404-302-24__

LOSS CAT FOUND by Tim Speeld, Atlanta, GA

WHERE ARE THEY NOW?!

⚡FOUND⚡
THE BEST LOST, TOSSED, AND FORGOTTEN ITEMS FROM AROUND THE WORLD

THE NATIONAL BESTSELLER

DAVY ROTHBART
CREATOR OF FOUND MAGAZINE

from the book *FOUND*
page 72

Whatever happened to Speckles? Did he make it back to Ward's house safely?

FOUND reader Neal Skorpen from Portland, Oregon drew up this comic strip which fills us in on the Loss Cat's adventures!

LOST STAFF

FOUND by Karin Rabe & Matt Gaffron

Houston, TX

This sign was hanging on all the mailboxes at our apartment complex. It was obvious to us that this poor kid was just writing down exactly what his parents had said to him. I think I actually know which kid this is—he's about 10 or 11 years old. I'm happy to say I've seen him playing outside since he had to post his sign, so I figure either his karate staff was returned or his parents relented and he's no longer grounded.

—K.R.

Lost...

This is a karate staff. It is a piece of equipment meant for training . I was not suppose to play with it outside but disobeyed my parents. Now I have lost it and am grounded until it is returned. Please help.

Benjamin

Lost the 2nd week in January. If found please return to #3455 or call 713-393-63_

242

ZURAWSKI

Not A Man
Be My Man.

I KNOW YOURE

FOUND; BUT WHAT AM I?
3455 CHARING CROSS RD.
ANN ARBOR, MI
48108-1911

FOUND MAGAZINE

FOUND MAGAZINE

Nov 1, 2004

A RELAXING
EVENING
AT THE
MOTEL
(A FLIPBOOK BY
BEN ZURAWSKI)

Dear Mr. Teacher, I was thinking of you over the weekend. So I have made up my mine to let you in on my thoughts.

First you know that I am married and anything I do that comes first! Now I like older men maybe that's because I am mature , but I must have order in everything that I do. If you have not thought of me in this way that's fine we can go on as if I never wrote you. If you have then please read on.

I am not as innocent as you may think, or is it that when you look at me, you can tell that I am not so innocent. If that is the case then lets state the things that we know I am 26, I go to school everyday for 2 to 4 hours a day. I love my husband and always want to be with him, but growing up around all males have made me a little selfish, it also has allow me to know my worth and that nothing is for free. But if you are a woman something's you can get away with.

If we are going to spend time together then there are a few rules that must be followed, and something's you need to know about me. The rules first, because you may not want to deal with me after you hear the rules.

Rule #1 You are never allow to call me so I must have a way of getting in touch with you.

Rule #2 You would never see my family.

Rule #3 You must know that it is a privilege to be with me ,for I have picked you for the purpose of fulfilling some of my needs that are not getting satisfied.

Rule #4 Understand that I am looking for some one to spend time with, maybe go to a movie, maybe just someone to talk to. But not a man to be my man. I have one of them already.

Rule #5 If we ever decide to have sex then I will only have sex in a hotel, you will have to pay for the room.(I will never be able to spend the night, but what ever time I spend with you it will always be worth it!)

Rule #6 Everything I do must have order there for meeting up with you will always have to be planed. You must also know that I may have to brake plans. But not likely.

Now, things I feel that you should know about me. I have been married almost 8 years, he takes care of me and his children.

244

While walking in the halls on a 10-minute break from my college art class, I found this zesty little note peaking from underneath a used coffee filter in the trash. I can't say for sure which 'Mr. Teacher' it was for, but I wonder if he accepted the offer.
—B.Z.

I have only been with 5 men in my life my husband was my 4th. I have had an affair one time that was about a year a go. It lasted a while but his feeling got in the way. So I had to end something that went on for over a few years. Now if you feel that I am a hoe then we need not get together. I know that I am not a hoe. If we was to have sex I would feel the need to know how many people you are having sex with not because I am jealous but because I am married and you already know who I am sleeping with. I will tell you if I start to sleep with any one else. (Not likely) But in the case that I feel that you are having sex with too many people I will end it. Not because I am jealous but because I am married, and I don't want to bring anything home. You will know more than my husband about my sex life. That's because you will be fulfilling things that he dose not.

Now, may be you think I wont be able to handle you ,but the truth is I hope not, I hope there are things that you can teach me for I am willing to learn. If not I hope you are not unwilling to learn what I like. Because I am a big girl and I do know what I like. I am not afraid to let people know what I like. I like to do things and I like to have it done to me. If you are unwilling to do the things I like ,then there is no need to get together. For the truth is its all about me, And if YOU want to please me. For in return you will always be please!

I also like to smoke weed most of the time before sex, or throughout sex it helps to relax me if you can't be around it that's fine but never ask me to not smoke. I will never have sex if I am not relaxed.

I know that I have given you a lot to think about. Therefore I will not ask you about this letter. You will have to make the first move . I don't know if you feel the same , or if you are willing to follow the rules(the rules must be kept.) I hope that it something that you will think hard and long about. Please don't start something you can't handle.

One of your students
I am a black female in one of you're a.m. classes.

P.S. I am not doing this to better my grade I am passing your class I got an A on the midterm if you think you know who I am call me into your office and we can talk about it. Tell no one I have just as much to loss as you. May be that's why I picked you. J.A.

FOUND Magazine. Let you in on my thoughts.

245

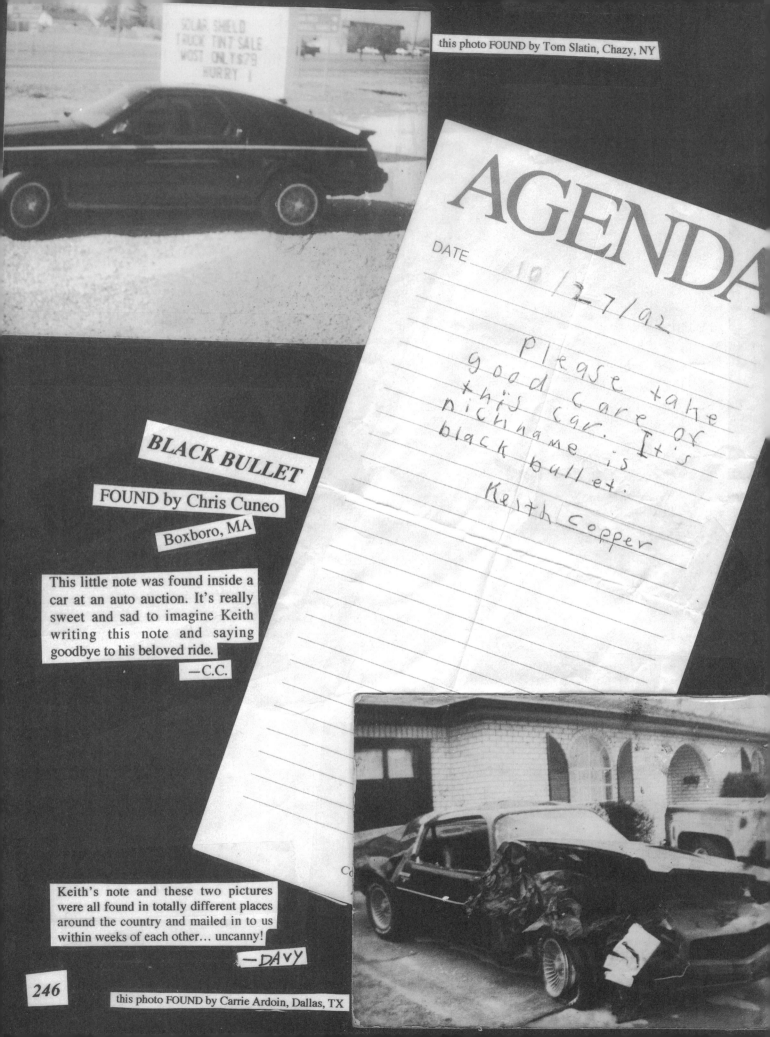

this photo FOUND by Tom Slatin, Chazy, NY

AGENDA

DATE 10/27/92

Please take good care of this car. It's nickname is black bullet.

Keith Copper

BLACK BULLET

FOUND by Chris Cuneo

Boxboro, MA

This little note was found inside a car at an auto auction. It's really sweet and sad to imagine Keith writing this note and saying goodbye to his beloved ride.

—C.C.

Keith's note and these two pictures were all found in totally different places around the country and mailed in to us within weeks of each other... uncanny!

—DAVY

this photo FOUND by Carrie Ardoin, Dallas, TX

Yo what's up?! This is Davy writing to you. So, I done went and wrote a book of stories — they're mostly about girls and jail and driving around the country. I would be thrilled if you wanted to read it, I worked really hard on the stories. You can probably find a copy at any bookstore or library. Let me know what you think! PEACE — DAVY

DAVY@FOUNDMAGAZINE.COM

Much like the lost, tossed, and forgotten items Davy Rothbart collects in his acclaimed magazine, his first story collection, *The Lone Surfer of Montana, Kansas,* captures the oddity, poetry, and dignity of everyday life.

"Davy writes with his whole heart. These stories are crushing."
—Arthur Miller

"A talented new writer. Rothbart writes with such energy, wit, and heart."
—Judy Blume

"A prodigiously talented young writer....His stories are full of a strange, nervous energy in which wisdom is also, somehow, always visible."
—Charles Baxter, author of *The Feast of Love*

"Davy writes with his whole heart. These stories are crushing."
—ARTHUR MILLER

THE LONE SURFER OF MONTANA, KANSAS

STORIES

DAVY ROTHBART

AUTHOR OF THE NATIONAL BESTSELLER FOUND

www.simonsays.com

TOUCHSTONE
A Division of Simon & Schuster

U.S. $12.00   Can. $16.50

ISBN-13: 978-0-7432-6305-4
ISBN-10: 0-7432-6305-7

247

FOUND Magazine's Jason Bitner kindly requests that you

SEND IN YOUR FINDS!!!

FOUND!

illustration by Ben Snakepit

249

"I'm white trash, bald head, skinny pothead/ with a love for this rap game until the day I drop dead" —Classified

You know what's cool? It's cool when you're doing something for just the second time in life and it already feels like a tradition. Here I am back in my brick-and-dirt basement sippin' the deuce of Olde E, celebrating the fact I finished this damn book ten minutes ago, 'bout to write these thank yous and shout-outs, so I can ship this shit off to amanda in NY tomorrow morning. See that find down there—A WICKED PARTY—I wish all of you, the whole entire FOUND family, was here right now to celebrate with me. Instead, I'll just crank the Classified, down this 22, and clatter on these keys. Soon enough me and Popcorn Pete'll be in your town and we can rock it in person.

The funny thing is, I just looked back to see what I said in the Thank Yous in the 1st FOUND book for guidance with this one, and I realize I kinda nailed it the 1st time: I feel enormous gratitude and love for every one of you who has participated in this project in any way at all—sending in your finds, telling your friends about this shit, or even just reading this book right here. Sometimes I stop off at my folks' house to pick up the mail and when I see the crate full of envelopes addressed to FOUND Magazine I start tearing up because it seems so surreal and ridiculous. It's so weird to see your idle dreams turned into reality. "Wouldn't it be cool if everyone could share what they were finding with everyone else?" One of those thoughts that crosses your mind for an instant, then darts away. But y'all motherfuckers are crazy enough for this shit to really happen! You crazy enough to actually do it, to find stuff, put it in an envelope, and mail it to us! Listen, that is so fuckin' cool. That's why I tear up. Gratitude, man. I can't tell you how grateful I am to everyone who has sent in their finds. It's a gift, and I'm tellin' you, I appreciate it. If you're reading this and you've ever sent in a find, I'm tellin' you, THIS BUDS FOR YOU—just ask me and I will buy you a drink when I come to your town, it will be a *honor*.

A WICKED PARTY

FOUND by Kara Race-Moore

Boston, MA

As I think I said in the introduction to this book, perhaps the best thing about this project for me has been getting to meet so many amazing people while we've been on the road. People like Rhonda J. McSween and Jacalyn in Birmingham, Alabama, like Matthew Latkiewicz in Montague, Mass., Peg Leg Meg in Indy. Rodney in D.C., Magan and Rose in St.Louis, MC Lava in Taos, Janelle in Long Beach, Andrea and Carlos Lama in Houston, Chip in Sac-Town. Infinite thanks to anyone who has ever given us a bed or a couch or a floor!!! Some folks we manage to invade on a constant basis—thanks for always having an open door, no questions asked, can't tell you how much we appreciate it—Eddie Fakotorovitch & Tammy in L.A., Mad Art Gallery crew, Liam & Marti Murphy, Bess Brodsky & Greg Goldstein in NYC, Chintu & Dina Kumar, Johnny "Cash K" Kovacs, Claire Reichstein, Seth & Smeeta, and Alex in the Bay Area, Adam Peltz, Abram Himelstein & Shana in NOLA, those down-ass chicks in Baton Rouge who we only give an hour's notice before we show up, Tamera Ford & Dora Silver in Denver, and of course Brother Mike and Amy in Madison. Thanks also to Frank Warren of PostSecret for risking the road with us, and to our lovely angel of a tour partner, Devon Sproule ("T.B.").

At this point, lookin' at 50 states in the rear-view, it's gonna be impossible to give love here to everyone who deserves it. But let me do what I can. First off, let me shout 6 bad motherfuckers and dear loved ones who brought this book to life, as well as all FOUND shit you might've seen. JASON BITNER—this man is crazier than I could've ever known, and that's the best compliment I could ever give anyone. He's a fuckin' menace, he's a madman, he's so goddamn beautiful I wish you could see it like I seen it. He works so hard to it. bring FOUND to you. Look, it's one thing to think something is cool, it's another to be so generous that you will dedicate your life to it. Seems neato at first, but ain't that glamourous sitting in your apartment people be lookin' at this shit, so he stays up all night most nights workin'. I mean, dude should be at the bar like Day every fuckin' day of the year. But Jason knows nineteen million people be lookin' at this shit. Check Dirty FOUND—if you dare. Haha. Check Jason's *LaPorte, Indiana* book. You'll get the idea. Thanks Jason! All right, then there's PETER ROTHBART—yeah, that's my brother, man. I'd use to describe J.B. are the words I imagine they'd use in some silly-ass TV ad for the U.S.Marines: Sacrifice; Discipline; Courage; Strength; Wisdom. This dude is *bringin'* it! The rest of us. Okay, sometimes he go to the bar, too. But I'm sayin', Classified has a funny song about sibling rivalry that I'm listening to right now. Love you man! At some point I realized that if I wanted people to send in finds from every land, I was gonna have to roll town to town and personally bully and harangue folks into participating. The tours have become one of the main parts of the whole FOUND project, and I could not pull off these tours without Popcorn. Champion musician, marathon driver, and serious baller. Poem Adept, y'all! I don't mean to be fan-boy, but I'm like his biggest fan. It's fuckin' amazing someone with you who's as diehard a Pistons fan as you. Plus, the music, *the music*! The only annoying thing about Petey is how after every show the girls gather 'round Petey to get to hear your favorite musician in the world every single fuckin' night—am I right or am I right?! and only talk to me to get to Petey. But that's what happens, I guess, when you go on tour with an international hearthrob. Still, we clocked 60,000 miles in 2 years—that, my friends, is commitment. I'm proud of you Pete, keep making music—the booty don't never stop. LaGrange or bust homey!!

AMANDA PATTEN—okay, this lady right here, she the one who put this book in your hands. You think a editor at some major label shit can just say to they bosses, "Yo, check out this cool 'zine, let's make it into a book!" No, she put herself on the line for me and for FOUND, she fought for this book to even be. I will always be the editor at Simon & Schuster or I guess they call it 'Touchstone/Fireside,' she the one who put this book in your hands. This year you gotta come on tour with us!!! For serious! Love you Amanda!! grateful for her vision, energy, and guidance. Thanks for stickin' with me kid, even when I fuck up.

- 12 bottles champagne.
- 1 jug wine.
- battle of captain morgans.

BRANDE WIX—what can I say about this man that hasn't already been said about Afghanistan? I love him to death, man. It's hard to believe how much he's given to FOUND over the last 5 years. If you ever ordered a FOUND Magazine online, it's pretty much guaranteed that Brande was the one who sent it to you. If you ever picked up a FOUND Magazine at a store, it's near certain that Brande was the one who unloaded the pallet full of mags off the truck, boxed 'em up, and shipped 'em to that store. I don't even know how the FOUND office works anymore. I mean, when I'm down there, I'm just basically getting in the way. All I know is I wake up and look out my window and I see his car parked out front, I go to the basement and he's there listening to reggae on WCBN or some revolutionary-type political records, and packaging up magazines to send to y'all. I'll be here at like 5, 6 in the morning, motherfucker gets off work at Pizza House and comes here to go to work. This dude work harder than 5 Detroit Pistons! Dr.Wix—I owe you 1,000 drinks. Much love. For life, G. DAVID MEIKLEJOHN—haha, let me tell you a funny story. Meikledong, me and Pete call him, also sometimes known as Old Gray Towel. Well, on the Lone Surfer tour, Peter and David and Javan kept makin' fun of me because I called every find we saw "sweet." I mean, some of these FOUND notes people gave us were fucked up, full of rage, hurt, brutality, but somehow it was the sweetness within these notes that always emerged for me. So, we were in Houston, and I forced everyone to go to a strip club called Legends Entertainment at 4 in the afternoon, mostly because Peter and David had never been to one and I wanted to make them uncomfortable. It was a sadsack dive, the strippers were making no money, and the half-dozen folks there were just kinda sitting there brooding over 6-dollar Sprites. Two kids in LeBron jerseys and sick jewelry bundled up the courage to approach the dancer on stage and put a couple bucks in her G-string. The next dancer was up, and an older guy made his way over from the bar and stood close to the stage for a couple minutes and got some attention from the girl, then picked his way back to his barstool. I started talking about how sweet and heartbreaking the whole scene was, the vulnerability of the patrons, the forced party-vibe of the dancers when they could've made more dough on a paper route. My friends made fun of me for this. But the best moment was ahead of us. First, you gotta know that Meiklejohn is a vegan, a punk-rock good guy, the kindest-hearted person in the galaxy, or at least the solar system. It was mildly upsetting to him when we forced him to go up to the stage to offer the dancer a few bucks. But to be a good sport, he did. He was shy. The woman said, "Come on, I won't bite." He inched closer, and that's when it happened—she shoved his face between her giant boobies and squeezed 'em together and rocked side-to-side. Oh, when David emerged eight seconds later, he was beet-fuckin'-red and had the most wild-eyed look of thrill and fright and amazement I'd ever seen. Best moment ever on tour. Thanks David! Okay, okay, if you insist, one more Meiklejohn moment. This is the story of how he got another one of his nicknames. David can look cosmopolitan when he wants to, but at heart he's a gutter-punk like me. Dirty black jeans, ripped clothes, painted fingernails, bracelets, chains, spikes… that's how he roll sometimes on tour. You know, folks at rest stops and in Indiana fast-food joints get nervous. So the funniest shit ever was when we rolled into my cousins Jon and Randi's house in Phoenix at 4 in the morning, they being cool like all the dozens of other kick-ass souls who put us up over the years without a second thought. Meiklejohn crashed out in the living room; I stayed up to do logistical emails; Pete went for a jog or something and then came back. 6 a.m., Randi comes out of the bedroom with her little, wobbling 1-year-old, Ben. He gets to the living room, smiles at me, smiles at Peter, then looks at the sofa, sees Meiklejohn stretched out there, and cries out: "Uh-oh!" Hahaha, so that's the nickname that stuck: "Uh-oh!" If you see Meiklejohn in your town, please greet him that way: "Uh-oh!" He also happens to be a talented writer and filmmaker. We're making a couple movies together and we'll be in your town soon to show 'em, so yeah, come out and visit. SARAH LOCKE—23 months ago, Sarah sent in a find (see pg.5) and drew a little picture on the back of the envelope of a stick figure couple exchanging a gift. "Oooh, just what I wanted," the recipient was saying, "it's the new issue of FOUND Magazine! I love you!" "Don't be silly," said the other. "I only got it because *I* wanted to read it!" 22 months ago, I met Sarah for the first time, this was at the Blind Pig here in Ann Arbor, the show which kicked off our 50-state Slapdance tour. The very next day, and ever since, Sarah has been working hard to bring joy to FOUND readers everywhere, pouring her heart and soul into this project. From reading every FOUND note that arrives here to decorating thousands of magazine covers, and in countless other ways, she's kept FOUND—and me—going. Nobody worked harder on this book than Sarah—every page bears her touch. Sarah, I could never have put this book together without you, and I feel blessed to have you in my life. I love you so much!!

Bich & Porter, what up! Dean & Mandy, Jeremiah & Natalie, what up!

Okay, I'm out of beer, I gotta go see what liquor I can round up from around the house. Be right back.

I'm back. I must be getting old or something. I skipped out on liquor in favor of a bottle of Odwalla Wellness. It's 5:30am. I got a lot more shit to say. I'm a pump some Metallica and stay up.

Significant thanks go to all FOUND staff and volunteers (who're we kiddin'—the whole staff is volunteers!), past, present, and future, who have generously given their time and energy to this project, such as Angella Petrella, Arthur Jones, Mike Kozura, Emily Long, Maggie Murray, Britten Stringwell, Vinh Nguyen, Mike Helferstay, James Molenda, Lauren Hart, Natalie Newton, Moira Saltzman, Holly Matthews, Timmy Smith, Michelle Angus, Genevieve Belleveau, Aaron Wickenden, Josh Noel, Jed Lackritz, Mike DiBella, Amanda Bullock, Jenny Cunningham, Emilie Goodhart—and way more good folks.

Ridiculous respect to everyone at Simon & Schuster and Touchstone/Fireside: Trish, Jamie, Betsy Haglage, Liz Bevilacqua, Cherlynne Li, Jason Heuer, Tricia Wygal, Marcia Burch, Amy Cormier, and especially London King, Trina Rice, and Kimberly Brissenden, who have always gone far above and way beyond the call of duty for FOUND: How many publicists you know gonna sign on to work a 136-city tour?! I can't believe how much magic these women are capable of. Thanks Trina!! Thanks Kimberly!!

Steve Chung went from being my R.A. at East Quad to being my legal advisor on this book—thanks for the help homey! He took time away from workin' for 50-Cent and the Game to help with this; he also made me change the name Steve to Dave in one note in this book, you can maybe guess which one if you go through these pages with some fine-toothed type shit. Thanks to Josie Friedman at ICM in L.A., love to Denise Shaw, and a blunt and a beer to my agent and friend Jud Laghi at LJK. I would be living in my van in the junkyard if it wasn't for Jud.

Thanks to the artists who contributed their amazing skills to this book—Dan Tice, Amy Thomas, Ryan Sias, Ben Snakepit, Jeffrey Brown, Matthew Thurber, Ayun Halliday, Melissa Gardner, and of course Rob Doran, who I love very much, and who is welcome to always call me Phil Knight.

Thanks to all the FOUND operatives who've done so much to spread the FOUND love in their cities, to the Street Team members, and especially to the All-Star Finders—you know who you are and you make life worth living!!! I know who you are even if I don't write back personally to each find you send in. I spend most of my nights laying in bed, listening to music, reading the notes you found and sent in, as well as the notes you wrote to me about them. It's kind of intimate, right? Just know you are fucking amazing and I will fill you with so many drinks when I see you on the road that you will end up passed out in the alleyway for someone else to find.

The indie bookstores who represent hard know who they are, too. And they know that I love 'em! Quimby's, Atomic Books, Clean Well-Lit Place, Cody's, Pegasus, Diesel, BookPeople, Chicago Comics, St.Mark's (hi Margarita!), Skylight (what up Kev! What up Darin! What up Steve and Kerry!), Casco Bay Books (what up Mark, Liz, Zoe, Isaac!), Chop Suey in Richmond, VA (what up Ward!), Politics & Prose (what up Cleve!), Powell's (what up Samp!), Regulator, Internationalist, Mac's Backs, Shaman Drum, Vault of Midnight, and all the other good, good folks fighting the good, good fight out there and giving shelf-space and love and support to indie writers and publishers like us. Thanks also to Loop Distro, Small Changes, Stickfigure, Carrottop, Central Books, the man of steel Clint Johns, Mike Brown, and everyone at Tower, and a big motherfuckin' FUCK YOU to JR Fesperman of Desert Moon—you still owe me 12 grand, it ain't over motherfucker, I know where you live even now and I know what car you drive, so watch your motherfuckin' back every second of every day… me myself, I'm a peaceful dude, but some of the other people you fucked over aren't so nice and I'm sending 'em your way.

GIANT thanks to every single daily and weekly newspaper writer and editor and radio & TV reporter, host and producer that has helped us spread word about FOUND! Special shouts to Matt Roberts and Eliana Salzhauer at Letterman, Ben Karlin at the Daily Show, T.Gross, John Mark Eberhart, Alex Kotlowitz, everyone at KUER, and Hillary Robe. R.I.P. Glenn Mitchell!!

THIS BUD'S FOR YOU

FOUND by Suzanne DeGaetano

Cleveland Heights, OH

I have ferocious appreciation to some folks who've looked after my health and constitution through some troubled times: Brooke Bailey especially, and also Heather and Cindy and Dr.Fivenson, plus that pimp Dr.Raymond Rion at Packard Community, and Dr.Taylor. Tangentially related, Jordan Stolte gives the best haircuts in the Ace Deuce.

Love to my families at This American Life, 826, McSweeney's, the Believer, SLAM Magazine, and GQ. Chris Young and WestCan—thanks for being so fuckin' beautiful and making our magazines look so nice.

Thanks to my dear friends for sharing life with me—all my boyz: Javan, Virginia Park ballers, Bryant School ballers, Manix, Sachin, Shyam, Mukri, Jiro, Kevin, and all the Gurus of Ultimate, Eldad, Mike the K, Brande, Devin, Seth, Mike D., Dan Z., Eddie, Tim Dogg, Tim-Pat, Tim M. & Rise Against, Jesse P., Jordan, Anvil, Will Sheff, Dan Tice, Abe Hurst, Don at Kosmo, Reda, Charlie, Steve & Co. at Bell's, Byron Case (keep ya head up) and also Cincinnati's Great Hope Alex B.—and my girlz: Nicole Schude, Alex Gross, Rachel Dengiz, Lauren Hill, Carrie Cecchini, Sarah Lidgus, Julia Leonard, Anne Gunnison, Meta Bodewes, Aimee McDonald, Shari Stadel, Rachel Frey, Shawna Lee, Janelle Gunther, and Monica Lams at Fleetwood. My roommates is Fila Fresh: Dorothy, Jacob K. & Meg Hopeman. Big love to my family—Petey, Mike & Amy, mom and dad, Mimi, and my wonderful aunts, uncles and cousins.

Yo—I know I'm forgetting mad people here, but it's 7:40am and the sun is up. Now I'm listening to Okkervil River. If I didn't give you love here and you know you deserve it, lemme know, and I'll owe you two drinks. Deal?

Lola Hurst and Lydia Bakopoulos too!

This book is additionally dedicated to Shyel Meisels, Blythe McIlrath, Ava Schude, Junior Wasik, Leroy Kozura, Blaze Haldeman, JoJo Rothbart, Edith Heinemann, and all my other barely-born nephews and nieces who represent the new generation of finders. Keep your eyes to the ground, squirts!

Finally, thanks to the authors of the notes in this book—they are us, we are them, slims with the tilted brim, one and all.

Peace out ch'all—see you in your city

LOVE DAVY

I HOPE YOU GOT YOUR LAUGHS

THE LAST LAUGH

FOUND by Crystal Brown

Paw Paw, WV

My daily commute to work takes me through the backwoods of West Virginia. A couple of months ago, I saw this sign in blue paint nailed to a tree by the side of the road. —C.B.